MW01469048

God's Vagabond

Autobiography of
Sadie Custer

Compiled by
Loraine Czarneke

God's Vagabond

© 2006 Sadie Custer.

Published by Lammermir House Publishers, an imprint of OMF Books.

All rights reserved. Printed in the United States of America. No part of this book may be used or reproduced in any form or by any means, or stored in a database or retrieval system, without prior written permission of the publisher except in the case of brief quotations embodied in critical articles or reviews. Making copies of any part of this book for any purpose other than your own personal use is a violation of United States copyright laws. For information and permissions write to OMF Books, 10 West Dry Creek Circle, Littleton, CO 80120-4413 U.S.A.

Published in 2006 by Lammermuir House Publishers, Littleton, CO. Printed in U.S.A.

ISBN: 1-929122-25-X

God's Voyager available from

   OMF Books, 10 West Dry Creek Circle, Littleton, CO 80120-4413 U.S.A.
   OMF Books, 5155 Spectrum Way, Building 21, Mississauga, ON L4W 5A1, Canada
   OMF Books, Station Approach, Borough Green, Sevenoaks, Kent TN15 8BG, U.K., and other OMF offices

COVER PICTURES (top to bottom):

Sadie Custer often traveled by sedan chair in China. Actually this day her Chinese co-worker (right) was riding in the sedan chair; Sadie was peddling her bicycle. But they traded places momentarily for Sadie to get her picture taken in the flimsy conveyance.

In her last term before retirement, in Taiwan, Sadie riding on the back of a motorbike among the Paiwan in the mountains.

Sadie during a furlough in mid-life.

Introduction

We were on our way from Muskegon to Allendale, Michigan. My three sisters and I were seated in the back "seats" of my dad's panel truck. The truck doubled as his milk truck *and* our family car. When converted to the family car, we kids sat on milk crates in the back of the truck. Since we didn't take a trip like this very often, it was always an adventure for us. We loved going to Grandma's house in Allendale. But this time it was even more exciting. We were meeting a very special person—Aunt Sadie. It was special because my sisters and I had never met her before. We had heard only stories about her. Aunt Sadie, my dad's sister, was a missionary and had been in China for the last several years. Little did I know that I was about to meet someone who would have a significant impact on my life.

On this particular day Aunt Sadie prepared a Chinese meal for the whole family. This was my first lesson in how to eat with chopsticks. But even more interesting than the chopstick lesson were the stories that Aunt Sadie eventually told us. She wore her Chinese clothes, and every story had an object lesson. Especially exciting, though, were the stories of her adventures. Aunt Sadie traveled in those days either by foot or varied conveyances: bicycles, motorbikes, rickety buses that would break down, or trucks that would fall apart along the way. Her journeys took her over rivers, dangerous mountain paths, noisy city streets and mud-filled streets. Sometimes rickety trucks traversed narrow mountain tracks with hairpin turns. We loved hearing of those travels. And she was so patient when we would ask for "just one more story" over and over again.

Even though I saw Aunt Sadie only when she was home on furlough, her stories and, especially her spirit, made a deep impression on me.

I grew up in a Christian home. At the age of eight, while attending vacation Bible school one summer, I accepted the Lord as my Savior. Later, when I was about twelve years old, I committed my life to the Lord. I wanted to be a missionary like Aunt Sadie. Sadly, however, by the time I was a teenager, I disregarded that promise and went down a different path. But I never forgot the promise I had made and, in fact, I felt very guilty every time I thought of it. It was through the prayers of my parents, Aunt Sadie, and a patient friend that I returned to the Lord. By this time I was an adult working as a social worker in an inner-city school. I worked with troubled families and their children. I finally realized that I was a missionary in a foreign land after all. I just didn't have to cross an ocean to get there!

Today, at 94, Aunt Sadie suffers from chronic pain caused by a deteriorating spine, and she has lost most of her sight. However, her mind is still bright, and her spirit is joyful. Her daily prayer is that God will be glorified in her pain.

God laid it on my heart to put Aunt Sadie's story together in book form after I learned that the family had preserved a suitcase full of the letters she sent home faithfully from the time she went to Moody Bible Institute to the end of her career. In addition, she had written in her diary daily all that time. When we decided to proceed with the writing, Aunt Sadie made it very clear that she wanted God glorified through the telling of her story.

Aunt Sadie also realizes that her work would not have been fruitful without the prayers of her faithful prayer partners back in the States. Her first term in China lasted from 1936 until 1946. Missionaries could not return home during that time because of World War II. More than once there were bombings within yards of their living quarters, but God protected them at every turn. She endured many hardships, but had a wonderful sense of humor through situations that most of us would not or could not have endured. She credits her protection and her stamina to God through her prayer partners. After her commission in China was over, Aunt Sadie continued to serve in Malaysia and, later, in Taiwan.

I believe the reader will be inspired to see how wonderfully God works when His children are obedient. My prayer is that the story of this remarkable woman will inspire readers, that it will encourage young people to give their lives to missionary work and others to commit to praying for missionaries.

To God be the glory! ೞ

A Word from the Author

The Lord has done great and mighty things for me, for which I am glad. As I sit in my rocking chair at Calvary Fellowship Homes in Lancaster, Pennsylvania, I praise the Lord that "His way is perfect... and it is God that girdeth me with strength and makes my way perfect" (Ps. 18:30, 32). If I could live my life over again, I would do it just the way the Lord planned it the first time.

When friends suggested I should write a book, my reply always was, "People don't have time to read." But then my niece, Loraine Czarneke, decided she would like to put together the story of my life from my letters over the years. My reply was, "I want it written only if it's not a story of what I did, but of what the Lord did." I wanted it to give God all the glory. I am amazed at how He took me, a young farm girl without a high-school education, and used me in building His church in China, Malaysia, and Taiwan. I often receive phone calls and letters from Christian workers who were students in my classes when I was in the field. Today they are pastors, Christian teachers in seminaries, and holding their own Bible classes. The seeds that were planted have been watered and continue to grow.

I am so grateful to all my faithful prayer partners and financial supporters, some who are still standing by me today. Without them this book would not have been written. I want to say thanks to Loraine for compiling and smoothing the text, to Fay Goddard for editing, and to Rachael Borne for proofreading. ❧

7

Table of Contents

Chapter 1

Bombs and Beginnings

"'Ye shall hear of wars and rumors of wars: see that ye be not troubled,'" read Superintendent Arthur Moore from *Daily Light* in his strong voice. "'God is our refuge and strength, a very present help in trouble. Therefore will we not fear, though the earth be removed, and though the mountains be carried into the midst of the sea....'" All of us in the Nancheng mission center that May 7th Sunday morning were gathered in the upstairs bedroom. On the bed our young fellow worker Helen Dalton lay unconscious with spinal meningitis.

Mr. Moore was still reading when the drone of approaching Japanese war planes grew ominously until the roar swallowed up every other sound. At least one aircraft was directly overhead. Suddenly a deafening *BOOM* shook the house, loosening plaster, shattering windows, and flinging doors open. Mr. Moore stopped mid-sentence in his reading. When a four-foot section of plaster began falling from the ceiling, I jumped on the bed and threw myself across Helen's head. Pieces of plaster pummeled my back. Some chunks just missed Helen's eyeglasses on the dresser. As the planes moved away, the air reeked with plaster dust and the smell of sulfur.

My mind raced. *Was this the end? Would more bombs fall? Would I die here? Was this the finish in China for me?*

When the dust settled and it was once again quiet, we thanked God that we were uninjured. Making sure Helen was all right, we filed downstairs and looked out the back door. What a sight! What had been the vegetable garden was one big hole—about thirty feet across and fifteen feet deep—and that bomb-created crater lay gaping only fifteen yards from the house! How close we had come to great harm, even death! Though we found pieces of shrapnel in the goat pen and by the chickens, the animals were not hurt any more than we were. I never expected when I, a simple Michigan farm girl, committed myself to becoming a missionary, that I would experience anything like the Sino-Japanese War firsthand.

As a family we were poor as church mice but we were a happy and hard-working family. My parents, Benjamin and Sadie Custer, and eventually eight of us children lived in a small house in Allendale, Michigan, a farming community. We children arrived in boy-girl-boy-girl order. Father used to say, "Others had eight, but mine were tailor made." I was born on January 29, 1911—number six.

My father—"Pop" to us—hadn't gone to school past the second grade. But he had taught himself, mostly through reading the newspaper. He could talk on almost any subject. He loved the Lord and read the Bible to the family every day.

I remember my mother as a quiet and contented person. In the wintertime we all played checkers and dominoes or listened to records on the old Victrola. Mother loved music. Everyone in the family sang and had musical talent, except me, though I was the one who would eventually need it most of all.

Being one of the youngest, I often spent my days outside with Pop, helping in the fields. My older sisters helped Mother in the house.

In front of the old house the summer of 1911, the year I was born, are (back row, left to right) Aunt Grace, Sister Dean, Mother with me on her lap, Father with Brother Ben, and Grandma Custer; (front row) Sister Julia, Brother John, Cousin Ben, and Brother Dick.

Being a close-knit family, we did almost everything together. In the busiest of times, even in the middle of harvest, we often took time after dinner for a ball game. Between the neighborhood kids and us, we had enough players to make teams! Mother usually watched from the porch while darning the never-empty basket of socks.

We girls all slept in one room and the boys in another in our small farmhouse. One winter, when I was just a little girl, everyone seemed to be getting sick with one thing or another. The doctor told Pop that if he would build a bigger house, he would have fewer doctor bills! Pop took that advice to heart and did, indeed, build a new house.

While the house was being built, the family lived in the garage and slept in the granary.

Not long after the house was finished, my grandmother, who lived with us, fell and broke her hip. Grandma spent the rest of her life in bed, and Mother cared for her as well as for us children.

In order of birth all eight of us Custer children pose in front of our new, larger house—Dick, Julia, John, Dean, Ben, me, Bill and Grace.

One of my earliest memories as a child was of the "great fire." We had just finished harvesting, and Dad had thanked God that we had such a good harvest and would be free and clear of debt. Then the barn caught fire. I can remember being wakened in the middle of the night. I can even remember—I don't know who it was, probably one of my brothers—but somebody picked Grandma up and carried her out of the bedroom because he thought the house was going to burn too. We watched, tousle-headed and almost unbelieving, from the big bay window in the dining room as flames roared through the structure. In my mind I can still see those burning cows and horses. We lost all the cows, the horses, the pigs, the hay and all the machinery.

Remarkably, the next morning Dad sat at the kitchen table with the eight of us children and said, "The Lord hath given, and the Lord hath taken away. Blessed be the name of the Lord! Nobody got hurt." What an attitude!¯since the loss meant that we had to buy everything new and start over. My parents managed to do such a good job with the farming, however, that when they retired some years later, they had enough to live on.

Hard work marked my childhood and that of my siblings. That

was my heritage, really. It was all part of God's plan to prepare me for what lay ahead. Years later, I received an email from Frank Moore‾son of Percy and Amy Moore and grandson of Arthur [the one reading *Daily Light* mentioned earlier] and his wife Esther. He knew me as "Auntie Sadie" when he was a little boy. He wrote in part: "I am beginning to fill out a picture which starts with [you] in China so long ago.... I read somewhere that the missionaries who stayed in China and withstood the incredible rigors of living out[side] of their cultural context were those brought up on farms."

As a youngster I wanted to be a bookkeeper as I liked working with numbers. I am sure the Lord was in that too. I couldn't go to high school because there wasn't one where we lived, and my dad wouldn't let us girls live away from home. I think that if I had gone to high school, I might have gone into business rather than going to the mission field. I went through the tenth grade, however, and was able to use my math skills at home.

My mother decided she wanted to contribute to the family income by raising chickens. My father wasn't so sure about that. But to prove her wrong, he bought her 500 or so chicks. As it turned out, Mum was very successful with her chickens, and I got to practice my bookkeeping skills. My father's reaction was to buy more chicks for Mom! Wise man!

Even though I was brought up in a Christian family, and went to catechism class, Sunday school, and church regularly with my siblings, I didn't come to know the Lord personally until I was about seventeen. My oldest sister, Julia, was a Christian and had already decided to become a missionary. When I went to live with her in nearby Grand Rapids, I met Dr. DeHaan, who had just started his work in Radio Bible Class. Until that time I thought that because I was in the church, had gone through the catechism, was baptized, and then joined the church that I was "in." When Julia took me to Dr. DeHaan's church, I didn't particularly like the church and didn't listen. Used to a quiet, reverent service, I thought the church was too noisy. I just wanted to get out of there. But when I got to the door, a lady said to me, "Sister, are you saved?"

Well, they didn't say "Sister" in my church! I answered, "I don't know."

The lady asked, "Well, are you born again?"

I didn't know the answer to that one either.

Well, at that, the lady just took me by the sleeve and said, "I'm going to call Dr. DeHaan to talk to you."

I didn't want to talk to Dr. DeHaan, but the lady held on, and Dr. DeHaan came and talked to me. Since my sister took her Bible to church, I carried one too. As our church had Bibles in the pews, we didn't have to take our Bibles. Dr. DeHaan said, pointing to my Bible, "Do you believe this is the Word of God?"

I said, "Of course I do, from Genesis to Revelation."

He said, "Do you believe Jesus died for your sins?"

I said, "Of course I do. He died for the sins of the whole world." Being a proud Dutchman, I thought I'd let him know I knew a little something and quoted John 3:16 to him.

He said, "That's right, and verse 36 says, 'He that believeth on the Son hath everlasting life: and he that believeth not the Son shall not see life, but the wrath of God abideth on him.' Now, Sister, do you have the Son of God or the wrath of God?" He nailed me! He said, "You go home alone with the Lord and just tell Him you want the Son of God. Ask Him to forgive you, and just invite Him into your heart."

The Holy Spirit then took over, and that was it!

While I was living in Grand Rapids, I worked for the Klingman family, who were well-known owners of a successful Michigan furniture factory. I cooked for this wealthy family and took care of their little boy. I had my own private room and bath in their home. I ate lunch with the little boy every day at noon; the family had their formal dinner at night. Oh, I just loved the beautiful spode china and the sterling silver and other lovely things. Every stick of furniture in their house was custom made. I just loved to polish the beautiful all-cherry dining room furniture. The living room was something else again. The bedrooms were just…well, the man of the house had designed the furniture himself. I was going to have a house like that myself someday, I decided, including all the bone china and all the silverware and all the furniture. I was *not* going to the mission field! I was sure I couldn't eat rice, and I was sure I couldn't eat with chopsticks! Those were my good excuses!

All this time my sister Julia was trying to talk me into going to Moody Bible Institute with her to study to become a missionary. Then our church had a missionary conference. At the end an invitation was given to anyone who had dedicated his or her life to God to stand up. Everybody stood up except another girl and me. She and I were pals, and we stood together as the black sheep in this church. Right at the end the speaker, CIMer Dr. Issac Page, said, "Now those who have never stood up and to whom the Lord is speaking, you stand up and tell the Lord you're ready to go." It was as if the Holy Spirit put His hands under my elbows and lifted me up. I couldn't have stayed seated if I tried. That night I dedicated my life to the Lord.

After the service we went to my brother's home, a hangout where the young people always went for a cup of coffee after church. Everybody there was excited about the meeting. "Now, Sadie, you send in your application first thing tomorrow morning," chirped Julia enthusiastically. "Get it in and then we can go [to Moody] together."

This was February, and Julia was going to leave in September. That Monday Julia took ill with the flu. The people she was working for tried to get her out to our parents' home in Allendale. But as a blizzard had blocked the roads, they rushed her to the hospital instead. Julia died during the night before anyone in the family even had a chance to see her.

After that I turned against the Lord. "I just *will not, I cannot* go if

I can't go with Julia." I fought my anger all through the summer. But the Holy Spirit spoke to me through my misery. My dad had always taught us as children, "You promise anything, you keep your promise." Since I had promised the Lord, I didn't dare *not* go. Yet I didn't *want* to go.

Finally in mid-summer I went to John Smitter, my Sunday school teacher. (His family owned Smitter's Men's Clothing Store in Burton Heights). I told him, "I'm so miserable I don't know what to do. I don't dare *not* go because I promised the Lord." I worried that I wouldn't even get to Heaven if I disobeyed the Lord.

Mr. Smitter said, "Sadie, don't worry about that. You pray that if it's the Lord's will for you not to go, He'll just close the door. If the Lord doesn't want you, He won't let you go." Nobody ever prayed harder for a door to be closed than I did!

But the Lord didn't close the door. I applied to Moody, and, wouldn't you know it, I was accepted. So when September came, I *had* to go.

I was at Moody only a few months when my money ran out. This would be the first of many times that my money would run low. On this occasion my brother Ben, who had borrowed money from me, made a surprise payment. Then Faith Leeuwenberg from China sent $5.00, which had been on the way for *months.* It arrived just at the right time. Then a missionary friend in Africa sent me $2.00.

That kind of provision kept me in Moody for the three years until graduation. It convinced me that I was in the Lord's will. The Lord's timing is perfect as long as we keep following. You've got to do His will because He's not going to do yours!

One Sunday after I had written a letter to the folks I did not have a three-cent stamp and had no money to buy one. I laid the letter on my desk and said, "Lord, if you want Mom to have this letter, then give me money for a stamp." I didn't tell Him what to do, but I might as well have, because I was sure someone would give me a nickel tip at work! That was what *I* thought would happen.

But that's not what the Lord had in mind. I was running downtown on Monday morning on my way to work and, there on the sidewalk, were stamps! I stopped, picked them up, held them before the Lord and said, "Thank you, Lord, I'll never doubt you again! You can do it!"

One teacher at Moody who especially impressed me was Kenneth Wuest. No matter what class it was, I sensed the Lord was there. I discovered the secret at our junior-senior banquet. Mr. and Mrs. Wuest were seated at my table. During the meal I thanked him for the blessing he had been in my life. He pointed at his wife and said, "There's the cause." He then told how, when he and his wife were young, they had applied to go to the mission field but were turned down because of health. After that Mrs. Wuest dedicated her life to praying for him as he trained young people to go to the mission field. He went on to say, "Every time I go to a class, my wife goes to the bedroom and prays me through the class. And there's the secret." That was a real lesson in the importance of prayer. It spurred me on to make conversation with God a significant part of my everyday life.

My schedule at Moody was a very busy one. On a typical day I would leave class at 11:20 a.m., run all the way downtown to work at the lunch counter at Woolworth's, change my clothes, eat a sandwich, and be on the floor by 11:45. I worked until 2:15 p. m. and then ran all the way home to study until 5:00. I ate early supper, then dashed off to the YWCA to work in the dining room. Mondays were my day off at the YMCA, so I would study all afternoon and go to the China Inland Mission meetings in the evening. I made only 20 cents an hour at my job, just enough to pay for my food but nothing else. I had to trust the Lord for everything—clothing, spending money, everything. One of China Inland Mission's principles was that its missionaries did not ask anyone for anything. I practiced that for three years at Moody, and that's how I learned to trust the Lord for everything.

Students at Moody were required to work in evangelism. Each student had to complete a certain number of assignment hours in factory witness, street preaching, mission work, teaching children, and reaching out to Jewish people before they could graduate. I had the joy of leading many people to the Lord through these assignments.

A special memory is one of leading a Chinese woman to the Lord. Though I was fairly certain that China was the place the Lord wanted me to go, I was not totally convinced. So for one term at Moody I decided I would not go to any China prayer bands. I went only to the South American, African, and Indian prayer bands so that I could soak in as much of other mission fields as possible. After that I told the Lord, "If you really want me to go to China, let me bring one Chinese person to Yourself." I had never done that—in fact, I had not even had contact with Chinese. Though I did not tell anybody of my prayer, the next term I was assigned to do my practical work in Chinatown. I was to teach Bible stories to the children and teach English to one of the mothers. This young mother I had the privilege of leading to the Lord!

As graduation day grew near, I was very excited. Again, money became an issue. I needed $7.00 for my graduation pictures. On June 21st I received $4.00 from a brother and $3.00 from Pop and Mom. Again, the Lord answered my prayers.

With her children clustered around her, the young mother I led to the Lord to confirm the Lord's leading to China.

In October 1934 I sent my first letter to China Inland Mission (CIM). I then claimed Deuteronomy 31:8: "And the Lord, he it is that doth go before thee. He will be with thee, he will not fail thee, neither forsake thee: fear not, neither be dismayed." When I received my medical papers from CIM the following March, I returned them almost immediately. But then in April I received a disappointing letter from the mission. CIM was not allowing any women to go to China because it was too dangerous. Communist insurgents in China had captured young missionaries John and Betty Stam and beheaded them.

I was, indeed, disappointed not to be able to move forward in my application to CIM. The devil whispered, "See Sadie, you're not going to China. The Lord doesn't want you in China."

But then that night I opened my Bible to my daily reading. God's answer to Satan's insinuations: "Behold I have set before thee an open door, and no man can shut it" (Rev. 3:8). ∞

Chapter 2

Promised Open Door

Finally on August 1, 1935, I graduated from Moody Bible Institute. What bittersweet feelings I had!—a mixture of excitement over graduating and disappointment at not being able to go on the mission I had been working so hard for! I claimed Philippians 4:19, as I had often before: "But my God shall supply all your need according to his riches in glory by Christ Jesus."

Then, to add more bricks to the barriers ahead of me, I received a letter from the new CIM Candidate Secretary saying, "We have read your letter, and I'm not satisfied with your doctrinal paper." My response? I studied doctrine like never before! I memorized Scripture for months on end! Once again, I was forced to cling in faith to the Lord's promise from Revelation 3:8: "I know thy works: behold, I have set before thee an open door, and no man can shut it; for thou hast a little strength, and hast kept my word, and hast not denied my name."

Returning to Michigan from Moody, I worked in Grand Rapids in a ladies hat and dress shop. I moved in with my brother John and his wife Dorothy. Because Dorothy was quite ill at that time, I helped take care of their three little boys.

In looking back, I find that these are the only months in this five-year diary that there are almost no entries. It probably reflects how despondent I felt. Then, praise the Lord, I received an encouraging letter from CIM on December 30th, 1935! My spirits soared. "His ear is not heavy that he cannot hear!" I wrote in my diary, reflecting my rejoicing and excitement.

At the beginning of 1936 I chose Psalm 27:14 as my verse for the year: "Wait on the Lord: be of good courage, and he shall strengthen thine heart. Wait, I say, on the Lord." And wait, I did. I was expecting great things from God.

Late in March the long-awaited letter from CIM arrived, inviting me to the Philadelphia headquarters for a candidates' course. My diary entry that night reflects my confidence in the way ahead:

> He cannot fail, for He is God;
> He cannot fail, He's pledged His word.
> He cannot fail; He'll see you through.
> 'Tis God with whom you have to do.
> (Source unknown)

Mid-June I boarded a train headed for Philadelphia. During my weeks at CIM headquarters my diary entries were full of Mr. and Mrs. Judd, the Candidate Secretary and his wife. They were the godliest people I had ever met. My days were filled with classes and studying. Learning Chinese was hard for me, but I continued to lean on the Lord.

During my time at candidate school, all the other young women were called in for interviews except me. I thought, *Oh, they're not even considering me*. I was still suffering from an inferiority complex from not having completed normal high school, although I did complete the entire high school coursework my first year at Moody. As all the other candidates had more education than I, I was sure CIM leaders were not considering me.

But then I did get called before the Council. Dr. Robert Glover, Home Director for North America, was first to question me. "Miss Custer," he said, "if you went to China and you met bandits and they took all of your things, what would you do?"

I said, "Well, everything I have belongs to the Lord. I guess He can do with it as He pleases." I wasn't expecting that kind of question. Perhaps the Council wasn't expecting that kind of answer either!

And then somebody else asked me, "Could you live with others?"

"Well," I said, "I come from a family of eight children, and we got along pretty well." To myself I thought, *Come on, get on with it*!

And then there was Dr. Clarence Mason from Philadelphia Bible College (I had been told that he was a crack on doctrine). "Miss Sadie," he said, "what do you believe on inspiration of the Scripture?" I quoted appropriate Scriptures.

"Miss Custer, what would you do if you didn't have anything to eat?"

"Well," I replied, "I lived at Moody for three years, and I trusted the Lord for everything. He hasn't failed me yet; I don't expect Him to fail me now."

And I was accepted! I could hardly believe it.

I returned home to prepare for the long journey ahead.

I marvel when I look back at how the Lord provided for me. My own church, the Open Bible Church, wanted to support me. In order to do so, however, the congregation planned to drop a couple that they had been supporting in China because they were not members of our church. They were also China Inland Mission members. I was just a farm kid and didn't even know if I could learn the language. I told the church I did not agree with their dropping this couple and that I would just trust the Lord. After I went out to the field my family wrote that they would take on my support. I wrote back and said, "I will not take your support if you're going to stop giving to your local church, because that wouldn't be fair." So the family decided they would double tithe. And that's what they did. The Lord's way is perfect! He never left me without support.

Early September 1936 I boarded a train in Grand Rapids to start on my long journey to China. Mom and Pop and several other family members accompanied me that day. I had never in my life seen my pop shed tears. Later a family member told me that, as the train was leaving, Pop cried and said, "I'll never see my Sadie again."

I must admit there were times in later years ahead⁻such as when the bombs were falling in Nancheng⁻that I too wondered whether I would ever see home again. ೞ

Chapter 3

The Journey

Friday, September 11, 1936, was the BIG day. At 3:30 that cool, but fair afternoon in Seattle forty other missionary ladies and I boarded a Japanese liner bound for China. Of the forty of us aboard, twenty were from the China Inland Mission, including my two cabin mates, Margaret and Maybeth. We scrambled excitedly to get settled for the journey up the coast and across the Pacific.

The ship churned its way from the docks at 4:15 in the afternoon. With the heavy salt air blowing against my face, I leaned against the rail and watched as the city skyline receded, replaced by hillside neighborhoods and then wooded areas with driftwood- and rock-strewn beaches. The cliff-marred shoreline and hills behind almost glowed in the late afternoon sunshine as we headed north. The journey along Washington's rugged coastline would be the last most of us would see of America for several years. For me it would be more years than I could imagine then.

On Saturday the ship tied up at the docks in Vancouver, where we took advantage of the opportunity for a few hours of shopping. When I reboarded the ship, I learned that my trunks were missing. We sailed off again at 2:00. As we chugged across the Pacific Ocean, we spent our time in prayer meetings, studying, hymn sings, writing letters and, of course, playing games, walking the deck, enjoying tea parties and other recreational activities.

Tuesday the 15th was a rough day on board. The rain pelted down, and the wind stirred up huge waves. My verse for the day was Joshua 1:6, "Be strong and of a good courage...." The tossing ship made sleeping difficult that night. I was up by 4:15 a.m. on Wednesday, walking the deck. Later I studied Chinese with several of the other girls. It was rainy and dreary all day. Thursday was another grand day (to me!)—nice and rough! Maybeth, however, didn't think it was grand as she was sick all day. She wasn't alone either!

Good news: they found my trunks!

The next few days were uneventful except that one evening we had our first Japanese dinner of frog legs. Just to be authentic, we all sat on the floor. On Wednesday the 23rd we were warned that a typhoon would be in the area by nighttime. We finally spotted land on Thursday. In the evening we attended a Captain's dinner and later enjoyed a hymn-sing on deck. No mention of the typhoon.

At last, on Friday, we steamed into the harbor at Yokohama, Japan. When our feet first hit the ground, the ground felt like it was moving. Once we got our land legs, however, we enjoyed a morning of shopping. In the evening we went to Kamubrun to see the big Buddha. I found the sight of the people worshiping this huge idol overwhelming.

The next day we CIMers boarded a train headed for Tokyo. We were twenty foreigners in a strange land. We must have been quite a sight to the local people!

On Sunday the captain of the ship came to Miss Lang, our chaperone, to inform us that the incessant rain had hindered their unloading of the ship. For this reason we passengers would have to take the train to Kobe to make connections with our next ship. We were to have our baggage ready for customs inspection in two hours—all 133 pieces of it!! Happily Miss Lang, by hard and fast talk, persuaded the company to have all our baggage banded through—except the cases we needed for that night.

The Japanese shipping company's representative took wonderful care of us. He not only met us and took us through Tokyo, the company paid every cent of our expenses that day, even the tips for meals and taxi fares. They sent five taxis to the ship to take us to the train station. The captain, purser, and chief steward all joined the company representative at the station to see us off. The captain even gave us a beautiful bouquet of flowers.

We traveled all day by train. How I wished my family could have been with us! I had never seen such beautiful scenery in all my life. As the country is very mountainous, the farmers had terraced mountain sides into small plots. Even if the fields were only an acre or two, they planted it in little sixteen-foot squares with a hedge or a row of flowers around each one. It was just beautiful, so neat and attractive. The main crops were rice, tea, mulberries, and small vegetables such as onions and radishes.

We enjoyed a grand four-course dinner on the train. I didn't know what some of the things were, but I ate them anyway. When we got to our station in Kobe, the shipping company had a representative there to meet us and to take care of our baggage. Six taxis were waiting to take us to the Oriental Hotel.

"Boy, oh boy, what a swell place!" was how I described that hotel in a letter at the time. We were two in a room, and each room was very large with a private bath and beautiful sitting room. We even had our own telephone. Sad part was that we had no one to call! The rate for our room was $10.00 a day! I could hardly imagine myself, a farm girl, in all this class! I enjoyed it to the full, however, especially since we didn't have to pay for any of it.

The captain of our new ship, the *President Grant*, said we were fortunate that we traveled by train, as there had been a fierce typhoon at sea. Out of full hearts we praised the Lord.

Sailing out of Kobe, we traveled the Japan Inland Sea for the next few days, headed for Nagasaki, then westward toward

Shanghai, China. During those final days aboard ship the sea remained choppy; the sunsets, beautiful.

As China came into distant view, our excitement mounted. We couldn't help but wonder what lay ahead. ☙

Chapter 4

Greenhorns in China

Mid-afternoon October 1, 1936, we caught our first excited glimpse of the busy Shanghai harbor. China at last! My first impression of this country was that coolies swarmed everywhere!

After a few days in the mission home in Shanghai we traveled to the language school in Yangchow City in the Province of Kiangsu. We left the mission home for the Shanghai train station in taxis—with all our bags and baggage. From there we took the train to Chinkiang. The trains were very nice, although not Pullmans!! Though the seats were simple wooden ones, I found them to be quite comfortable. One advantage the Chinese trains have over the Japanese is that the spittoons were under the seats instead of in the middle of the aisle.

Hungrily we watched the passing scenery as we rumbled through the countryside. Most of the houses we could see seemed small, one-story buildings made of bamboo covered in mud with bamboo roofs. They appeared to have only one room. Just outside each house was a small bamboo canopy under which an ox might be trudging along, turning a worn millstone. The farmers still used oxen and buffaloes to work their ground.

In Chinkiang we climbed into an old Ford truck for the ride to the river. Perched in back on seats eight inches wide and running lengthwise, we hung on for dear life as the driver tore down one-lane streets and careened around sharp corners. I thought the trip lots of fun and enjoyed it to the full.

Our truck reached the river just in time for us to clamber onto the ferry. I sat on the edge of the crowded vessel, way up in the front point. The river water was yellowish about the color of navy bean soup! We managed to get across the river safely and then heaved ourselves onto another truck. This truck took us to a channel, which we had to cross on a little barge so loaded that everyone had to stand up. Two men pushed us across with long bamboo poles.

When we reached Yangchow, we discovered that the only means of travel were wheelbarrows and small buggy-like rickshaws, both man-powered. We were supposed to finish our journey in rickshaws, but because we thought we looked too conspicuous, we chose to walk. While a few of the five- or six-foot-wide streets were cobbled with stones, most of them were just plain mud, made muddier by people throwing all their wash water out in the street. Ten-foot high walls lined the mess and tangle of streets with no street running straight for more than a block. Square openings in the walls led to shops and homes.

The daily activities of the people spilled out into the street. As we walked through the city, we saw women doing their family laundry, squatting in the street and using only a little basin of water in the process. Others were cooking, sewing, knitting, or kneading bread. It was a marvel to me how the people lived, with their houses jammed one right next to the other in one solid mass.

Yangchow would be home for us, at least for a few months. When we reached the language school premises, the women in charge of the home gave us a warm welcome. What a treat it was that first afternoon to pull our clothes out of suitcases and hang them up! But best of all, my friend Evangeline Kok was my roommate. Evangeline and I had been roommates at Moody and had become good buddies. I was sure we would have a good time together.

Over the months we discovered the city of Yangchow to be one of the most backward in China. The old city wall had thirteen gates. The sights and smells assaulted my senses.

When out for a walk, we noticed that most of the older women hobbled around on bound feet. Their feet had been bound when they were babies so that as adults their feet were only three or four inches long. One day I even saw a man with an old-fashioned "queue." His hair was all shaved off from the front of his head, with a long braid dangling down his back.

The children stopped their play to watch us curiously with their pretty dark eyes surrounded by smudged faces. Even in October many of them were already in their wadded gowns for the winter.

Eventually 52 young women of many different nationalities settled into life at the Yangchow language school. But the building was large and accommodating with classrooms and a big dining room downstairs and twenty-five bedrooms upstairs. Our room was large with a door opening onto a porch. We each had a cot bed with a straw tick for a mattress. I slept like a log. We had a wash stand and had to carry our water up every night. The bathtubs were big tin ones. We bought our hot water from the street for our weekly bath. We each had a kerosene lamp in our room. Electricity was on only at certain hours. Every night we would take our flashlights and make a parade to the outhouse. I was amused by the reactions of the girls who hadn't been brought up on a farm.

Early in our sojourn at language school the Chinese tailor came to measure us for Chinese gowns. Even so, wearing the gowns we must have looked most peculiar to the Chinese. Within ten minutes of going out for a walk we would attract a crowd. Some were looking at our big feet, others at our green or blue eyes.

Yet I was perfectly happy because I knew I was in the place God had chosen for me. I wouldn't have traded places with anyone.

Language school was difficult for me, however. Even though I loved learning the language and studied from morning until night, I did not do well at first. About three weeks into the course three ladies who were China-born were promoted to a more advanced class. A couple of weeks later another group was put in a class by themselves. That left only two other girls and me. Then to add to my self-doubts, the temined not to let her comment discourageacher said to me one day, "I don't know why you ever came to China. You're never going to get the language." I simply thanked her and kept on struggling, determined not to let her comment discourage me.

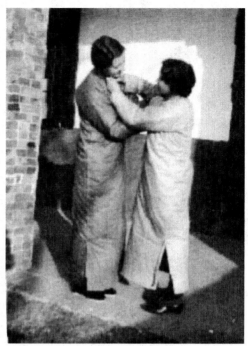

Evangeline Kok (left) and I help each other button our wadded gowns in language school.

From the book They Called Us White Chinese *by Robert N. Tharp. Used by permission.*

I think I had difficulty learning the language because Chinese is a tonal language, and I did not have an ear for music. I couldn't distinguish one tone from the other. As it turned out, what I learned at language school did not help me much when I got to my assigned center. I couldn't understand a word because the people spoke a completely different dialect. So I had to start right from the bottom again. Actually I learned the language best of all right from the people.

As hard as the tonal spoken language was for me, I was fascinated with the Chinese characters used in the written language. For example, the word "come" shows the whole crucifixion story: it is a cross with a man on it and a man on each side. For the word "happiness" you put God first, then yourself and next your possessions. The Chinese language also provided a good opening to talk about God to the people. For example, the word for "ship" is a boat with eight people inside. I could ask an educated man, "Where did that word come from?" He would tell me that it was an ancient character and then tell me a story of a great flood. That would lead right into the Bible story of Noah and the ark.

We had to dress warmly, as the temperature was between 30 and 40 degrees. We wore wadded gowns and hand-made Chinese shoes and during study hours wrapped ourselves in our steamer rugs. With a little oil burner going in the middle of the room, we were really very comfy!

One day on an outing several of us walked up on the city wall for about a mile. It was the first good look I had into the homes of the people. Such poverty! In one place we counted thirty-one homes packed into a space about the size of my parents' yard back home. They were made out of straw and were only about nine feet long and six feet wide. Even so, judging from the number of children we saw, families seemed to be large.

I wa struck by the sight of so many mothers holding babies in their laps with hardly enough clothes to keep the babies warm. In spite of the poverty, the women were smoking cigarettes. I had read that the aim of one of the American tobacco companies was "to put a cigarette in the mouth of every man, woman, and child in China." They certainly had come a long way in accomplishing that goal. How wonderful it would be if Western Christians would tend to their business that well and make an effort to reach every Chinese at least once with the Gospel!

I was surprised to see the conditions in which the people lived. I thought that this city would be fairly modern as it was quite near the coast. I discovered that very few cities in China were as old or so far behind the times. Seeing the poor of the city made my heart bleed. Some of the beggars were suffering from leprosy. Parts of their faces or hands or feet were terribly distorted with the dreadful disease. They would bow with their faces to the earth, bumping their heads on the ground seeking in this way to obtain some favor with their gods. We could only stand and look at them and pray for them; in the first weeks we were unable to say a word. We pleaded with the Lord to give us the language quickly. ෩

Chapter 5

Beginnings in Xin Ji

When CIM leaders told me that I would be sent to Shensi Province, the news floored me. I knew absolutely nothing about Shensi. Nevertheless, I said, "Thank you, Lord. I asked you to choose, and I believe you did, and I'll go."

Secretly I had hoped to be sent to Gansu, because that's where my good friend Faith Leeuwenberg was. Faith was from my home church and was the only missionary with whom I had regularly corresponded. But I promised the Lord I would go wherever He sent me. I knew He would not make a mistake.

After I moved to the village of Xin Ji in the province of Shensi in late May 1937, I came to realize that this place was exactly what I wanted. I fear if I had gone to Gansu, I would not have lasted more than a couple of years. Liangchow, Gansu, where Faith was, was an old, established center. The original missionary there, a very wealthy Englishman, had spent all his money on building the place and providing things for the Chinese. Xin Ji was a new place. The village boasted just one old baptized Christian man, Carpenter Chin, and a handful of other believers. Carpenter Qin (we spelled his name Chin) was uneducated and couldn't read, but he had so completely changed that anywhere we missionaries went to tell about the Lord, the people would say, "Oh, that's the religion of Carpenter Qin."

The mission's plan was to rent a house for ten years with the goal that the church would be self-supporting at the end of that time. Thus right from the beginning, my co-worker and I trained the people to trust the Lord just as we did. My fellow worker was Bertha Silversides, an experienced missionary from Canada.

Carpenter Qin in the courtyard in front of our quarters in the house the misision rented for us in Xin Ji. Our dining room was to the left with my bedroom above it. The sitting room, with Bertha's bedroom above it, is to the right.

When Bertha and I traveled the 18 English miles from Nancheng (now Hanzhong) to Xin Ji my first time, we came in sedan chairs because the weather had turned very hot. In nice weather we would walk. Sedan chairs were boxlike conveyances with a seat inside and were carried on poles resting on men's shoulders. (See cover.) Bertha was riding ahead of me. The road much of the way was a narrow footpath running along dikes between fields—some of them flooded rice fields. I watched Bertha as her men carried her through creeks or tried to jump over a ditch with her, and I wondered what would happen when my men came along with their heavy load. I must confess I felt more comfortable when they let us get out to jump over the ditches ourselves!

Our gatekeeper was supposed to come out to meet us, but he was so busy preaching that when we passed him, he didn't see us at first. Then he came running to meet us.

My, it was good to meet the Christians in Xin Ji! Mrs. Wu¯ a dear Bible woman about fifty years old—worked with us. Although she had little bound feet and could hardly walk, she still went out from early morning until late at night preaching the Gospel. She was almost blind and, though she could not read, could she ever quote Scripture! She planned to go for some eye treatment. As soon as she could see, she let us know, she wanted to learn to read. Our gatekeeper spent most of his time preaching too. They were pleased to see a new missionary. Together we were a great team.

Mrs. Wu especially was valuable to me in my greenhorn days. Unlike some Chinese shy of foreigners, she was not afraid to correct either my language mistakes or other, sometimes more serious blunders. Early on, for instance, I had given a well-memorized version of the way of salvation in Chinese, when Mrs. Wu drew me aside after we were out of earshot and scolded: "Teacher, you told about Jesus dying on the cross for our sins, but you didn't tell about the resurrection. You left Jesus *dead* in these people's minds—you left Him in the grave!"

Our team in 1938 in front of the entrance to our Xin Ji quarters: (Standing, left to right) Mrs. Tan, househelper; Mr Yang, evangelist; Mr. Cheng, cook; and me. (Sitting) Bertha Silversides of Canada and Mrs. Wu, Bible woman.

That was a lesson I never forgot.

Sunday was a highlight of the week. By the time we finished breakfast about eight o'clock, some of the folk from the country were already gathering for service. The benches were about three feet high and six inches wide. We sat through the whole service from shortly after eight o'clock until twelve. My bench felt as sharp as a knife by noon, but the Chinese did not seem to mind in the least. In fact, some of them were still there when we finished our dinner. Old Carpenter Chin stayed until dark. The next morning he was back on the scene when we had our Chinese prayers at six-thirty.

All the people that came to service in Xin Ji were persecuted by their families. Their love for the Lord showed on their faces. In the early days twenty-four of the cutest children and a few adults turned up on Sunday afternoon for Sunday school.

My new home in Xin Ji was a rare one just like I had always wished I might have. It was a mud house. Three of our walls were also the walls of our neighbor's houses, and the front wall was the street. You can imagine how packed in we were! There was a place in front and in the back where we had openings in the roof to let some light in. The room against the street was a street chapel where meetings were held every other day—on market days. For our own use we had a dining room and a sitting room. Bertha's bedroom was above the dining room, and mine was above the sitting room. Our kitchen was a stove in the open place in the back.

We had to improvise a lot for dishes and utensils. A pretty pink powder jar received as a gift before I left home became our butter dish! Bertha had lost all the things she owned when the Reds visited her three years before. Before my things came through from Shanghai we were in a fix when we had company! It was really great fun; I loved it.

The day after market day, especially if we were expecting company, we sometimes had a rooster tied to the leg of the wheat grinder. We had to buy a live chicken for our meat. We could not kill it when the weather was hot because we had no way of keeping it fresh. We had some great fun with a rooster crowing away all day!

We had some other critters in the house too. Living so close to our neighbors, we had no way of keeping the rats out. We would wake up at night and find them playing tag on our beds. All we had to do was shine our flashlights on them, and they would scram! A lady in Nancheng told how she had made some blackberry tarts and put them away in her cupboard. She woke up that night and found two rats sitting beside her bed having a party on blackberry tarts.

I often woke up with my flashlight in my hand. My brother Bill did not know how much I appreciated his gift. We used those flashlights all the time as we had no electricity. We couldn't walk around much in the dark because we also had some snake friends who called on us occasionally. I did not see any, but Bertha said they were there, and I believed her.

As our walls were all whitewashed inside, everything looked nice and bright. With the few pretty things I brought from home, my room was very cheery. My bed was a wooden frame with ropes across for a spring. I found it quite comfy!

One of the first weeks that I was in Xin Ji the eldest son and wife of one of our church members had a newborn daughter. We went to congratulate them and pay our due respects. Because the Chinese made much of these events, of course, we had to do likewise. We had the gatekeeper go out and buy the gifts a little flour, a few eggs, a live chicken, and enough material to make the baby a dress—dark green with big pink flowers! Bertha and Mrs. Wu were going, and I was pleased when they said I could go along! Can't you just see us walking along the road with these things—especially the live chicken?!

This family lived a few miles out in the country in a one-room mud house with a straw roof. They were extremely poor. I had never been in a darker hovel in my life—not a sign of a window. The lady was lying on a board bed in one corner. It was so dark we could just manage to make out her face. We couldn't see the baby at all. In one corner of the house there was a big pile of wheat, and above that was a scaffold with a bit of straw. I think that was the grandfather's bed. The only bright spot was the group of Gospel posters pasted on the wall where there had been idols before the grandfather became a Christian.

It almost broke my heart to see such poverty. Yet I had never seen a happier man than that old man. After we arrived, the family served us a big bowl of eggs cooked in water. We sat on little wooden benches about a foot high to eat. With the flies trying relentlessly to share our meal, my dislike for eggs was greatly increased. Nevertheless, I must say, the eggs were cooked well and were not half bad.

Mrs. Wu talked to the lady for a while, as she and her husband were not Christians. Only the grandfather and his youngest son were believers. The old man had all the say in the house, much like in Bible times. When the sons married, the wives would come to live in their home.

About a month after I arrived in Xin Ji I experienced first hand the effects of the Sino-Japanese War. One night two Chinese soldiers came marching into our home and said they wanted to stay in our place for the night. We told them this was a Gospel hall, and we had no room for soldiers. They looked over the house and decided there was plenty of room, then left with the promise that they would be back in a few minutes.

After about five minutes around eighty soldiers shouldered their way in with all their paraphernalia. They filled the preaching hall and the househelpers' rooms and took complete possession of the whole front part of the house. They tried their best to get back in our rooms, but we managed to keep them out. The next morning a fresh batch came in and *demanded* our rooms for their officials, but we told them that that would be breaking the etiquette of their honorable country as we were only two women and could not have any men back there.

Of course, our visitors were good Chinese soldiers, so there was no great danger. These armies were always on the march. When they came to a city, they had absolutely no place to stay except in the homes of the people. Everybody had to put up a few of them. But we could not go outside of our rooms while they were in the house. If we had, they would have swiped everything they could lay their hands on. They borrowed plenty as it was.

Our househelp suffered more than we did because they got all the cursing and swearing. But they stuck up for us and took good care of us. No matter how tired they were, they would not go to bed at night without first properly locking us in. And dear Mrs. Wu, our Bible woman, was right on misbehaving soldiers' heels telling them where to get off! She was a regular mother to us.

We kidded about being well protected because we not only had eighty soldiers to watch out for us, but there were three policemen on guard all the time. Of course, they were for the officials, but we pretended they were for us. Not a soul could come inside of the building. One of the Christians tried three times every day to get in to see if there was anything we needed or if he could do anything for us, but the policemen would not let him in.

Happily the soldiers left after three days. When they had all gone, we felt like birds let out of a cage. We celebrated by going for a long walk out in the mountains.

Even though I was still struggling with the verbal language, I was most eager to start teaching Sunday school. I continued to practice by going out with Mrs. Wu every chance I got.

I had not yet received my trunks from Shanghai because the soldiers were using all the trucks. The mail was piled up at the post office at Paoki 3,000 bags high. It would take weeks to sort through it all.

We could no longer send letters by airmail because we were cut off from all communication from the coast. I had one letter from Mr. Gibb, director of the mission, but that was the only mail we had for several weeks. That letter was written August 25th, and in it he said conditions were getting serious.

We had heard rumors that the American consul had given orders for all Americans to leave, but no direct word had come through to us. I hoped it was not true as we had such high hopes for our work in the fall. If conditions were really that serious, of course, we had no choice but to obey orders. We patiently waited for more news.

I doubted whether any of my letters were reaching my family either. I felt so sorry for them. I knew they would be worried about me. I wished that I could fly over momentarily and tell them how safe and peaceful we were. Since that couldn't be done, all of us had to rest in the Lord.

One day Bertha and I went to visit the city official in Nancheng to find out how conditions were. He said it was safe to travel and gave us a letter to take to the city official who was under his charge, asking him to inform us in case of any trouble and to provide proper escort to return home in case of any brigands or other dangers. He did not profess to be a Christian but was always very kind to us. I was eager to get back to Xin Ji, but we were not able to leave Nancheng. A large band of brigands was operating near the city now that the soldiers had left.

When the way opened to return to Xin Ji, we had quite a time getting home. When our *hua-kans* (sedan chairs) came, they were all old rickety ones, and we did not think any of them would hold up until we got to Xin Ji. As there were no others available, we had to take a chance. We started out and got as far as the Nancheng city gate. There the soldiers stopped us and made a big fuss because we did not get out to go through the gate. While that used to be the custom, we were told that no one practiced it anymore. After we got out and showed our cards, they told us to be on our way.

By this time the sheet I had stretched over the *hua-kan* for protection from the sun came down, and I had to take it off. Bertha went a bit farther and then had to take hers off as well. The road looked like and had the consistency of a luscious caramel pudding that did not quite thicken.

Bertha's men entertained themselves by swearing at each other all the way. We had to cross six rivers and streams, and sometimes our carriers would stop in the middle of a river to curse each other. Bertha once looked back at me and remarked, "It'll be a miracle if they don't throw me in!" I could not help but laugh at her.

My men often fell down. First the front man fell in the middle of a creek and left me with my feet dangling in the water. Shortly after that he slipped in the mud and went down into the rice field beside the road. This ruined him for the whole journey, as he was nervous. The very sight of a slippery place almost made him fall. With the mud about a foot deep, each time one of the men went down, they left me standing in mud that came over the top of my galoshes. The front man went down five times, and the back one twice. I was a sight for sore eyes when I got home. My gown, stockings, shoes—everything was one mess of sticky clay! The men looked even worse.

Just after we had finished our breakfast one day one of our little Sunday school girls came running in screaming for all she was worth. She ducked inside the door with her father right behind, waving a big club. I never saw a man so mad in my life all because his chicken had run away, and the neighbors killed it and ate it. The poor girls in China had to take the blame for everything. Ordered around like slaves, they were often treated worse than the dogs on the street. This poor girl ran into the househelpers' kitchen, behind the stove and yelled bloody murder! Mrs. Wu held the man and got in between him and the girl. By this time we were all out there and simply forbade the man to beat his child in our home. Mrs. Wu held him until the girl could get away. He took after her, and I was afraid she received the beating after all.

In October I went on my first mountain trip. Early in the morning Bertha and I, plus Mrs. Wu and the little lady that helped us in the house, started off. Mr. Chin came along too and carried a load for us. We made quite a parade as we marched the eight miles to the foot of the first mountain, then filed along the narrow mountain trails. Once we reached the mountains, the scenery was beautiful.

We must have crossed the same river about a dozen times. I thought it was fun! There were no bridges, but in the shallow part big stones were placed strategically. Bertha and I jumped from one stone to another easily. Mrs. Wu, with her bound feet, would get on a stone in the middle of the river. Then, while putting forth all her effort to keep her balance on the stone, she would call us, "Oh, *Chiao-si,* (Chinese for "teacher") come quick and pull me over." Back I would go to get her. She had a keen sense of humor and just kept us in fits of laughter all the way. If she or anyone else fell in, she always thought it a huge joke.

We found that the old man in whose home we were to stay was very sick. He had been a Christian only about a year. The first few months he came to church every Sunday and often brought others with him. He had broken off his opium smoking and had taken down all his idols. Those near him were keen to hear the Gospel.

But he had been sick now for months so ill, in fact, that I was afraid he would die before we left. The oldest son decided that since the old man was going to die anyway, he wanted the idols back up; so they were back in their old place. Discouraged, the old man thought that God did not or would not answer his prayers. All the folk who had been eager to hear the Gospel were now afraid to believe. They thought the former gods were punishing him for becoming a Christian. The old man had heard so little of the Gospel that he couldn't defend himself. We were praying that he would get well and still be able to win those folk for Christ.

Though we walked into a rather difficult situation, the people gave us a warm welcome. I wish you could have seen these folk as they had their first look at a foreigner. They would feel of us, inspect what we were wearing, ask what we ate, etc., as though they couldn't quite decide whether we were human or not!

As soon as we arrived, they made a dinner for us, consisting of *mien* (narrow noodles made only of flour and water) along with green pepper and a vegetable that looked a little like spinach but tasted like weeds. I managed to get three bowls of that down; Bertha had two, and each of the Chinese had seven or eight. It is most embarrassing not to be able to eat as much as they do because they think I don't like their food.

For the people in the mountains cracked corn (much like we feed our chickens) cooked to a mush without any salt was a staple seven days a week. They ate the *mien* they served us only on special occasions. They ate too few vegetables, often only a bit of very hot green chili pepper.

This day the women in this mountain village were all sitting around a huge wooden tub shelling corn. We joined them and, while the corn was being shelled, Mrs. Wu preached almost constantly. They marveled that a foreign teacher could shell corn! By the time dusk was falling, several of the neighbor women had heard that foreigners were in the town and came to have a look.

When at six o'clock and darkness had moved in, we went to our room, feeling quite ready for bed. But, lo and behold, the lady of the house came in with a bowl of fat pork boiled with some turnips for us! By this time the men were all in from the field, and crowds of people were standing around to watch us eat. Before we finished the first bowl the old woman came around with a second one for each of us. By this time we were more than ready for bed. Then the old gentleman announced that there was to be a meeting in our bedroom! About thirty people had crowded into the room by this time. Once more we pulled out our chorus sheets for a sing, and Mrs. Wu preached. It was nine o'clock before the last of the people were ready to go home.

The next question was how to get undressed and into bed. A large opening served as a window. It had no glass, no paper, nor even a curtain of any kind, and *always* curious eyes were peeking in to see these funny creatures. I felt as if I were a monkey in a zoo! Mrs. Wu and other women also slept in the same room. They stretched out on a straw mat on the floor. The bed assigned to Bertha and me looked like a big wooden box, six inches high and just wide enough for the two of us. A bit of straw covered the bottom. As the two of us had each brought a quilt, we spread one under us and one over us. We put out our light⎯just a little iron dish of vegetable oil with a string in it for a wick⎯slipped off our top gown, and slid under the quilt for the night.

I slept like a log, and never heard a thing all night. Bertha was awake several times. One baby or another apparently cried most of the night. And since a full moon was shining brightly that night, the men were plowing by its light. Every hour or so they came in to have a smoke, walking right through our room.

The next morning we got up and cooked our own breakfast of *mien* and a little vegetable with vinegar and salt for flavoring. Because the people were so very poor, we had brought some of our own *mien* and vegetables. We did not take a bit more along than necessary. As it was, they thought we were millionaires!

All that day Mrs. Wu, Bertha, and I visited the mountain homes. To get from place to place, we had to climb up and over lots of large rocks. Sometimes we had to crawl on all-fours. In every home we asked if they had ever heard of the Gospel. None had. Since travel was difficult and since all the women and girls had tightly bound feet, very few of them had ever been out of their own village.

We visited one man who had been coming to services and seemed to believe. With his elderly mother he lived about half way up a mountain in a tiny one-room mud house with a straw roof. What a joy to visit the man! Neither he nor his mother would let us leave without eating. While he ran to the neighbors for some bowls and chopsticks, his mother cooked some rice and sweet potato. Several other people came in while we were there.

When we were ready to leave, the mother wanted to give us some persimmons to take along. The son determinedly insisted we could not carry them and told us to go ahead, and he would bring the fruit to us. We got home about four o'clock and found the man waiting with a big basket of persimmons. He brought them into our room and sat down. We then realized why he was so eager to bring the fruit to us. He was full of questions. He wanted to know how he should live, what he should do, what he should eat, etc., now that he was a Christian. When we were in his home, he was reluctant to ask us in front of so many neighbors.

Another night we had a service in our room. Mrs. Wu had to do nearly all the preaching because Bertha could not make the people understand, much less me! The language in the mountains was quite different from the dialect we spoke.

The next morning, just as we were crawling out of bed, the lady of the house came in with a bowl of bean curd. It was beans ground to a powder, soaked in water, and then let set until it jellied. It was the foulest stuff I had ever tasted! But that was just an appetizer! When we went to eat our breakfast, she came along with a big bowl of corn porridge.

After breakfast and a brief service we started for home. We traveled a different way, a few miles further, but a lovely trip. In several villages along the way we found people who had never heard the Gospel. We preached in some of the villages and only left tracts at others.

This road we took went straight up one side of a mountain almost to the top, then circled around the top, and came straight down the other side to the valley. We would climb for about half an hour, then sit in the shade of a tree and eat persimmons. It was like being on a picnic. The whole path all the way up and down again was stones and, oh, so steep. After five hours we arrived home tired and with blistered feet.

My first year in China went so quickly that it was over before I knew it. It was a wonderful year because it seemed the Lord was nearer and more precious than ever before. Of course, I missed my family. I marveled that the Lord ever counted me worthy of the privilege of bearing His name in China. If it were not that He can use the weak and foolish things of this world to confound the wise, I should never have had this privilege. ◌

Chapter 6

Travel Adventures, War, Rituals and Rats

1938 began rather quietly for us. We still had to deal with rats trying to eat our food. Mosquitoes and fleas pestered us to no end in the warm weather. And mail delivery was ever so slow. I still loved my work, however.

We never knew what we would have to deal with next. One day the mud wall around our toilet caved in. We hired a carpenter to come and replace it with a wooden wall. The tools he had to work with were rare! Building the enclosure took the man more than four days. First he had to make his own boards. Next he put them together with wooden pegs. After that he made beams for the top and bottom with grooves and carved grooves for the boards to fit into—so the whole structure went up without a single nail!

My trips with Mrs. Wu always proved to be interesting. One day to get to the first village we had to cross a river on a pole about two inches thick stretched across the water and anchored to trees on each side. Wobbly we inched our way across. On the way back, we had to do the same thing again. This time, though, we had an audience of about twelve curious people. Mrs. Wu stood by as I cautiously mounted the pole, advising, "Don't be afraid,

Chiao-si just look straight up!"

On a typical day of teaching we would start off for town right after breakfast. Mrs. Wu came armed with a bag of tracts and posters. Often the way took us along narrow footpaths between rice fields, forcing us to go single file. If we met others, we would have to wait at a cross-path for them to pass.

If it were market day in Xin Ji, a great number of folk would be making their way along the paths. We might meet a group jammed up behind an old woman leading a poky pig to market. Among those behind her, ahead of us, or crossing our path might be a man with a huge basketful of charcoal strapped to his back, perhaps a man with a basket of rice dangling from each end of the pole across his shoulder, perhaps a couple of men shouldering a log between them, a little boy carrying live chickens tied up by their feet, or a man staggering under the weight of a bed. We would tag along in the parade or wait for people to pass and then continue on our way.

Sometimes the people we visited were very interested and listened; other times they appeared to be interested but then would ask questions like, "How much did your shoes cost? Is this [Mrs. Wu] your mother?" or "Why are your eyes green?"

One day on our travels Mrs. Wu asked an old lady we met if she had ever heard the Gospel. She said no and sat down on a stone beside the path while Mrs. Wu and I took out our posters and proceeded to preach to her. Since folks were just coming back from market, we soon had a large crowd of people listening. Most had found a stone for a perch. When we finished, the people begged us to preach all over again. Instead, we invited them to go back to the preaching hall, where an evangelist and others usually preached all day on market day.

In Xin Ji we held our first short-term Bible school, then a second, and also organized Christian Endeavor. Following our second Bible school, some of the new Christians, who had never before witnessed publicly for the Lord, started sharing their testimonies. Besides five new people attending services, a number of young believers were ready to be a part of our first baptismal service. What an encouragement to see how the Lord was answering our prayers!

Meanwhile, the Sino-Japanese war was still eating away at China like a giant cancer, inching its way closer to us. We were not afraid that the Japanese would visit us, as Xin Ji boasted nothing worth bombing. But one Sunday while I was teaching the class, the house suddenly began to tremble. Bertha came dashing out shouting, "An earthquake!" A little while later news came that nine enemy planes had dropped several bombs outside Nancheng..

The next day I was hanging up clothes when we heard the sound of airplanes again, very different from the ordinary ones. They did not go over us but we could hear them in the distance. This time twelve planes gave Nancheng another "shaking." We learned that they were trying to blow up the place where the gas was stored. We hoped they were satisfied and would not return.

Happily the Moores, our supervisors, and other folk in Nancheng were all safe. The first day their house shook so that part of the ceiling came down. But apart from that, the bombs did little damage to the mission center and nothing major to the city.

I wondered if my family had read in the newspaper that Nancheng had been bombed. Just in case, I quickly wrote to them to relieve their minds and let them know that I was still okay.

The Catholic missionaries were ordered to leave the country. Our Chinese friends were worried that my co-workers and I would have to leave as well—it had become very dangerous for some. We assured these kind people that we would not leave.

Life went on as usual for us. Yet we never knew what to expect next. One day Mr. Meng, a Christian, came to us very distressed. His sister-in-law, who lived in the same compound as he did, was very upset because her son had become a Christian. She blamed Mr. Meng because he had invited the missionaries into his home. She was afraid she would die without anyone to chant for her, burn paper on her grave, or perform any of the other heathen responses to a death. She warned her son that if he dared come to service again, she would bury him alive. To get at Mr. Meng, she filed false reports about him to the authorities. He had already been beaten once. He feared for his life. He was not afraid to die, he said, he just wanted us to pray for him.

At around this same time, while visiting one home, I witnessed one of the worst sights I had seen since coming to China. Two small children in the family had masses of ringworm spots as big as saucers from head to toe, and pus was just pouring out of them. The mother was calmly sitting by pulling off the scabs and rubbing on some awful-looking black medicine. I watched her for a little while, but it made me so sick that I almost fainted. The poor kids were wailing in terrible pain.

Another time I was sitting outside to study when a woman came up to me and asked me if I would buy her little girl. It was the season of the year when the Chinese in those days became very poor. They would sell almost anything to get food. Among the first things they would sell were their little girls. The usual price for a girl was twenty dollars and a piece of meat. People who had little boys would often buy these girls and keep them in their home until their sons were old enough to marry them. The life of the little girl was, indeed, a miserable one.

One time we picked some flowers that looked something like our lilacs. The Chinese had some superstition about those particular flowers and thought we were crazy for keeping them in our home.

The people of this area had a certain date when they took off their wadded gowns. By April that year, because the weather had turned very hot, we removed some of the layers under our wadded gowns. As hot as it was, the Chinese around us were still wearing their heavy winter clothes simply because the date had not yet come for taking them off.

The good news was that many people were so eager to hear the Gospel that they would walk miles and miles in all kinds of weather over all kinds of rough terrain to come to service. One

Sunday it rained so hard that we did not expect anyone for service. We were surprised when twelve men and three women came. Because they were covered with mud, first in the order of service was foot washing.

We were eagerly looking forward to the annual field conference for missionaries. It was supposed to be held in Sisiang in May. But because of the flood of refugees passing through the mission premises in Nancheng, where we would need to stay on the way, we wondered if it would occur. The Moores were hosting forty people there at one point. Happily the conference was held, and we were able to attend. We thoroughly enjoyed the fellowship of other English-speaking missionaries. We also got some much-needed rest.

An added blessing came in the form of rain. It rained so much after the conference was over that we could not travel and had to stay a few extra days. Although we were all eager to get back to our stations, that gave us more wonderful times of fellowship with each other and with the Lord in times of prayer. I can't tell you the joy that I felt—I saw Christ anew in all His love and beauty.

Traveling in China was never easy, and the trip home from the conference was no exception. We left Sisiang Monday morning, all traveling by sedan chair. We made quite a parade as ten chairs filed through the streets. Because of one of my carriers' inexperience and my not-so-light weight, I had to walk most of the way the first day—over fifteen miles. Monday night we stayed in an inn. Our crowd was quite a source of entertainment for the whole town!

Tuesday morning we were all up about three o'clock. We wanted to get away early as the sun was terribly hot. As we took time to get different carriers for me, we didn't get away from the place until seven o'clock. I had one new man, but he wasn't much better. I walked about ten miles that day and, oh me, the mountains! Some were so steep we almost had to crawl up on our hands and knees.

Tuesday night we were in the mission station in Chengku and, believe me, we were glad be to where we could have a good wash and good food. Mr. and Mrs. Strange lived there. They had a phonograph and entertained us by playing records in the evening. It did sound good.

Wednesday morning we were all up at the crack of dawn again, hoping to get into Nancheng early. When the carriers got into a scrap in the morning, we fired the whole gang and came the rest of the way by rickshaw. The road had been flooded, then deeply rutted by mule-drawn carts while the road was still muddy. It had dried into one mass of bumps. We were nearly shaken to bits! That evening we got in to Nancheng at six o'clock feeling very ready for bed.

Renewed rain forced us into staying in Nancheng a couple of more days. We used the time to wash our clothes, buy supplies, study, and write letters.

Saturday morning we started for Xin Ji about five o'clock. As Bertha was not feeling well, I insisted she ride while Mrs. Wu and I walked. When we got to the river, we had to wait a full hour for a boat to take us across. A Christian from another town traveling with us kindly helped us all the way. Because the

A Chinese companion and I cross the River Han on bouncy planks.

riverbank was all soft, sticky mud, two and three feet deep, we had to be carried into the boat. When we could not find anyone to carry us, this Christian man offered to do it. The poor man went down with me. We just took a gentle slide right into the mud! The boat was overly crowded with people, horses, sedan chairs, bundles, and all manner of strange cargo. The water was racing along at a break-neck speed. I was really scared that the old thing would go over. Believe me, we prayed hard!

We got across safely and then found that the land was all flooded for about a half a mile. What a sight it was to see the men all file through this flooded field, the water above their knees. Some were carrying huge loads of cabbage or other vegetables, others had bicycles on their backs, and others were piggybacking several Chinese women as well as the three of us. When I managed to get onto a man's back, he said, "Just hang on tight," so I hugged him as tight as ever I could. Off we went! He had to hold me so high to keep my feet from dragging in the water that sometimes I thought I could take a good summersault right over his head! The man just in front of us was carrying a load of cabbage; he slipped and fell into the water. I was afraid my man might do the same, but he was a good carrier and got me safely over.

We found the road washed out in several places and had to be carried again. I guess I had at least a dozen rides that day. At one place we could find no one but a beggar. As it wasn't a very wide place, we let him take us. While I was on his back, I discovered his hair alive with bugs. Not only so, but his face and neck were covered with sores and here I was with my arms around him! I searched later but, happily, didn't find any creatures in my hair!

We got home about three o'clock that afternoon. What a mess we came home to! As my room had leaked, the mud from my ceiling was on the floor. Everything was green with mold. A rug of green moss covered the mud floors. Getting the place cleaned up took us hours.

In June we heard that the Japanese were making a drive for Hankow. We hoped they wouldn't get that far. The news was that the dykes of the Yellow River had been deliberately bombed, causing a flood over an area of 30,000 English square miles. It made our hearts ache for the poor Chinese who lived in that area. This would mean another lot of refugees. Later we learned that many of the missionaries who were ready for furlough would not be able to leave also, that many missionaries who would like to come to China would not be allowed to come.

In July we were asked to go to Ningkiang to care for a missionary who was ill. We decided that Bertha would go ahead, and I would come later. When I did leave, my trip, as usual, was eventful. I was fortunate enough to get a truck to take me there. My seat was in the front with the driver. The road was so bumpy that after eight hours of that abuse, my backside was black and blue. The mountains we crossed were so high that the truck often had to rest two or three times to get to the top of a pass. The water in the radiator would boil, and the engine would overheat. The curves were so sharp that several times the driver would have to stop and back up in order to get around. The road was just wide enough for one car with a mountain of rock on one side and a great deep cliff on the other. I held my breath for fear another vehicle would come around the corner to meet us. The driver was pretty careful, but I think I would have felt more comfortable if I had had one of my big brothers driving!

While we were in Ningkiang, the people there were fasting in hopes that their gods would send rain. During the two weeks of fasting we could not buy pork. Each day during this time young men with leaves tied on their heads and hardly any clothes on would run through the streets throwing water over themselves, trying to fool their gods. In one parade they carried two of their gods in chairs. Following that was a man who was tied to a kind of platform. He had a big knife in each hand and was cutting his face until the blood poured down.

On the return trip home we intended to leave in time to spend a day with our former househelper. This dear soul had worked for us the previous year, but had to leave because she had tuberculosis. She had been baptized at our last service. We wanted to visit her one more time before we came on home, but, sadly, she had died before we got there. One of her relatives told us that she had kept calling for us. Just before she died, she had asked someone to come and give her a bath and put clean clothes on her. Then she had lain down and said, "I am all ready now. Come, Lord Jesus, and take me." She said that five times and was gone with a great smile on her face. We comforted ourselves with the knowledge that this member of the Xin Ji church was up in Heaven waiting for the rest of us to follow. At that time none of her family had yet accepted Christ as Savior, but she had borne such a good testimony all through her sickness that her eldest brother expressed his desire to become a Christian.

We wondered if our being away so long might affect the crowd for Sunday service in Xin Ji. Actually we had a bigger crowd than ever. That first Sunday 24 men and 18 women attended worship, plus 35 children in Sunday school. The lady who helped with the work, being good at teaching children, had kept the Sunday school going for us. As the church could not hold the women's classes while we were away, the old evangelist turned that time into a special prayer meeting for rain. The farmers desperately needed rain. All the heathen's fasting and other rituals to attract the rain gods did not work. When they stopped, the Christians started praying. Praise God, He sent rain. We then held a Thanksgiving service to thank Him for answered prayer.

Mrs. Wu received the disappointing news from the doctor that her eyes were too far gone for surgery. This meant she would never read her Bible again. She had memorized about half the Bible, a hymnbook, and the entire catechism book, but was not satisfied. When we went out in the country together, she would often quote whole chapters of Psalms at a time. Sometimes she just quoted a verse here and there and asked me where that verse could be found. Oh, me, how it showed up my ignorance! Sometimes I didn't understand enough of it to even know what the verse was!

Late in summer we had planned a day of prayer for China. We did not expect any of our folk to be able to come because of the rain. Imagine our surprise when six men came—some had walked several miles. They stayed for the day. We had one service in the morning and another in the afternoon. It was a good day. During the afternoon service a terrific crash and then a rumble shocked us all. *An earthquake!* we thought. Instead our neighbor's house had collapsed! One never knew when these mud houses would just decide to "sit down!" We had ours all braced with beams inside, and tiles protected us from over-soaking in the rain.

The Lord had truly blessed us that year. How we rejoiced over the many people who had come out for Christ!

Since Mrs. Yang, was baptized, the poor dear endured the bitterest of persecution from her relatives with whom she lived. When her husband was taken off to be a soldier, she was left with her three children, and relatives made sure her life became even more miserable. They assured her that she would get no help from any of them. With her oldest child only seven and without adult help, she had no way to get her rice harvested. Her relatives said these things were happening to her because the gods were displeased with her becoming a Christian. We suggested to the Christian men that they give her a hand.

I pose with the growing congregation at Xin Ji in 1938.

What years my first two years in China had been! I missed my family. Often I felt like I would just like to take a quick run home and have a little visit with them! Yet I was fully happy because I knew I was in the place of the Lord's appointment. One of my greatest joys was the fact that my loved ones had such a great share in the work there. I knew the Lord would reward them for every prayer offered and every dollar given.

One day we heard the little girl next door crying for all she was worth and pleading, "Don't! Don't! Don't!" We tried to figure out what the trouble was. We could hear several people talking. We decided they were binding the child's feet. If ever there was a wicked practice, it was that one.

When we went out to the country, we found that nearly every little girl had bound feet. Here in the city some had ordinary feet. It was bad enough when the feet of babies were bound, but sometimes they bound the feel of little girls of eight and ten years. First they broke the bones of their feet, then bent the bones backward and bound them. The pain the poor girls had to endure was beyond words. The old women were proud as peacocks of their tiny feet. Some of the old women that came here to service had feet no more than three inches long. They would hobble along two and three miles to come to service.

The mail had not been coming through for months perhaps because of washed out roads and war conditions. So I was very excited in September to receive a bundle of mail. I also received a newspaper from home that told me more about what was going on in China than I had heard before. I had ordered an English-language newspaper. It came the same day as the one from home, but was even older!

In addition to mail, the boxes arrived that were supposed to have come with me to China over a year ago! They were waiting for me in Nancheng. Wrote a friend who had seen them: "Take the spoiling of your goods joyfully! Mold and wet have done considerable damage. Everything is sopping wet, locks are broken on boxes, and everything is in need of a wash."

The British consul had advised folks who held British passports to stay on at their stations for the present. I heard rumors that the Americans had been ordered out, but as it was not official, we did not plan to move until we heard directly from the authorities.

One morning I picked up courage and began taking Chinese prayers. I was to have them every Saturday at 6:30 in the morning. I studied all week and then managed to talk about ten minutes. This was my message the first Saturday:

> One thing I do (Phil. 3:13)
>
> One thing is needful (Luke 10:42)
>
> One thing have I desired (Psalm 27:4)

When I was all through the first time, it seemed like a dream that I had really taken a service in Chinese!!

In September Mr. Moore sent a circular letter telling about the short-term Bible school at Sisiang. In it he told the story of one of the students that impacted me then and still blesses my life today. I quote:

> The youngest member [of the student body] was Tsu-Pen-Tse. He was very quiet and studious and didn't mix much with the other students. Then, too, he was physically weak. Spiritually he was well above the others, and everyone thought a lot of him. When he fell sick, no one thought it was serious, until one day he went into a coma. He died on the following Sunday afternoon. He had told all the students at the beginning of the term that he was going to die at Sisiang....
>
> Tsu-Pen-Tse had written on a slip of paper a set of texts and a poem of his own composition. The poem was in the center, "Jehovah-Jireh" on one side, and "Jehovah-Ropheka" on the other. At the top GOD'S PURPOSE and I Samuel 3:18 written alongside. He believed that God had a purpose for his life, and he lived accordingly. How it rejoiced our hearts to see God's working in this young life! A friend has kindly translated the poem for

us:

If illness come, and daily pain,
My body weak and life doth wane.
I breathe my soul to Thee again,
Thy will be done.

Holy Spirit, filled with Thee,
I have peace though weak I be,
Life is fleeting—choose for me.
Thy will be done.

Renew my heart and will each day,
In close communion all the way,
And make it easy then to say,
Thy will be done.

From this scene of tears and grief,
I shall soon find sweet relief,
Singing yonder my belief,
Thy will be done.

At around this same time we received the bad news that Hankow had fallen to the Japanese. We wondered how that would affect us. Would the mail still go through? Because we were a small town with absolutely no military objects, we did not worry about being harmed.

September brought good news, too. The Christians in Xin Ji had been discussing the need for the church to get a building of their own for services. We were thrilled at this. That was just what we had been praying for. We didn't mind having services in our house, but we didn't expect to stay there forever and wondered what the people would do when we left. The place where we had been staying was leased for ten years, and it had already been six years since the beginning of the lease. Our hope was that when the ten years were up, the church would be able to take care of itself, and we would be able to go on to some other place where the Gospel was not being preached.

In November we visited some of the mountain villages again. In one village a crowd of people were waiting for us when we arrived and responded well to our teaching and preaching. Later we went right up over the top of a high, stony mountain. Sometimes the path was so indistinct that we could hardly make it out. The people at the foot of the hill said there was no use going up there as few people lived up there. But we went anyway. Because women in the mountains never left their homes, they never had a chance to hear the Gospel. All with tightly bound feet, they couldn't possibly walk over the mountain trails. Actually we found quite a few people, men and women. We visited in seven homes and must have reached about fifty people.

A week later we went up into the mountains again. This time we went to a town called Big River Valley, also known as the "Brigands' Nest" because it was often visited by brigands. It was twenty miles from where we lived—twenty miles of mountain climbing. We expected to find quite a big city and, lo and behold, we found only six or seven houses in the whole town. We thought the people would be very poor, but instead they were all quite well to do. Recently the brigands had been going to the school, kidnapping the children of the wealthiest people, and demanding a big ransom.

We got the shock of our lives, however, when we walked into the church and discovered that the gatekeeper was an opium smoker. Our bedroom had been rented to a medicine seller and, since he was out of town, he had left a false god there to look after his medicines while he was away. Our bed was a counter and table pushed together, each about 18 inches wide but different heights. They put a little straw over the top and then an oilcloth. It wasn't altogether comfortable but we managed to sleep on it anyway. The rats were even worse than in the last place we had visited. The wretched things would climb on top of a high cupboard that reached almost to the ceiling and then jump on to the bed. The poorest jumpers landed on our feet, others hit the middle of our stomachs while the champions came tumbling in summersaults over our heads! Some nights we hardly got any sleep.

As someone had told us that we would be able to buy rice and vegetables in this town, we did not bring anything with us except a few bundles of dough strings for the first night and next day's breakfast. When we got there, we found we could not buy anything. The first night we had just a bowl of dough strings —they tasted awful! We could not imagine what was wrong with them. Then, on the third day we found out that the water our helper used to cook the dough strings was from a filthy old hole near the house instead of river water. After that Mrs. Wu and helper went just a few feet further to the river for our water.

Thanksgiving Day we had a bowl of dough strings for breakfast and a bowl of plain cooked rice for supper. We were fortunate to get three eggs for dessert for the four of us! Mrs. Wu and I had been out preaching all day and had some good times. The people all listened well. I was afraid the mountain folk would not be able to understand anything I said, but surprisingly, I could understand them quite well, and they understood me. Happily on Friday our helper managed to buy some turnips and potatoes for the rest of our meals. On Saturday I was reading in Psalm 78:25,"Man shall eat angels' food; and he gave them meat to the full." After that we were invited out to one meal every day and had meat and vegetables at each place! Through leanness and plenty, I was totally happy where God had placed me.

In Xin Ji one day I dropped a tangerine on the floor and could not find it. As I was in a hurry, I just left it. That night as I was going to bed, I found the tangerine on my pillow with the top eaten off and all the juice sucked out of it! Having got used to sleeping with rats running around while we were out in the country, now I was brave enough to sleep without a net at home!

When oil became very expensive, we started to use Chinese lamps during the daytime, using our good lamp only after supper. Local lamps were simply vegetable oil in a little tray with a piece of weed-like "lamp straw" for a wick. I woke up one morning to find that rats had eaten the entire wick and about half of the oil. Though the lamp was on a stool just beside my bed, I never heard those four-legged thieves! I began to feel like a real missionary!

Ministry opportunities were endless. Mrs. Chang came to service every Sunday bringing a crowd of her relatives and neighbors with her. They were all very keen—we just couldn't seem to preach and teach enough for them. As they kept begging us to go to their home, one day Mrs. Wu and I decided to go visit them. As soon as we got there, Mrs. Chang gave us a bowl of sweet rice with eggs. To me the sweet rice was sickening, but I managed to get it down. After we had preached for a short time, one of the other relatives came with another bowl of the same kind of rice! Mrs. Wu gave hers to one of the kids, but they wouldn't take mine.

How we enjoyed seeing these people in their homes! As one of the husbands could read, he had taught the whole family the content of all the tracts and Scripture verses we had given them. Not only so, the group had memorized two pages of the catechism! Even the grannies and the little kids could quote these things from memory. As soon as we got there, they wanted us to teach them some more. I taught them a song that was written out in tract form. It had four verses. Ten or twelve women and girls learned the whole thing.

When we went to leave, Mrs. Chang said, "You must pray for us; we women all believe, but that is not enough. We want the men to trust in Jesus too!" They tried to insist that we stay for dinner. We had to pull ourselves away by force. When they hid our umbrellas, thinking that would keep us from leaving, I said, "Please bring our umbrellas to church with you on Sunday. That way you will have to come to service!" When they saw we were really going to go without the umbrellas, they brought them out.

We had a grand time celebrating Christmas. The only thing that would have made it perfect would have been to have all my family with me. But this year I had received big home mail with letters from all of them along with some Christmas cards and Christmas gifts. Nothing could have pleased me more. I told

Bertha that was the Lord's "exceeding abundantly" for us. We were so happy we burst out in singing the chorus:

> How good is the God we adore,
> Our faithful, unchangeable friend,
> Whose love is as great as His power,
> And knows neither measure nor end!

But God had something much more significant in store for us to stoke our praise in direct answer to many prayers, especially those of the women of the village we had just visited. Instead of the traditional Christmas program, we decided to have a testimony service. My, how it thrilled me to hear those folk get up and tell how they had come to believe! One young lad from that country place we had just visited gave his testimony for the first time. Then as the evangelist was preaching, he asked the congregation several times if they believed that Christ was the Son of God, and if they believed that He came for them? Two other men from this same village who had just started coming to service answered these questions with a hearty, "I believe!" From the expressions and big smiles on their faces, obviously they were really experiencing much joy in believing. What a way to finish the year!

Yet, with Japanese forces still eating at China's heart, we wondered what the year ahead would bring. ❧

Chapter 7

Air Raids, Bombs, and Miracles

By 1939 my ability to speak and understand the Chinese language had improved significantly. I faced the new year with expectancy.

The dedication of fellow workers to preaching God's way of reconciling mankind to Himself often amazed me. One evening the evangelist invited us to a special feast. When we sat down to eat, he was missing. We were told he had gone out preaching at the market. His explanation: "Eating doesn't matter; preaching the Gospel does!" That evening he preached until the crowds had gone home. Then he came back and had his dinner!

Interacting with so many people day after day, we constantly learned local customs and medical "remedies" new to us. For example, for sore eyes, we were told to wash our feet in water that had been boiled then to wash our eyes in the same water! I couldn't figure out how that remedy could possibly work.

We learned of another remedy one day when the wife of one of the Christians came to borrow the gold ring my mother had given me. This woman had taken her little month-old baby to see a doctor. He told her the only medicine that would help would be to boil a gold ring in water and then make the baby drink that water. I noticed that the baby's hands were bleeding from acupuncture.

Some customs had their roots deep in non-Christian beliefs. When, for instance, some time later Bertha revisited the mountain village in which the elderly Christian man was so very sick, she discovered that he had died shortly after we left. Yet the family had still not buried the body. They were waiting for a lucky day. They had the coffin in the house and had plastered it with a coating of mud on the outside to keep the smells in. Since the days before Chinese New Year were considered "lucky days," those days were full of funerals, weddings and other celebrations! Those were also days when non-Christians chanted for the dead.

In one house where a death had occurred just a couple of doors from us, the family chanted from early morning until late at night. Along with the chanting they beat drums and tin pans. When I woke up at five in the morning, they were still banging. By midnight the following night my ears were ringing.

Letters from home came very slowly. Sometimes it took three or four months for them to get to me. However, I had to give three cheers for the Chinese post office; at least they eventually got all the letters to me. The folks at home and I numbered all our letters so that we would know if one was missing. Sometimes the mail piled up at the post office for weeks. When they were finally ready to deliver mail, they just took the letters off the top. This meant that the most recent ones would often arrive before earlier mail.

The Chinese Christians continued to be persecuted. Mrs. Tan, one of the ladies who had been coming regularly to services for almost a year, came to ask us for prayer. The family had bought a pig for ten dollars, a pile of money to them. Unfortunately, the pig died. Then her husband became sick. Her neighbors all blamed her, insisting that these things were happening because she had become a Christian.

Mr. Meng, who had been beaten recently, returned to Sunday

service again. We wondered if his experience might keep some of the new Christians away from services. But they were there in full force. When we spoke to one of these new believers about Mr. Meng's being beaten, the man said, "Oh that is nothing; it will help him to be a better Christian!"

The evangelist gave the folks a heavy lecture about buying and selling on Sunday. Keeping the Lord's Day was one of the hardest things for the Chinese. Every other Sunday was market day, and they liked to bring their baskets when they came to church so that they could buy things before returning home. It was amusing to see those who had brought their baskets with them! Some of them tried to push their baskets off onto the next fellow. One woman was asked if she was going to market after the services. She said, "No, seeing I can't go and buy thread today, I might as well stay here and play a while!"

We had seventy-nine kids in Sunday school by January of '39. It seemed to get better every week. They were a handful, however, especially since I couldn't speak as freely as I would have liked.

Before leaving for furlough, my good friend Faith Leeuwenberg came for a short visit. I was thrilled to see her. Since she was from my home church, she could tell my family how happy and peaceful we were. It was easy to forget that a war was tearing people's lives apart elsewhere.

Yet the war wasn't that far away¯near enough to hear the noise and feel the vibrations of exploding bombs. In Sian bombs had destroyed the part of the post office where parcels were stored. We wondered whether we had lost anything.

Bertha was also preparing to go on furlough. I didn't know if someone would come to replace her or if I would be left alone. I reminded myself that I would not really be alone, for the Lord is *always* with me.

In March I received a bicycle. Since I had never ridden a bicycle before, learning to ride was a new experience for me. My first trip was quite an adventure. Because the first ten *li* crowds of people were going to market, I couldn't pick up enough courage to get on and ride at first. When I finally did, I passed a group of soldiers standing by a house drinking tea. One of them was carrying a basket on a pole and swung the basket in front of me. In my effort to miss the basket, I sprawled myself across the road. When I quickly gathered myself up and wobbled merrily on my way, the soldiers gave three cheers!

As the second ten *li* was very rough, I had to push the bike most of the way. The last thirty *li* the road was good all the way, and I went sailing along. Still, I couldn't count the times I had to jump off. Although we had a new road to Xin Ji, the farmers still thought nothing of digging a ditch across the road if they wanted to drain their rice fields. I simply got out of the way of unpredictable donkeys with their bulky loads. I took an awful spill trying to pass a *hua-kan* and nearly knocked one of the carriers over. However, I did the last three miles in fifteen minutes and got home almost two hours before Bertha. By the time she pulled in, I had a nice fire going, the water boiling and dinner ready.

In April I traveled to Nancheng to see Bertha leave for furlough. There I learned I would be alone in Xin Ji. Actually I was given a choice to go to a station in Fenghsien in the north, but I did not feel right about leaving Xin Ji. At the same time, I did not think I could face going back to Xin Ji alone. However, Mr. Moore insisted that I come to Nancheng every two or three weeks to spend a day with them for fellowship and advice. True, now that I had a bike, I could ride in to Nancheng in a hurry. The morning that I was to return to Xin Ji, my Bible reading for the day was Judges 6: 14-16, where God commanded Gideon: "Go…have not I sent thee… I will be with thee." How marvelously the Lord made His presence felt to me!

In the months that followed I took Percy and Amy Moore up on their invitation to spend an occasional few days with them for a break. I had no idea of the impact I was making during those visits on their little boy Frank. In 2003 he began email correspondence with my niece Loraine (who spent months and months creating this book out of a suitcase or two of my letters and diaries). Frank is now a white-haired retired schoolteacher teaching English in China. I have read his emails, letters, and other writings with intense interest and enjoyed a visit from him immensely. In an early email Frank wrote:

"I see Sadie now sitting in the doorstep of the old mission home…engaging with me. …She parried with me. I was a curious and skeptical little boy who…didn't fall into line quietly with my parents' wishes. I asked a lot of questions. Sadie was particularly 'cool' about my questions and my kind of sassiness. I used to go quite crazy with excitement when I heard that Auntie Sadie was on her way from Xin Ji and would be arriving any moment on her bike. I'd rush out to meet her and just hang around her. Sadie made the presence of God into a palpable fact. …She was a sunbeam….

I have often wondered what impact I had on Chinese children during my years in China. They would be among the older generation today. Frank has given me a tiny glimpse of the answer through friendship with a man he first knew when they were both children. Gou was one of a group of boys who used to chase Frank as he raced on his bike around the military parade ground near the mission home in Nancheng. Frank often eats with Gou, his wife, and Gou's mother. Not long ago the wife told Frank (recorded in *The Chefoo Magazine*, 2004):

When I was a little girl, I lived over the river in Nancheng County. My parents were deacons in the local church, so I knew the missionaries very well. *Chen Jiao Si* (Sadie Custer) from America used to play with me, and she gave me a nickname…*Xiao Kuai Le* (Little Happiness). I was so proud of this name.

In the spring co-workers organized revival meetings in Nancheng. Sixteen of us from Xin Ji joined in. It was hard to say who enjoyed the meetings most—the Chinese or the foreigners. The last day of the meetings a woman stood up and beamingly praised God for the blessing she had received, at the same time asked us all to pray that she might bear a good testimony in her own home. A few days later local missionaries found her in a nearby village exhorting her mother to become a Christian.

In response to the messages, one young man and his wife were going to go right home and prepare a family altar.

In May I was helping with the care of critically ill Helen Dalton in Nancheng, when bombs fell on the city. That's when the bomb obliterated the garden. I detailed this close encounter with the Sino-Japanese War in the opening paragraphs of this book.

I thought I could never stand to go through an air raid, but it was marvelous how the Lord gave us all perfect peace. Not only so, but the Lord continued to show us His tender care. Helen desperately needed serum. We could not buy it in Nancheng. When the doctor came on Monday morning, the day after the bomb made a crater out of our garden, he said there was nothing to do but to let the disease run its course. Yet that very afternoon the serum came in from a neighboring province. Had it been a day later, Helen would not likely have survived. And later on, when complications set in that were almost as life-threatening as the meningitis, the Lord brought Helen safely through that episode too. Shortly after that Helen was moved to a hospital, and I returned to Xin Ji.

My trust in the Lord continued to grow as I considered how He miraculously protected us in that dangerous situation. Later, when I was on my first furlough, I went to visit a prayer partner who was in hospital. In comparing stories, we discovered that at the very time the bombs were falling in Nancheng, she was praying for me!

Back in Xin Ji, I was relieved not to have to worry about air raids. I returned to find Mrs. Yang, a lady whose husband was taken for a soldier, in a desperate state. Her husband had left the army and tried to return home. But he was caught, then killed as punishment for deserting the army. Poor Mrs. Yang was having a horrendous time. Forced by the circumstances to give her two little girls away, she struggled to find ways to support herself and her one remaining child, a little boy.

Shortly after I returned home to Xin Ji, someone started rumors about the missionaries that four big men with long black beards and who wore black gowns were living in our household! The rumormongers said that we took people in and gave them poisoned breads or tea that put the people to sleep. Then we roasted them to get some fat. It was reported that we could get one pound of fat off of the fat ladies, a half pound from boys and a quarter pound from babies. Can you imagine? As a result of these stories, not a single child came to Sunday school for two weeks. They were simply scared stiff of missionaries. Even when we went out on the street, the children ran from us.

That whole business lasted until an order was sent from Nancheng forbidding the people to believe these tales or to speak about them. We wondered if someone was paying people to start the stories or if the idea of our roasting people had roots in people's misunderstanding of the evangelist's announcement on a Sunday that the missionaries were going to *kao-ren*, meaning "to examine," them for baptism. The words for roasting people sound almost the same. It took a couple of weeks to get things straightened out. We surely were relieved to put it all behind us.

Xin Ji was particularly hot that summer. The flies, fleas and mosquitoes were worse than any year since I had been there. As a result almost every home suffered sickness. People were dying by the scores with cholera. As the government had ordered that everyone be vaccinated, a nurse stood at the city gate and "stabbed" everyone that came along! The worst of it for us, besides our dismay at the number of deaths, was that we couldn't eat anything raw, and the watermelons were just getting ripe!

Several people were baptized that summer—both men and women. I was especially pleased because I had helped teach the women among them from the time they first began to come. For some of these women to be baptized took courage as they had unsaved relatives and friends who came along to see the show!

The Moores insisted that I come to Nancheng during the summer months because of the heat in Xin Ji. While I was there, Mrs. Moore became very ill with dysentery. I helped with her care as well as assisting in the running of their very busy home. More air alarms occurred while I was there. In fact, we all kept a little bag packed with washcloth, towel, soap, comb, passport, and purse for when we might have to flee to the country. I included some paper and a pen so that I could use the time to write letters. We also brought along dark-colored clothes to cover ourselves with when the planes came. Once when we had a false alarm, I was pretty miffed to think we sat in a cornfield from 10:30 p.m. until midnight when we could have been home snoozing in our beds!

One day in August thirty-three planes flew overhead and fired their machine guns, but dropped no bombs. The next day the Moores and I and another family spent the whole day in the country for fear that the Japanese would follow the strafing with a bombing run.

In September I learned through a Chinese newspaper that England had gone to war with Germany. How I hoped America would keep out of it! After all the awful bombings that China went through, I prayed hard that the U.S. would never experience that.

It was now three years since I had left home. They had been very happy years. I had to admit, though, the stress and strain of air alarms, visitors coming and going, caring for the sick, and helping with the running of a busy household were all taking their toll on my energy level. I would have loved a good swim in Lake Michigan, as I used to do with my family in the summer time. I was needing a vacation. By the next summer, I would be halfway through my seven-year term. I suspected that if I didn't get back to civilization once during my seven years, I would be so old-fashioned that my family wouldn't recognize me.

I was not to leave Nancheng, however, without another air alarm. When it came, Mrs. Moore got into her rickshaw, and the rest of us hopped on our bikes and away we flew out to the country. As the alarm sounded just before dinner, the cook left the dinner on the stove when he ran for a safer place. After the all-clear signal I returned to the mission home on my bike ahead of the others and found the chicken all cooked. The potatoes had cooked so long that only the top ones were still edible.

As the visitors were leaving the Moores' house, I decided to go home too. I was anxious to see my house before we had another rainstorm. The last time I was away someone had reported hearing a crash and thought my bedroom ceiling had come down. Because the house was locked and I had the keys, they could not get in to see. That time I had found my rooms all okay. What folk had heard was the neighbors' house collapsing!

On arriving home I did get one surprise: I found the preaching hall packed with soldiers! As I entered, I said, "What's going on here?" I didn't wait for an answer, but as I came through the hall, I heard the soldiers whispering, "The *Chiao-si* has come back." A few minutes later they came and asked the evangelist to preach to them! They cleared out the same night, but not before one of them took suddenly ill. They were sure he was going to die. They called in a quasi doctor, who gave the sick man a few shots with a needle. That sort of revived him, and the soldiers left, dragging their patient along with them.

I was glad to be home again. I had missed having services with Xin Ji people on Sundays.

Milk became a precious commodity, and I didn't like going without it. My solution: I would keep a goat. But I saw only one place to keep it—in the *kitchen!* In a corner I planned to have a pen made with a cement bottom so that it could be scrubbed every day. I thought it was a fairly good plan. It turned out, though, that when a new co-worker arrived, she didn't see it my way, and I had to scratch the idea.

Missionaries learned to make a lot of things through the war: soap, vinegar, coffee, quasi Grapenuts, peanut butter, refined sugar, clean salt, shaving soap for men, puffed rice, etc.

As the summer of 1939 ended, Mrs. Moore came to spend a few days with me before she and her husband would leave for the States for furlough. I was glad she had an opportunity to rest before making the long journey. I knew I would miss the Moores in a mighty way. They had almost become like surrogate parents to me. I looked forward, however, to the folks at home meeting the Moores and getting to know them.

About this time Helen Dalton to live with me. I was thrilled to have someone with whom to share the work, but especially someone with whom to share meals again. As Helen was around the same age as I, I hoped we would be a fairly good match stamina-wise. With Helen also having a bike, we would be able to travel together.

Shortly after Helen's arrival, we had a very sad experience. When we returned home from preaching in the country, one of the Christian women came to us with her little boy, sick with scarlet fever. The father came to service on Sunday morning, and while he was there, the boy died. It seemed the devil was doing his best to discourage the faith of this young couple. They had had six children, and this was the only one still living. His being a son, they felt especially grieved. We asked the father if they would have a Christian funeral for the eight-year-old. He said, "No, we just threw him out on the hill for the dogs to eat!" Though that was the heathen practice, we didn't expect that from this family. Later when Mrs. Wu and I went to visit them, the poor mother was weeping her eyes out. We assured her that the Lord really loved her and that if she loved Him, He was coming soon to take her to be with her child. Mrs. Wu told them they should not have thrown the boy's body out like the heathen do. The father said he wrapped it in a little straw and a straw mat. That having a funeral for a child would be proper never crossed their minds.

On a happier note, we went to a home one day where a middle-aged woman was sewing. The woman's little boy often came to Sunday school and said he believed. Sometimes he couldn't come because this mother (or grandmother, I wasn't sure which) wouldn't let him come. Helen and I sat down by her and started to preach to her, but she would have nothing to do with our message. When I noticed that the woman was having difficulty threading a needle, I said, "Please, old lady (a very respectful way to address an older woman in China), may I thread that needle for you?" The woman looked up, surprised. She let me thread the needle. After that she listened and even promised to come to service on Sunday. Sometimes it was the little helpful things that we could do for people that opened the door for them to listen to the Gospel.

Before winter, Helen, Mrs. Wu, and Mrs. Tan (pronounced Dan), and I all went on a long visit in the mountains. We went to Ta Ho Pa (Big River Valley) and, my, but didn't we have a good time! I thoroughly enjoyed going out now that I could understand more of what was being said.

We left home early on a Thursday morning. When we heard it raining during the night, we wondered if we would be able to get away or not. As it stopped raining about seven, we started out. Though it did not rain again down on the plain, the farther we got up in the mountains the wetter it got, and, oh, the roads! By the time we got to the top of the mountain, it was pouring. The road going down was very steep and *slippery*. When we reached our destination, we looked like little kids that had been playing in mud puddles all day!

We found a new friend there—a cat. Our old friends the rats had all done the disappearing act. We had a big Chinese bed given us this time, with some bamboo poles for a spring and lots of nice fresh straw. I slept like a log every night. Only one midnight I was jarred awake by Mrs. Wu calling Mrs. Tan to tell her that the brigands had come. We could hear a man yelling outside. Scared, I was deciding what I should do, when the lady of the house called over and said it was just a carrier who had been delayed on the road and who was just coming in.

The next day I went out with Mrs. Tan, and Helen went with Mrs. Wu. Some of the Christians we visited seemed spiritually cold and to understand very little of Christian doctrines. Yet in one of the first homes we visited we found a young woman who said she wanted to believe. She seemed very keen and earnest.

Mrs. Tan and I did some tall climbing that day. The trail over one mountain seemed to go right straight up and down again. In spots we followed little tracks through what had been cornfields. We pulled ourselves up grabbing onto the corn stubble. We made it to many homes and in every place got a good hearing. In one home the man said, "Don't start to preach until I get back. I want to invite my neighbors to come and hear too."

Another day Mrs. Wu, Helen, and I went out together. We climbed and climbed that day until finally we could see just one more house at the very top of the mountain. As Helen found climbing the mountains rather difficult, she waited while Mrs. Wu and I went up. We found a young couple living there. The woman was beautiful. Though her parents were Christians and she knew the Way, she did not believe.

Saturday night it poured all night. We were tempted to wonder why the Lord would allow it to rain just this one Sunday when the Christians there finally had an opportunity to attend church. Instead we praised the Lord, guessing He may have sent the rain to keep away evil men. About 15 children came in the morning for Sunday school. Afterwards fifteen or so people came to the adult service. Our cook preached the sermon. In the middle of it a pig walked up to the front and smelled all around our feet, the preacher's included. A chicken strutted through next, followed by the cat, and then a man got up and walked to the front to peer at our chorus sheets!

We had planned to go home on Monday, but went to the market village of Fu Ch'uan instead. What a lovely trip that was! We traveled through the most beautiful scenery I had ever seen. The mountains were one mass of trees and shrubbery. We could hardly find the trail through it in some places. The changing colors of deciduous trees contrasted with evergreen and holly. We brushed by bushes with red berries and some with bright yellow. And wild chrysanthemums everywhere added cheery color. I longed for a camera that would take colored pictures!

As Monday was market day in Fu Ch'uan, crowds of people milled the streets. Being the first foreign ladies to visit this place, we were objects of special interest. The people simply thronged about us. One said, "Look at her big feet!" The next one said, "Look at her high nose!" and another, "What funny eyes she has!" The last one asked if Helen was my husband! Helen had had her hair cut short when she was sick, and being much taller and heavier than I was, she did look a bit mannish.

We took our posters outside and tacked them up on the wall where everyone could see. Mrs. Wu and the cook preached for about two hours with great crowds listening. Helen and I sold Gospels and books, gave away tracts, and talked to people about their need of reconciliation with God. We sold everything we had in about an hour and could have sold more. It was a wonderful opportunity as very few of those people had ever heard the Gospel before.

We rented a room in an inn that night. We found only one room, and it was mostly enclosed with a mud wall. We had the benefit of that room because someone had died in it, and the local people were afraid to sleep in it. When we arrived, two wide boards on forms served as a bed. When we got ready for bed, however, the lady of the house came and wanted the boards as they were the doors to her house! We found ourselves let down on a little straw in the corner on the mud floor! I really slept well there too, but poor Helen not only didn't sleep well, but caught an awful cold. The woman, being a vegetarian, was angry when she learned we had contaminated her cooking pot with pork fat. She asked us to leave the next morning. Because brigands were lurking all around, the Chinese were keen that we foreigners should leave anyway. Though Helen and I did leave, Mrs. Wu and Mrs. Tan stayed on.

On our return trip we were near the top of the mountain when we met two men who told us brigands had been on that road in the morning. We prayed, asking God to send his guardian angels. Just then two big flocks of wild geese put in their appearance, and the peoples' attention was all drawn to them as they flew over in formation. We quietly and quickly walked on. We can't say for certain that there were brigands there just when we passed, but we would not be surprised if God sent His birds for our benefit!

In early winter we held a conference in Xin Ji. We were all ready to start the conference on a Saturday afternoon. Because it had rained all day on Friday, we wondered if any of the folks would be able to get through. We were pleasantly surprised when nearly all of the folks came, in spite of the weather.

Mr. Liu from the mountains was the first to arrive. He had walked thirty *li* (10 miles) along an awful road! What sights he and others were—they were soaked and covered with mud. One old lady evidently had quite a few sit-downs in the mud from the looks of her clothes! One man and wife were worth a picture. The man was carrying two baskets with a carrying pole across his shoulder. In the front basket were their baby and blankets for all the family and in the other basket he had their rice and Bibles and hymnbooks. His wife tagged along behind. Instead of stockings, she had just a bit of cloth wound around her feet—which you could not see for mud! She had her trousers rolled up to her knees, was wearing a huge straw rain hat, and carried a long walking stick! Though we all laughed at them, we could not help but admire their courage for coming out in such conditions. We had about thirty people staying here at our place, one happy family. The first thing on the program was a foot wash and a change of clothes!

The theme of the conference, "We Would See Jesus," was also Mr. Wu's first message. Mr. Wu was the Bible woman's son, who had graduated from Bible school and was a good preacher. He came in the rain and was soaked. He had only straw sandals on his feet. Because the sandals were coarse straw, they had rubbed sores on his feet in several places. We had also asked a Mrs. Ma to take the women's meetings. A sixty-five-year-old refugee from Hopei, she had been with foreigners all her life. She had been taught in a mission school and was more like us than like the Chinese. Happily she was very "hot-hearted," as the Chinese say. She loved the Lord and His work. Quite a wealthy woman, she wrote beautifully, could sing either alto or soprano, and played the organ. When we gave her foreign food, she handled her fork and knife just as well as her chopsticks.

The Chinese were determined that Helen and I should take some meetings, but we finally persuaded them that we were constantly preaching, and it was our turn to listen for a change.

During the conference we had evening meetings in the street chapel. We opened the doors and invited the neighbors to come in. Mrs. Ma had charge of the meetings because Mr. Wu had a sore throat and three meetings a day was all he could manage. Testimony time in the evening meeting was interesting, sometimes amusing. Some of the men talked too long. When their time was up, Mrs. Ma would stand up behind them. Instead of saying a polite "Amen," she would say in a loud voice, "Enough!" It tickled me so much I had to bury my face in my hands so the people couldn't see me laugh.

Young Mrs. T'an, had a husband with TB. He had been sick for quite some time. Though she preached to him, he would not believe. The week before the conference at prayer meeting she prayed: "Lord, you know my husband. He won't believe. Living he won't live, and dying he won't die. I beseech You, Lord, not to allow him to stop me from coming to conference; that I might come peacefully and with a full heart return!" The day after the conference closed Mrs. T'an came to say her husband had died. She said that just before he died he called on God to have mercy on him. This brave widow had him buried with none of normal heathen practices. As soon as he was out of the house, she destroyed all the false gods. She maintained a wonderful testimony through it all. We judged the conference a wonderful success.

I wanted to start a knitting class for some of the older girls. We had been trying our best to reach them but without much success. The Lord in His graciousness helped us. One Monday a lad came in and asked if we had any books for sale. I sold him *A Traveler's Guide*. In a few minutes we had all the school children in and our stock of fifty books was sold out in no time. The next day as Mrs. Wu was going out, a child asked her for a Gospel.

She sold it to him, and we had the same experience as on Monday. After the Gospels were all sold, I kept the kids for a time, sang a couple choruses, and had a little preach. Then I invited the girls to come on Wednesday for a knitting and Bible class. Wednesday morning they came on their way to school and asked if they could bring their Gospels along. They wanted me to teach that! In the afternoon about eighteen girls came. I was thrilled.

The girls had to bring their own needles—all homemade ones. Some were so big, coarse and rough that a person could not possibly push any thread over them. One girl brought four pieces of coarse wire, no points on them! Others, however, had theirs made beautifully smooth, like any bamboo needles sold in the store. Most got on well with their knitting while others were hopeless. The strugglers' work looked like just so many knots, reminding me of mine when I was first learning.

Sunday afternoon most of the little girls of my knitting class came to Sunday school, and I invited them to stay for the service for the older folks. They stayed, and as they were leaving, one little girl said, "*Chiao-si,* I want to tell you something."

"What do you want to tell me?" I asked.

She said, "Four of us girls would like to believe on the Lord."

I can't tell you what joy it gave me to hear those words. Twelve of the girls were back for the knitting class on Thursday. They were more interested in the study of Mark's Gospel than in their knitting. When I asked them why they wanted to believe, they said because they were sinners and Jesus could forgive their sins. They seemed to understand.

Mr. and Mrs. MacIntosh, a missionary couple from New Zealand who had come to China the same year that I did, invited us to their home in Nancheng for Christmas. We planned to go, providing there were no more air raids. Otherwise the MacIntoshes would come to our home in Xin Ji for Christmas. As it turned out, all the folk came back to Xin Ji because Christmas occurred at full moon, and air raids often took place during full moons. We had a wonderful Christmas after all. We put up decorations, exchanged gifts, and enjoyed great fellowship.

On the last Sunday of the year we had thirty-three women and twenty men at our service. That was about the biggest crowd we had ever had‾definitely the most women. When I first came to Xin Ji, we had about fifteen men and three or four women. The present group of women were all keen too. I couldn't help but love them. What a work the Lord was doing there!

As the year 1939 drew to a close, I could honestly say that the longer I was in China the better I liked it and the happier I was. The Lord was wonderfully near and precious. ❦

Chapter 8

Death, Weddings, and Water Dragons

The year 1940 came in with a blast of snow and brutal cold. The snowstorm lasted several days. Though I feared few people would make it to Sunday service, the storm did not stop most. We got through the Sunday school okay as we could divide up and get into our little rooms, but when it came to the big service, we had to sit outside. When the evangelist stood up to preach, he was all huddled up with his hands up his sleeves to keep warm. "It is too cold, too cold. We will have to have a short message this morning lest you freeze," he said. Everyone was glad that he preached for only about twenty minutes. To myself I said, *I just hope the Christians will get so cold they will decide to get a church building. I am sure they could get one if they tried hard enough.*

Monday the snow was still coming down in big flakes. Remarked Mr. Tang, the evangelist, "This is the Lord's work. Who can do the Lord's work?" He sounded just like Abraham or another of the Old Testament saints.

Our Sunday school attendance continued to climb. We broke our record with 78 children. We had to squeeze them into our tiny little courtyard. As there was not enough room for everyone to sit on the little benches, half of the children had to stand up, but no one complained.

I received sad news from the family back home: My two-and-a-half-year-old nephew had died of spinal meningitis. On a brighter side, the same brother and his wife had a baby girl the previous May, and from all the descriptions I was getting from home, I thought she must be a "perfect baby." I wished I could have the little Loraine for a while. It was hard not being able to comfort family members in their grief or greet new nieces and nephews as they arrived or watch them grow up..

In February I received the news that both my father and my brother John had been on the sick list. Even though I was fully happy in my work, when news like that came along, I sometimes wished I was a little bit nearer my family. I would have liked to be there to help. My one comfort was that I knew it was the Lord who allowed these things to happen, and He would see my loved ones through them.

The night after my birthday I dreamt about Pop. In my dream he was sick and dying, and I had gotten home just in time to see him. He recognized me just for a minute and then said, "The Door is opening."

When I asked him who he saw, he said, "The Lord, and there is Julia, and my mother and father, and there is Ronny, too. But who are all those yellow faces I see coming?"

I told him those were the Chinese whom he had helped to win for the Lord. He smiled and was gone.

When I awoke, the dream seemed so real that I felt something must really be wrong at home. The next morning as I was combing my hair, I remembered this dream and thought that if it was true, I would soon be hearing from my family. That afternoon Helen brought me a letter from home. The letter said that one of my sisters was sick. My family had kept pretty well, but now it seemed that sickness was coming all at once—first little Ronny's death, then my sister. Next my brother John, and now Pop was apparently going off mentally. How I wished I could know how Pop was *right now! How awful!* I thought. I knew Pop's condition would be a real trial to those who were with him all the time. I fretted until I remembered that "He gives more grace" was still true, and I knew the Lord would care for them. I prayed especially for Mom. It was a great comfort to me when a sister wrote, "Don't worry about Mom—we kids are sticking close by her." Even so, how I wished I could have been there!

At around this time we received an order of goods from Shanghai. I gasped when I saw the bill—$400 in Chinese currency! I need not have worried (as usual) because the Lord always provides. The very day after we received the large bill, I received a letter from home. In it was a gift of $30.00 from a friend at home, worth $385 in Chinese dollars, and another gift of $14.00. So the Lord paid my bill. The prices of the things bought in Shanghai were very cheap compared to what we had to pay in Xin Ji, but the cartage was twice the cost of the products. They had to come way around by French Indo-china, Yunnan, and on up.

The weather in Xin Ji continued to be bitterly cold with mounds of snow, reportedly the coldest winter in twenty years. Numbers for Sunday services were understandably down somewhat. Yet several people continued to come in spite of having to walk considerable distances.

I received no letters from home for several weeks after that. The Japanese had blown up the French railway in Yunnan. Repair was going to take a month.

On another of our trips to the country Mrs. Wu and I happened to hit a hard neighborhood. Most people were not keen to listen. One woman seemed frightened of us. She told us to go away as she didn't want to listen. Another man said, "I have heard this over and over again, and I don't believe in any God."

The dogs in that neighborhood were about as unfriendly as the people. My guess was that they didn't like Mrs. Wu's walking stick. The dogs knew beggars by their sticks and always barked at them. I think they took Mrs. Wu for a beggar, perhaps me as well.

While in meetings in Chengku, the service had just started when a telegram for me arrived saying that my father had passed away. He died on March 8th after just five weeks of illness. The whole family, except one brother-in-law in the military and me, was with him at home as he passed into God's presence.

I was glad I was in Chengku when the telegram came; the folk there were all so very kind to me. I wished only that I could have been home with my family all during Pop's illness. Family had all done so much; I had not been able to do anything.

I knew the family would all be missing Pop a lot, and I prayed that the Lord Himself would fill every vacant place and would be their constant companion. I did not think the separation would be for long as I felt surely the Lord was coming soon to take us all unto Himself. Then we would be a *complete* happy family once more.

When I heard of what Pop's illness did to his mind, I hoped everyone would forget the last few weeks of his life and remember him only as the good father he had been to us all. I was glad I had kept two letters that Pop sent me since I came to China. They were precious to me now. After I returned to Xin Ji I kept reading them over and over.

Heading out on a country trip one morning, we got a late start and found ourselves climbing the hardest part of the mountain right at noon. Was it *hot!* The trail took us seven miles up one side and then three miles down, almost straight down. By the time I got to the bottom, my toes felt as though they were coming right straight through the ends of my shoes! The mountain was very bare with nothing but stones and rocks. About the only living things we saw were a few snakes slithering around on the stones.

We arrived at our destination about four o'clock. We knew of only one older Christian man in the city and went to his home first, hoping he might be able to take us in. We did not stay there, however, as he had only one very small room, and his daughter was there with her two children. One child was sick with measles and the other with scarlet fever. Before we left the mother became sick too. For five days she had a raging fever—we thought it was typhus. Though we had dinner there, we sat outside to eat. A crowd of people soon gathered to watch us. Their bright remarks about us foreigners came close to giving me the giggles.

The Lord wonderfully gave us a nice place to stay. It was a good location—not right on the main street, but a place where all the people passed by to come to market. The landlord and his wife were very kind to us. The house was a big building with one room partitioned off in the center for a bedroom. This was our room. As there was no door to our room, the people as well as the livestock had free access to us. The first night we were awakened about midnight by the pigs coming into our room. The landlady came after them and cursed them for not knowing this was the guestroom! Mrs. Wu and I were completely tickled over her scolding and laughed into the night.

Daylight was fading by the time we got settled in the day we arrived, and we were hoping we could get to bed early. That was not to be. Just about that time the schoolboys were coming out of school and came over to have a look. They crowded into the room, and I taught them choruses for about an hour. When they left, Mrs. Wu was rejoicing because she thought we could go to rest. But just then a crowd of women came. We had a good preach to them, and before they were gone some men came in. It was quite late before everyone left. We had a crowd in almost every night, and sometimes Mrs. Wu and I went to bed before the last ones left. We just pulled off our top dress and crawled into bed Chinese fashion.

Tuesday was market day. I think we must have preached to almost a thousand people that day. All I needed to do was to go outside and sit in front of the house, and before long we had crowds to preach to. We preached until about three o'clock in the afternoon and then went into the market square and preached there.

Wednesday we began visits to a very densely populated string of villages in the country. In the first village we perched ourselves on a stone in the middle of the town, and many people came out to see and hear. Fifty or more listened well. We did the same in each community we visited.

It was a thrill to preach to these people. They seemed to drink in every thing we said. Surprised looks sometimes came over their faces when they heard that there was a living God.

We did not stay out very long our first full day, though, as the Christian man in town had invited us for dinner. I was not a bit keen on going, but we could not get out of it.

After dinner some military people invited us into a home. The wives seemed of a higher class. Preaching to them was a pleasure, and we stayed until almost dark. After that day they often came over to our room for more lessons.

Because Thursday was market day again, we preached on the street. The soldiers all left the city on this day. After the soldiers had gone, the people lived in fear of brigands. We did not know just what to do, but decided since we were there, we would stay. If the brigands came, we would just run to the mountains with the people. That morning my verse was, "It is better to trust in the Lord than to put confidence in man." Marvelously the Lord kept it quiet and peaceful all the time we were there.

Friday, because several of the women wanted me to teach them and said they were coming to where we were staying, I decided to stay in our room. The cook and Mrs. Wu went to the next market town five miles away. I was busy all day preaching and teaching choruses. The landlady was very kind and invited me to eat dinner with them. At night Mrs. Wu and the cook both came home sick—one with a sore back and the other with a headache. They both suffered these ailments occasionally and were usually laid up for two or three days. I didn't know just what we were in for. If ever I prayed for the sick, I did that night! The next morning they were both better. I tell you, all of us were thankful!

Saturday was another market day. When the night turned cold, we built a fire on the dirt floor in the middle of our room. Quite a few folk came in, and we had a good time singing choruses.

On Sunday we had a service. We invited the people to come and bring their own benches. As there was no building, we sat in the street in front of our rented quarters. I wish you could have seen us. People came from everywhere, plopping down wherever they wanted. The cook did the preaching. The singing consisted of a quartet of the 80-year-old local Christian man, the cook, Mrs. Wu, and me. A herd of pigs passed by, and men followed with big bundles of wood on their backs. It was the first time either attenders or passers-by had ever seen a Christian service.

The last two nights we could not sleep for bites of one kind and another. After we got home, the cook picked the bugs off my quilt and showed me which were head lice, body lice, bedbugs, etc.! If ever I appreciated a bath and a clean bed, it was on that Monday night! The cook celebrated our homecoming by putting on a grand Chinese dinner.

Our neighbors were building a new house, attached to ours on the side. We could watch all the building from Helen's bedroom window. In fact, Helen's window opened right into the new house! When workmen were about to put up the very top beams, the home owner killed a chicken and rubbed the blood all over the beams. After that they shot off a lot of firecrackers to scare away the demons. They also had a table festooned with ten long strips of red cloth. On the table were two piles of bread—about twenty little loaves. After the priest came and chanted for a time, someone gathered everything up. A while later the carpenters were served a chicken dinner!

In May my brother Dick wrote informing me that our sister Grace was quite ill and had been taken to the hospital. Again I had to deal with the worry of a loved one while so far away and feelings of helplessness. It was not easy at a time like that to praise the Lord, yet I knew that Romans 8:28 was still true. Surely the Lord was working in love and for our good.

In June the cook got married! For a Chinese man not to be married was unusual. Cook was 45 years old and had never had a wife. He married a widow who had a little girl of about four (but looked more like a two-and-a-half-year-old.). Cook was almost beside himself with excitement. We were happy for him, but concerned that he would not work for us any longer—and we were right. Shortly after he married he gave notice that he would be leaving. I was worried about what to do because we had a lot of company coming, including fellow workers returning from furlough. The MacIntoshes were already with us. I would have to stop preaching for a while and do the housework. It took a lot of time to do the cooking because we had to boil all the water, refine all the sugar (and sometimes the salt), make all our own coffee and porridge, and render out lard. Soon it would be time to make jam to store for the winter.

Most of the guests left us by July. Only Mr. and Mrs. McIntosh and their two children were still with us. We tried a new cook but he was so untidy in the kitchen that, when he left for a rest, we did not ask him to come back.

I went to Nancheng for a few weeks after all the guests left. When I returned home, my house was a mess. *Everything* was covered with disgusting mold. I spent several days cleaning it all up.

Letters from home were still very slow in arriving. Sometimes they took two or three months. As mail was being censored, we all had to be careful what we wrote.

In mid-fall a fellow missionary by the name of Miss Dickie and I decided to visit a mutual friend in Tenguang. While there Miss Dickie took sick. Because she was getting progressively worse, we decided she should go to Sian. Renting a cart, I made up a bed in it for her. Unhappily, riding five hours in that springless conveyance over dreadfully rough roads was very tough on her.

When we got to the area of the train station, I rented a room at an inn and put my patient to bed until train time. When the train arrived, it was packed. We managed to get a seat when a kind Chinese lady offered to move so that my companion and I could sit together. I made our seats up into a bed for Miss Dickie, and she was quite comfortable at first. But the farther we went, the worse she felt.

I feared I would not be able to get my patient off the train. When we got to the station at Sian, the two of us managed to walk to a waiting rickshaw. A kind coolie came along and took care of our luggage. Because the missionaries in town were not at home, no one came to meet us. We arrived at our destination at 1:30 a.m., very tired and relieved to be let in.

The next day we called the doctor, but she could not tell what was wrong with Miss Dickie. That night, when Miss Dickie's temperature shot up to 104 degrees, I took her to the hospital. The doctors there diagnosed her illness as typhus. I was very relieved that my sick fellow worker was where she could get proper care. Typhus was carried by lice. Miss Dickie must have been bitten on our trip. It was a wonder that I didn't get it too as we slept together in the same beds in the inns.

A few weeks later, when Miss Dickie recovered, we headed for Xin Ji. The trip home was quite an experience. We took a train from Sian on a Thursday afternoon and got to Paoki about one-thirty in the morning.

When we got to Paoki, we thought we could stay on the train until morning. But train officials would not let us as we did not have sleepers. I went to look for a man to carry our baggage, but could not find one. Finally I asked a policeman if he could get one for me while I went to look for a rickshaw or something for Miss Dickie. The foreigners there lived over a mile from the station, and Miss Dickie was still weak. When I could find nothing in the way of a conveyance, I went back to the train. By this time the policeman had found a coolie for us. He had carried our things out of the station and parked them in the middle of the street. There we sat.

After a time I left Miss Dickie to watch our baggage while I walked through the city to look for help. I finally found a man with a wheelbarrow to carry the baggage, and we walked the mile to where our friends lived. We got there about three o'clock in the morning.

It took us a half-hour to wake the household. We yelled, banged on the door, and were about to settle ourselves outside the gate for the rest of the night when finally our friends came to let us in! By that time poor Miss Dickie was just about dead. She stayed in bed most of the next day.

On Saturday we hitched a ride on the postal truck and, oh, was that grand compared to the truck we had ridden when we went to Sian! Only three of us sat in back among all the bags of letters. I had my quilt with me and just rolled myself up in it. It made a comfy seat.

We spent that night in an inn. Since it was quite cold, we decided to have a little fire in our room. When I undressed, my skirt evidently hit the fire and I didn't notice it. I put all my clothes in a pile, and a few minutes later we smelled smoke in the room. We didn't think anything of it as the men next door were smoking. Just a thin paper partition separated us, and the paper had holes in it! When we blew out the light, I saw a red blaze in the darkness and realized it was my clothes. The fire burned a big hole in my spring coat and about a foot off the bottom of my skirt. I knew Faith would say, "Goody," when she knew I wouldn't be able to wear that skirt any longer. It was so old-fashioned that she was embarrassed to have me wear it in Sian!

We got to Nancheng on Sunday, and I gave the remains of the coat to Mrs. MacIntosh, thinking she could make something for her little girl out of it. I came on home. A few days later here came my coat out to Xin Ji; Mrs. Mac had taken out all the facings and used them to patch the hole. I didn't think it could be done, as the hole was about 18 inches long and a foot wide.

I came home to the dirtiest house you ever saw. Before I went away I had had all the curtains, doilies, and linens washed, thinking they would be all clean and ready to use when I got back. Well, I found the rats had made a nest right in the middle of them. They gnawed a hole through the cupboard. Some of the curtains had such big holes chewed in them I couldn't patch them. Other things were filthy. It was good to get home anyway.

Since Bertha was coming soon, I decided to whitewash the living room. I did the rest of the house during the summer but did not get to the living room. When I finished, it still did not look very grand. I papered the ceiling, but, because the weather was cold and damp, it took too long to dry and turned yellow. Then I decided to make the room look pretty by putting a blue border around the top. It was quite a dark shade of blue when I first put it on. The second day it dried to a pretty shade of blue. I was so proud of it. But the lime was evidently too strong for the coloring because then it faded to an odd shade of lavender. As an interior decorator, I would make a good ditch digger!

December arrived and with it came thoughts of my family. I wondered if they were all together for Christmas—or had some of the boys been called to the front? *What a grand day it will be when the Lord comes*, I thought, *and there will be no more separations and no more wars!* ❧

Chapter 9

Eventful 1941

The year 1941 was to be an eventful one. But it started for me with a little rest. With Bertha graciously taking over the cooking, I was able to play "lady of leisure" for a few days. I spent most of my time catching up on correspondence. Letters from home were taking a long time to arrive, probably because they were coming by once-a-month boat. In fact, by March it had been six months since I had had any letters from the U.S. How I longed to hear what was happening with my family!

Early spring I went to Sisiang to help the superintendent's daughter-in-law, Amy Moore. She was cooking for the new lady missionaries who had come for language study.

When one of the workers became sick with appendicitis, I was elected to accompany her to Sian for surgery. We started toward Nancheng by truck about nine o'clock in the morning. About eight miles into our journey something went wrong with one of the wheels. Because the truck carried no tools, the driver had to walk back to Sisiang to fetch some. Meanwhile my charge and I sat on the truck and waited. We didn't get going again until three-thirty in the afternoon. It was dark before we got out of the mountains. Just as we neared the top of the last hill we had a flat tire. That meant another delay. We got to Nancheng about midnight. Since the city gate was already closed, we had to sleep in an inn. Though my patient was in quite a lot of pain by this time, she never once complained. I got her settled at the hospital early the next morning and then walked to the McIntoshes' for breakfast. They were really shocked to see me trotting in at that hour. After I had rested a day, a co-worker and I walked the eighteen miles home to Xin Ji¯ in four hours and fifteen minutes!

Mid-March Mrs. Wu and I went up into the mountains for several days. What a grand trip! Our destination was about thirteen miles from our home. Hiking over the passes between mountains we struggled up one side and scrambled down the other. In the lower valleys narrow mountain streams cut their way through steep banks covered with a solid mass of light-blue violets—gorgeous! Further up lilacs were blooming, also other wild flowers like little white pincushions with red pins. Scattered among big evergreens of all shapes and shades were fruit trees—peaches, cherries, pears, and quince—all in full bloom. My, what a sight to behold!

While in the mountains we stayed in the home of a Christian family named Liu. They lived in a tiny mud house almost at the top of the mountain. Old Granny Liu was about eighty years old, but was still a hearty soul. She claimed to believe, but how well she understood the Gospel I wasn't sure. For a living she spun thread from early morning until late at night or sometimes made straw sandals. Granny's daughter-in-law seemed to be kept busy making meals, gathering wood or helping in the fields. She and Granny's son had the cutest little three-month-old baby boy. Though he had a rather long thin face, big dimples appeared in his cheeks when he smiled. He was thoroughly grubby, but I loved him all the same. Though the younger Lius had had six children, this little boy was the sole survivor.

We got there rather late on Monday. We had dinner, and when a few children came in later, I taught them a chorus. That was about all we accomplished that day.

It was frightfully cold—even snowed at night. The wind seemed to blow right through the house. Our bed consisted of three boards about three inches apart, balanced on high benches and cushioned with a thin layer of straw. Because we thought the straw would be adequate, we didn't use our oil sheet the first night. Shiver! Shiver! Oh, but we were cold! The next night I put the oil sheet under us. We were much warmer.

The second day people kept coming in all day except for about ten minutes when we started to eat our dinner. Some people were still there at night when darkness fell. One young girl about twelve years old learned a verse and some choruses and seemed really interested. Also three men and a woman listened for a long time.

The third day, Wednesday, we visited the homes in the valleys. The very first country trip I ever made was to this place. We visited the home of the old Christian man with whom we had stayed on our first visit. He had died three days after we left. Well, his wife pretended not to be interested when we were in their home this time, but after we left she came along and followed us to two other homes and listened very well.

On Thursday we climbed right up over the top of the mountain. At the top some of the rocks were much taller than our heads, and the passes in between were so narrow that we could just squeeze through. We visited in homes where the people had never heard the Gospel or seen a foreigner. While some listened attentively, others could see or hear nothing but our queerness as foreigners. One family asked us all sorts of questions about the Gospel. The next home we visited the people would not listen at all. We were about to give up hope when a young boy came around who knew all about the Gospel—he had heard it at the market.

When we returned to where we were staying that evening, we found Mrs. Liu had made a meal for us. We had brought them a piece of meat when we arrived on Monday. By Thursday it had quite a strong smell. Mrs. Liu dished it up to us with rice and corn. I got by with eating only one bowl, but even that was hard to get down. Since I had no ill effects from it, I guess it did me no harm.

When we walked into our bedroom that evening, we found a

chicken doing a tapdance on our bed! I had evidently spilled a bit of rice, and she was doing her best to find it!

In the morning I was sitting in front of the door writing a letter while waiting for breakfast. Just in front of me was Everlasting Life, a little boy about three years old, doing his business, and the dog just behind him doing the mopping up operations!

By the way, the breakfast menu consisted of rice with mixed spinach and garlic and cold beans. Supper, our other meal of the day, included rice, garlic and pickled beans.

This was the season when people worshiped their ancestors at gravesides. On the way home we passed a little graveyard in the center of the town. About a hundred people were milling about— mostly young men—all dressed up in their best clothes. Each one brought a big basket of special red paper, dumped it in front of the grave, and set the mound afire. As the paper burned, they dropped on their knees and bowed three times. In just a few minutes the cemetery was a mass of smoke and flames.

The end of March I got a great lot of mail—most of it from the previous October through December. I was thrilled to get home news—a brother and a sister had gotten engaged; my mother was doing very well. I was especially appreciative of the copy of the *Reader's Digest* that family sent me regularly. When I finished with it, I would pass it around the district for others to read.

One Sunday morning rain began to fall just before breakfast. We didn't expect many for service, but had quite a crowd in spite of the wet weather. Those who lived the farthest away (five to ten miles) had started before it began to rain, and they would not turn back. We had decided we would drop the Bible class and just have the big service so that they could get home before the road was too bad. Nothing doing! Since they had come through the rain, they wanted to get all they could before they left. We had all our classes as usual!

It had been four years since I arrived at Xin Ji. It seemed more like four months to me. When I thought of the folks at home, however, it seemed like many years since I had last seen them.

One Monday Bertha went to see a man who had been very sick. He had not eaten anything for a month and was nothing but skin and bones. Though too weak to say much, he pointed to Heaven and said, "I'm going up." He died the next Tuesday.

The funeral on Thursday was held in the courtyard of the home and was a long drawn-out affair. Local people always put on a feast at a funeral. I felt sorry for the wife as she was so busy getting food ready that she didn't attend the service or even see her husband buried.

Old Mr. Yang took the service, and while he was speaking, some of the heathen relatives got up to light their pipes. Others were busy running back and forth with food. As Mr. Yang continued to speak, the sun got pretty hot. One of the relatives, a dear old woman, went over and very gently put a big straw hat on the old man's head!

After the service was over, the family served the first course of the dinner. Since we had to sit outside, they came around and put straw hats on each one of our heads as well. We hoped there was no livestock in them! As Bertha said mine came off from a bald-headed man, I felt fairly safe!

As Chinese coffins are made of very thick boards, especially the lid, they are frightfully heavy. It took ten or twelve men to carry the coffin this day. Right after the service they brought it to the courtyard. The door of the house was barely wide enough for the coffin to get through let alone for the men. What a struggle they had! A Christian man was lifting in the front, and he would say, "Praise the Lord, we are getting it out." Then a heathen relative would shout some curses at another fellow for not lifting hard enough. After they managed to get it out, an awful argument arose over which road they should take to the gravesite behind the house. Finally they got two long, wooden poles and tied them to the sides of the coffin. The men all maneuvered their shoulders under these, and, heaving and pulling and shoving and shouting, they struggled to their destination!

In June there was another bombing in Nancheng—the worst yet.

I praised God that all my friends as well as the mission premises escaped without injury. We could hear the bombing very distinctly in Xin Ji—the house shook as if there were an earthquake.

Because farmers were very busy during the early weeks of summer, to go out preaching was almost hopeless. They simply didn't have time to listen. They were harvesting winter wheat and then quickly had to get the fields ready for rice. If they didn't plant the seedlings right away, the little rice plants would get too big and couldn't be transplanted. This year they had had very little rain, nowhere near enough for the rice. Consequently the rice fields all had to be flooded before the rice could be transplanted.

Farmers were crying for rain. "If your God is so wonderful," they would ask me, "why doesn't He send us rain?"

"The trouble is," I told them, "if God did send you rain, you would not thank Him, but go and offer up gifts of thankfulness to your false gods."

The weather got hotter and hotter and still no rain. The farmers were getting desperate because they couldn't plant their rice. Some had a bit of water and planted out the little rice plants but the ground was drying up and the plants were all dying.

One day I saw several men parading shirtless and with trousers rolled up, maneuvering a "water dragon" through the streets. They were hoping to persuade the gods to send rain. With green branches tied to their heads, they all hung onto a long rope that had more branches tied onto it and waved the whole thing above their heads. Ahead of the procession were a couple of men beating drums. The people gathered along both sides of the street to watch. Sometimes they threw water onto the rope dragon. In this way they hoped to fool their gods, or please them, I really didn't know which. How we longed for them to turn and worship the true God!

Our Sunday school had almost come to a standstill. Schoolteachers wouldn't let the children attend. Some of them even held school on Sunday to keep the children from coming. We had twenty-five children one Sunday, which was a bit more encouraging. Most of them were little "rag-a-muffins" who didn't go to school, and a couple of them were older schoolboys. We wanted to plan a daily vacation Bible school for the children as soon as school was out, but we didn't dare announce it for fear the teachers would not give the kids a vacation!

Mid-summer we held our first week of DVBS. We had as many as 45 children one day—little tots ranging from babies to eight or nine years old. They were a handful! By the end of the week several of the children could recite all the memory verses and answer questions about the stories. We taught the older children the following week.

By the end of July there was still no rain in sight. We had two or three cloudy days and that gave a little relief from the awful heat. It was very muggy, but since the nights were a bit cooler, we were able to sleep in our bedrooms.

Meanwhile, the people of the city were doing everything imaginable to produce rain. They put on all kinds of theatricals, carried the rain dragon repeatedly through the streets, and even stopped eating meat for several days. All of it was useless!

One afternoon Bertha and I saw another group of people trying to make the rain gods cooperate. First a ragged-looking priest ran along carrying burning incense. Behind him came several men with green branches tied around their heads. They were beating drums and cymbals for all they were worth. Following the men were four others carrying a sedan chair trimmed with red paper. Inside that more incense and some candles burned. Gyrating behind the chair was a man possessed with a demon, slashing himself with two huge knives until blood was pouring out. Other than a red rag tied around his head, he had on almost no clothes. Surrounding him were men with spears to keep him from running wild. To look at him made me almost sick. As this group ran through the streets, the people all quickly lit incense in their homes. It was a horrible sight all around and made us realize anew that this city remained largely in the hands of the devil.

The following week still brought no rain—and along with that came a strong anti-foreign feeling. I suspected that if it once rained significantly, things would probably clear up. The ritualistic processions continued on, and the man with knives continued to cut himself. It was a wonder he did not get blood poisoning in those awful wounds or suffer the effects of blood loss.

The man who organized the rain procession also forbad the butchers to kill pigs unless they paid tax on each pig they killed. Eventually the tax collector came around and said if they didn't kill pigs, he would demand taxes anyway. Talk about a lose-lose situation for the poor butchers! In the end, the butchers killed the pigs and, when the demon man came around, they hauled the meat inside the house and hid it until he was gone!

For the rest of that year I received almost no mail from home and the letters I sent home were all lost. With the loss of those letters went the details of the months leading up to the shocking news of the Japanese attack on Pearl Harbor on December 7th. What little we knew of the widened scope of the war cast a shadow on our Christmas plans and beyond. Much depended on whether or not the war continued and what its outcome would be, especially now that it had a more global impact. The uncertainties sent shock waves that threatened to unsettle our hearts. Yet the year ended for me, not only with snow on the ground muffling the sounds outside, but with peace in my heart that I was exactly where God wanted me to be. ❧

Chapter 10

Preparing Xin Ji
for Independence

Because of Pearl Harbor and the broadening of the war to include
the United States, the mail hardly moved. People, too, struggled
to travel from one point to another. The last missionaries to come
from Shanghai took *nine months* to reach Nancheng, and they
still had a month to go before they would reach their stations.
The Moores' daughter Jessie and her husband, David Bentley-
Taylor, a part of that group, were bound for Kansu. The senior
Moores were making better time, we were told, and were due in
Nancheng soon.

Everyone was excited at the thought of having the Arthur Moores
back. Since most of the workers in the district were young folk, it
would be like having our China father and mother back. The
MacIntoshes had felt the burden of responsibility very greatly.
They had come to China the same year that I did, and both of
them were absolutely worn out and in need of a furlough. Only
the Lord knew when they would get one. Furloughs had all been
canceled. Helen and a married couple from Nancheng had
planned to start for home the following month, but they would
perhaps have to wait until the war was over. It was hard telling

when I would be able to go home. We were hoping the war would not be a long, drawn-out affair.

That year, instead of making long trips into the country, we planned to concentrate on the work in Xin Ji. By having all the Bible classes we possibly could, we hoped to establish the Christians. This was part of China Inland Mission's ten-year plan. For the first year of the plan, in each church that had a pastor the church paid one-tenth of his salary and the mission paid nine-tenths. The second year the church paid two-tenths of his salary and the mission paid eight-tenths, and so on until by the tenth year the church was completely self-supporting. When I arrived at Xin Ji, the church was already about halfway through the ten-year plan. In fact, by 1942 they had already taken over the complete support of their pastor. This was surely evidence that the Lord was in this work. Bertha and I shared the teaching in order that we might concentrate particularly on the growing number of new Christians in the Gospel.

At around this time one of the Christians gave her home to the Lord for a church building. Praise the Lord, at last we would have a place to worship! It needed a bit of fixing up. Because it was in the country, we would have to walk five miles to service each Sunday, but we were thrilled. The church was planning to move back into the city when the war was over. Hopefully prices would go down then.

In the spring we decided that the single lady missionaries in our district would go to all the surrounding stations to hold special Bible classes for women. My lot fell to go to a station fifty or sixty miles away. A Chinese lady and a new missionary who came to China the past year were to go with me. We would be responsible for six days of Bible classes. We would also be there for a Sunday, and on Monday the church would conduct special evangelistic outreach. It looked like our days would be very busy.

As soon as the meetings were over, I came home to Xin Ji. My duty in Xin Ji was to have a class in personal evangelism every day. The Christians usually went out in bands to preach on

Sunday afternoons. Actually, some of them didn't even know how to give a good testimony, to say nothing of preaching. We hoped to give them a bit of help.

The Moores did not arrive when we expected them. They were due on a Tuesday or Wednesday, but we learned that their truck had broken down. Mrs. Moore said in a letter to us that they were very eager to get to Xin Ji. They had been nine months on the way from Toronto, Canada, and she was "aweary from the journey." Mr. Moore said, "Half of our load is the love we are carrying from your family to you!" My, how I looked forward to seeing them and hearing some news of my family back home! I had not received any letters from home since the Pearl Harbor attack on December 7.

I had been looking forward to a promised vacation. The promise, however, was given before the U.S. was drawn into the war. I doubted now that it would be possible for me to go away. If I went anywhere, I wanted to go to see Faith. I would have to wait and see what Mr. Moore would say when he returned. It was costing us about fifteen dollars a day to live at the time. With traveling expenses on top of that, vacation would be very costly. I had saved enough money to cover my expenses fairly well, but the problem would be to draw out that much money. The Lord had most marvelously supplied all our needs thus far. We lacked nothing. And we looked to Him, trusting Him to supply for our future as well. My verse on my birthday was, "Thou crownest the year with thy goodness."

In August I did get the vacation I was hoping for. Faith and I went to a place called "Restwell." Though our travel there went safely, we witnessed some disturbing accidents¯two trucks overturned, a soldier boy killed when he fell off a truck, and then another truck wheels up. To add to the danger, a blizzard dumped six inches of snow on the ground in the higher elevations¯in August, no less! Fortunately, though the road through the mountains was treacherous, we had very careful drivers and a good bus, and when we arrived, we found Restwell to be a beautiful place. While there I enjoyed fellowship with Faith, went for long walks to the top of the mountain, rested, and wrote letters.

The last Sunday we were at Restwell, Generalissimo Chiang Kai Shek and Madame Chiang visited the place and invited all of us to a tea party held in the Governor's garden at four o'clock. Everybody arrived looking their best. The garden was a huge place with lots of trees and flowers. Under a big white awning was spread a beautiful red Oriental rug. Lovely easy chairs and davenports surrounded the rug. People sat around and talked until the Generalissimo arrived.

When Chiang entered, everyone stood up to greet him. He apologized for his wife, who was ill and could not come. After he had greeted us all as a group, he led us into the hall where the tea was served. A long table in the center held a variety of cakes and a large tea urn. Around the sides of the hall were small tables all laid with beautiful linen, china and silverware. Chiang sat with the governor and a military general at the head of the table. The first course featured cakes, tarts with fish, steamed dumplings with dates, candy, and tea. The second course was chocolate ice cream and fruitcake!

After tea the General made a speech followed by one given by our hospital doctor. Afterwards the Generalissimo went around to shake hands with each guest. A very gracious man, he was dressed unpretentiously in a plain khaki suit without trimming of any kind. His smile and his peaceful countenance held my gaze. I think he impressed everyone. I was glad for the privilege of meeting him. I wished only that Madame Chiang had been there.

When we left Restwell, Jeanie Dougan (Faith's fellow-worker) and I walked down the mountain for the first part of our trip. It took us about four hours. We traveled the rest of the way by raft. The river was quite high, and we did enjoy the ride. It was the first time I had traveled any distance by raft. We surrounded ourselves with baggage at the back and sides and then put our quilts down in the middle to sit on. It was like sitting on an easy chair. We arrived at Lanchow about three o'clock.

Faith and I had both planned to leave Lanchow on Friday of that week. Faith got away, but I didn't. I had the beginning of a siege of five boils on and under my arms. Also my ears had been troubling me, and the doctor wanted to have another look at them. The week prior the doctor had punctured my eardrum. As I was given chloroform for this procedure, the operation was quite painless. Even afterwards I could hardly feel that the doctor had done anything to my ear. I had taken a course of sulfanilamide for several days and hoped that would mean my trouble was conquered. The hole in my eardrum made me deaf temporarily, but I was told that that would gradually fill in, and my hearing would return to normal. It did.

I left Lanchow on September first. Traveling together were five foreigners: two YMCA men, a YWCA lady, another CIM lady and myself. Halfway home another man joined us. We were on a passenger bus, not an open truck. The drivers were usually careful. Only three of these buses made the run each month, but those runs were worth waiting for. We had one slight accident going around the corner¯a head-on collision with a truck. As neither vehicle was going fast, damage was limited to just a fender and bumper bent flat against the truck's wheel. Drivers put a rope around the damaged parts of the truck and hooked it to our bus, backed up quickly with a jerk, and pulled it free. That was the end of that! The whole trip took only four days.

We got to the village outside of Nancheng at one o'clock in pouring rain. When a coal truck came in from the city and dumped off its load, the passengers from our bus piled in for the ride into the city. We arrived about five o'clock. You can imagine what we looked like—covered with wet coal dust! I didn't much care what I looked like¯I was at the mission center, lifted by the Moores' wonderfully warm welcome.

Next morning I returned to Xin Ji. I was glad to be home and with Bertha again. The two of us were very compatible. Mrs. Wu told some Chinese ladies that she had never seen even two sisters who were as close as we were.

Once I had settled in again, Mrs. Wu and I went out together. Though we had planned on visiting the homes of two or three Christians, we got to the first place and stayed for the day. The women said they had not seen us for such a long time that they just did not want to let us go. We read the Sunday Bible lesson over with them twice and had prayer with them.

The next day we visited a woman whom we had nicknamed "Tonic Wang" because she was always so cheerful. We found her out in the field in her cornstalk hut, guarding her corn.

One Sunday morning about this time a man came to us and reported that his old mother was very sick and about to die. So the next day Bertha, Mrs. Wu, and I took the long trek out to see her. We expected to find her breathing her last. But, no, the old Granny was very much alive. In fact, she walked out to the gate to meet us. She sobbed a little when we first came and told us how miserable she felt and how bad her cough was. She told us she felt sad because she thought she was going to die without seeing me again. When her son came back from service the week previous, he told her that I was back. And there she was, too sick to come to see me. Well, she was so cheered before we left that she even said if we had a conference soon, she might manage to come.

In spite of the fact that letters did not get through, my family's support payments continued to come through regularly. How glad I was that they were sharing with me in this work! I was sure that for some of them their sacrifice was greater than mine. I *knew* what it meant to them to put up so much money for me every month—and the Lord knew too.

In November I was delighted to receive a good batch of home mail. That month, too, Xin Ji was pleasantly cool, just cool enough that we started wearing our wadded dresses but not so cool that we had to put up our stove‾a good thing as charcoal was terrifically expensive. We planned to do without as long as we could.

No end of activity and interesting events filled our days. One week, for instance, old Mrs. Chao asked Bertha to ask God to help her buy a pig. They went to the market and for $104 bought a foot-long piglet, which soon proved that it loved to eat and grow. We all praised the Lord.

One regular attender brought his wife and baby with him to service one week and, since there was no one home to watch their dog, he brought that too for fear someone would steal it. The wretched little pup kept running around my legs while I was teaching, and during the service it went up and lay at the preacher's feet and slept until the meeting was over.

Speaking of pets, I saw a little boy going to market with two little kittens one morning. When I asked him how much he wanted for them, he said $70 each. I suppose if I actually wanted them, I could have negotiated the price down some.

One Sunday late in the year while we were having Sunday school, a plane went over. Frightened, several of the children ran out. One sweet little girl, a refugee from Shansi, had evidently gone through some bad raids and was terribly frightened of planes. When she saw the others running, she said, "What are you running for? Can't the Lord Jesus protect us here?" When she said it, she was white with fear. Deciding it was probably only a Chinese plane, we went on with Sunday school, and soon the children were all quiet. We hadn't had a raid in this district for about a year, although scout planes went over occasionally.

When someone gave us some buckwheat, we decided to try our hands at making buckwheat pancakes. They didn't taste quite as good as the ones Mom used to make for us, but it was probably because we didn't set the yeast rising the night before as she did. Actually we didn't have any yeast. We just used baking powder. Cheng, our cook, was making our own syrup. We had made one kind from sweet potatoes, but he was making rice syrup. He was going to try corn syrup one day soon too. One day we put down a piece of bacon in brine. I thought maybe we were faring just as well as the folks back home. We read in the newspaper about all the rationing in the States. Home now probably would not have even seemed like home to me, since so many things had changed.

Another change was coming. Bertha and I had less than a year in Xin Ji before we would have to move. We didn't know yet where we would land. We had only one request, and that was that we would have Chinese fellow workers wherever we went. We didn't even know if we would be together. There was some talk of opening a new station in a city on the motor road. A lot could happen in a year, however. The Chinese people in Xin Ji wanted us to stay, but I didn't expect that would happen. If we did stay, we would move out to the country where the church meeting place was located.

But life went on. One Saturday in December a lady came to the door and yelled for Mrs. Wu to come quickly as she had urgent business. This lady was a Christian. Since she had not produced any children for her husband, he married another woman and moved to a neighboring town. Now, because she had not paid her taxes, the authorities were going to put her in prison for a couple of days. A church member had heard of her predicament and offered to fetch her grain for her to pay her taxes. Unwilling to pay the fellow for carrying it, she wanted Mrs. Wu to go and sit in prison for her for a couple days while she went to get her rice herself! She had neglected to pay before because she thought her husband might help.

Sunday I was at the gate when the delinquent tax payer said she was going to the place where she had paid her taxes to get her receipt. When I reminded her that she should not do such things on Sunday, she said, "Service is over, doesn't that finish it?" I asked her if the Lord came back today, would she like to be found in the tax office? I left her standing at the door while I talked with others who were leaving. A few minutes later she came to get her Bible and said she had decided not to go.

As Christmas neared, my thoughts flew home ever so often. I wondered what my family members were doing. I wondered if they would all be home with Mom.

As the church decided to have a conference Christmas week— including Christmas Day—we weren't able to do much on December 25th. We ended up having a bowl of rice porridge for breakfast with sweet potatoes and beans cooked in it. Dinner was rice with peppers and some turnips. We decided to celebrate Christmas the next Saturday. I planned to have stuffed chicken, mashed potatoes, carrots and dried peas, and a jellied tomato salad. Apple-crisp for dessert sounded yummy. In the afternoon we would have tea and Christmas cake. What we actually ate I can't remember.

We were so peaceful; it was hard to believe there was so much sorrow and suffering in other places. Everyone seemed to be encouraged. We hoped the end of World War II would soon be in view. Things would be very different once it was over. *Things* didn't matter so much. I was longing to see my family. ☙

Chapter 11

Demons, Xin Ji Triumph, and Bicycle Woes

The fall of 1943 would mark the tenth anniversary of CIM ministry in Xin Ji. At the end of August our lease would expire. As the new year dawned, we and the church became very much aware that we had eight months to prepare for our departure and the church's taking full responsibility for its own affairs.

Bertha and I were away over the New Year's Day weekend, probably for CIM's usual year-end day of prayer and a bit of a break. As Bertha needed two or three more days of rest, I came home to Xin Ji alone on Monday. On the way I pedaled my bike to Miss Haslam's place to deliver a bottle of milk to her as she had bunged up her ankle and couldn't get out. I carried the milk tied in socks around my neck. Nicely this veteran missionary treated me to dinner before I continued homeward.

Arriving home, I was greeted by the news that on Sunday the church had given $2,100 for renovations to the home that had been donated as a future church meeting place. I was thrilled. The next week the figure rose to $2,575. What an encouraging start to the final countdown to our departure! The actual renovations began with the first warming days of spring.

Our Bible classes took on new urgency as we prepared the

church for their launch to independence. We desperately didn't want to leave them vulnerable to "every wind of doctrine," as the Scriptures describe spurious teaching. Attendance held up encouragingly as the year progressed. My diary records 83 in my class one Sunday¯20 men, 26 women, and 37 children. And beside these Sunday classes, I was going weekdays to homes in various parts of the city, when church folk would gather friends and families for basic Biblical teaching. In spite of my wobbly start in learning Chinese, God was giving me new-found ability to communicate the truth. I loved it.

At Chinese New Year's time thousands of people swarmed the streets. Church people, nearly en masse, joined the crowds to help preach the Good News. We broke up into four bands. What a great opportunity for people to use what they learned in my classes on evangelism!

Mid-April Mrs. Li came smiling into our home with the news that her husband Cheng-Yong was home safely after a couple of years on the front lines. But a cloud soon darkened his homecoming. He was either mentally ill or demon-possessed. We were first aware of this when, five days after his arrival, he came to us wild-eyed and yelling, "The devil is after me!" We wondered if there was a connection between his present state and the fact that he had unwisely torn gods out of temples in his young fervor for God.

The next day Cheng-Yong was back, sure that the devil was after him again. He wanted food and a bath alternately. Mrs. Wu waited on him all day. Later he quieted down somewhat and spent the night sitting on a chair in our tiny sitting room.

The third day we fed our overnight guest and then called a special meeting to pray for his deliverance. He spent a good part of the day sitting on the same chair where he had spent the night, singing strangely and making motions similar to what we teach children in acting out choruses. His wife took him home in the evening.

In May we began packing for clearing out of our leased home.

Everything would have to go by summer's end.

July 26 the church moved benches and the rest of its furnishings and equipment to the new church building. Sunday, August 1st, the church met there for the first worship service and several baptisms. Percy Moore of the China Inland Mission, and Mr. Tseng, head of the group of CIM-founded churches in the area, came by bicycle to help us celebrate the opening of this new facility and the independence of the Xin Ji church now set to be fully self-supporting, self-governing, and self-propagating. What a day for rejoicing! We had to swallow hard to hold in our emotions as we looked around at the hundred or so people that filled the newly refurbished church building. We would soon be leaving these who had become so close to our hearts.

That evening Bertha and I slept in the church with the women. We strung our hammocks between benches. The Chinese ladies slept five to a mat on the floor. Li, feeling his new responsibility, came to see that we were safely tucked in. Quiet chatter and giggles persisted into the darkness as we enjoyed the camaraderie of being together.

About this time Mrs. Wu, who had been our invaluable companion and co-worker these past years, retired to her home church. We would miss her; we had become one in heart. In fact, Mrs. Wu had become like a mother to me.

On the late-August morning of our big move to Nancheng, our cook was up at 4:00. We had breakfast at 6:00. The exodus began at 7:00. Folk from the church turned out in force to shoulder our stuff, some of them pairing up to move bigger pieces (trunks and furniture) on poles. Even those who couldn't carry anything came along to escort us. What a parade we made as we filed out of town! At the Han River we piled onto boats with our baggage, sharing the space, not only with other people, but with horses, pigs, and chickens.

In a town just outside the city of Nancheng we all enjoyed a cup of tea together and said our goodbyes. Leaving Xin Ji and these people was like leaving home and family. Tears would not be held back.

The past year or two of concentrating on teaching a series of Bible classes had revealed my gifts in this area. Now CIM leaders were assigning me the task of itinerant Bible teaching. At conference time the churches, sensitive to their people's busy and slack times in planting and harvesting, would draw up my schedule. I would conduct informal two-week Bible schools for each congregation in turn. I didn't know it then, but itinerant Bible teaching was to become the focus of most of my ministry for decades to come.

Conducting short-term Bible schools from church to church sounds cut and dried. I found nothing cut and dried about the program certainly not the travel nor in the variety of homes and church premises in which co-workers and I stayed.

The first assignment for Bertha and me was an October-to-December circuit of Bible teaching and preaching, beginning in a distant place called Shihchuan, where Norman and Amy MacIntosh had once ministered. To get there, we had to travel through Chengku, Huangshapu, Shahokan, and Sisiang. It seemed like the end of the world.

After a delay because of washed-out roads, Bertha and I left Nancheng on a mild October day. After spending the night in Chengku, we were within a few steps of Huangshapu, when one of Bertha's bike's wheels locked. That was the one place where there was a man who repaired bikes! Bikes were rare in those days. It took the man just a half hour to take the wheel off, fix the problem, and put the wheel on again. Then just before we got to Shahokan, the halfway place, my bike succumbed to the pounding of the rough roads. A screw fell out of the back wheel, and the fork broke. I was quite prepared to walk and get to Sisiang about midnight. But a cart man came along and wired the thing together so that I could at least coast down the mountains by riding the pedals. We arrived at the Sisiang mission center just before dark.

We left Sisiang at eight the next morning, happy with the special bread tucked in our gear, sent along for our journey. But we no sooner got to the top of the first hill when my bike collapsed the frame broken in three pieces. We praised the Lord that it happened before I started coasting down the mountain. We sat down and ate our lunch and then turned back to Sisiang.

A couple days later we left for Shihchuan on foot. This last leg of our journey was beautiful, especially the flowers yet unspoiled by frost and splashes of bright red berries against the changing foliage. We made three steep climbs and three sharp descents before the crowded houses of Shihchuan came into view.

After days of living with only what we could carry on our bikes or backs, we were glad to see our suitcases and teaching materials. A CIM man and his Chinese co-worker had brought them by boat and dropped them off for us as they passed through.

In Shihchuan we stayed in the church premises. Also making her temporary home there was a Chinese lady refugee who had worked for the American consulate in Beijing or Shanghai. She had fled from the advancing Japanese. When she saw us eating with just a bowl and chopsticks, she quickly loaned us silverware. She also brought us treats such as coffee and chocolate, things we hadn't tasted for a long time. We relished each other's company as well, enjoying wonderful times of fellowship.

As we traveled from church to church, whether just emerging or well established, some of the short-term Bible schools were very encouraging with a good number of people attending. We reveled in sharing the Word of God with people showing a hunger to learn. But sometimes we felt the presence of Satan, with few people attending and a deadness of spirit. Those times reminded me of trudging uphill through deep mud.

Various hardships tried our commitment. We often walked as many as twenty miles in one day. Roads were often dreadful. On one trip I completely wore out my straw sandals. One day smoky fires made our eyes burn, and tears streaked our cheeks. Another time four big dogs attacked me, tearing through three layers of clothes not hurting me, but frightening me half to death.

By November the weather had turned bitter cold. My hands nearly froze as we traveled. At one point I even had to take off my shoes and stockings to wade through the icy water in a river.

Were our efforts worth the discomforts? Looking back at what the future held for these people, we would someday have not the slightest doubt. Even then we felt the Lord's seal on our work. God's provision of travel expenses and His strength and grace day by day were beautifully evident. I knew I was right where He wanted me. ∝

Chapter 12

Home!

Oh, what excitement started the New Year, 1944! Mission leaders not only granted my furlough, but instructed me to leave as soon as possible! I was so excited about seeing my family again that I didn't know what to do with myself.

In a telegram General Director Frank Houghton asked me to escort Miss Haslam, who was going home to retire. Elderly and heavy set, she suffered a stiff, painful ankle and shoulder from fractured bones that had never been properly set. I was to accompany her as far as India. Travel, I knew, would be difficult for her. She had been very kind to me. Now I was glad to help. I wanted to do all I could to make the first lap of her trip as easy as possible.

I planned to go to Miss Haslam's station the very next week to help her pack and clear up her stuff. From there I wanted to go to Xin Ji for the last Sunday of January to see the folk there again.

We hoped to leave for furlough early in March. It would take a week or ten days to get to Chungking, then 12 hours by plane to Calcutta. What with waiting for passes, visas, vaccinations, planes, buses, boats, etc., I reckoned I would do well if I got home by the 4th of July. It was all so sudden and exciting that I hardly knew where I was.

As soon as I got the telegram, I dropped everything and started packing my suitcase. I cut about a foot off my coat and some of my old dresses to wear for traveling. I was allowed only 30 pounds of luggage, not much when taking clothes for winter as well as summer. It took very careful sorting and planning.

Early that year all the churches in the district gathered for a big conference. Four meetings a day left little time for anything else. Special for me, though, was meeting lots of the folk who came in from the places where we had had classes.

Miss Haslam and I left our station early on a Monday morning in March. The church had farewell meetings for us the day before, and when we left, the whole church came to the bus station to see us off. They also gave each of us a small gold heart-shaped pendant. I still wear mine most of the time these decades later.

In a portrait taken during my first furlough I am wearing the pendant the Xin Ji church people gave me. I still wear it.

When our bus tickets were purchased, the agent assigned us the back seats. We prayed about those seats as they were very difficult to get in and out of and, of course, back there riders felt the bumps of the rough road so much more. I didn't mind for myself, but I was concerned for Miss Haslam as she suffered from arthritis. I didn't know if she could bear all the jostling. When we got to the bus, we found the two front seats reserved for us. A man in the telegraph office had kindly managed to get our seats changed.

During our dinner stop we went to a restaurant. As we were finishing our meal, a gentleman came to us and introduced himself as a magistrate from one of our northern districts. He said, "I am a Christian. I was baptized last year." After talking a while, he paid for our lunch and walked away.

Our ancient bus kept breaking down. Darkness hid the landscape before we reached Kuangyuan, where we were to stay the night. Our driver kindly managed to get a man with a wheelbarrow to take our luggage to the mission house while we walked.

Getting a bus from Kuangyuan seemed almost impossible. Ill with typhus, the resident missionary could do no more to help us than give us a letter of introduction to a bank manager. In the end a friend of the bank man introduced us to the bus stationmaster, and by the fifth morning we were on our way again.

It took three long days of travel from dawn until dark to reach Chungking. We stopped only once a day for a meal. We ate our supper after we got in at night. The wooden seats of that bus felt mighty hard by the end of the third day. We were thankful when we reached Chungking safely and could have a few days rest in wartime CIM headquarters there.

April 6th we left China by plane and flew over the awesome Himalayas—otherwise known as "The Hump." Most of the way only five passengers were aboard—two men from the British Embassy, one American Consulate man, Miss Haslam and me. The two British men shared an oxygen tank. Since the American man was sick when we started, he made up a bed on the floor. Miss Haslam and I felt quite well the whole time and enjoyed the journey. "The heavens declare the glory of God, and the firmament shows His handiwork" certainly true at 19,000 feet.

"If only we did not have to do this long journey in one hop," Miss Haslam kept saying, "I would not mind it so much." The Lord granted her desire. As the airfield in Calcutta was under repair, planes could not make night landings. So, instead of going on, we spent the night on a tea plantation after landing in Assam. The next morning our pilot came in a jeep and took us to the airport. Noon of that day found us in Calcutta. In one day we went from cold weather in China to the mid-summer weather of India.

In India we stayed at the Lee Memorial Mission. There a pleasant surprise awaited me: a telegram from my dear friend, Evangeline Kok Tharp. She invited me to come visit her. She and her husband were working at the British Ministry of Information in New Delhi. I thought they were in a Japanese concentration camp in North China. Here they were in India! During a weekend with them, I saw the sights of New Delhi. From there I spent a week with a missionary from my home church. That visit gave me a glimpse of God's work in India. The Lord planned our journey perfectly. During this time Miss Haslam was able to find transportation home to New Zealand.

On May 8th I boarded a ship for the U.S. that had taken 93 days to come from the States. After three days of waiting to sail, my fellow passengers and I were ordered to disembark. I felt the change was of the Lord, that He had something better for us. I was right. After a couple more weeks' wait, we were allowed to board a fine American troop ship. Though sidetracking to Australia, she brought us home in a record twenty-seven traveling days.

I simply can't describe my feelings when I put my two feet on U. S. soil. Everything looked so beautiful and clean, a land of plenty and still free from the ravages of war. Wonderful!

Red Cross ladies brought me and the young Chinese couple whom I was escorting to our China Inland Mission home. How good it was to see the friends there! A home never looked better.

We tried to make reservations on the train, but found that no tickets were available until August 3rd. Most of the many Chinese students on our ship were traveling east. The Chinese Consulate managed to have an extra car put on the Santa Fe Limited for them. Happily, since I was escorting Mr. and Mrs. Yeh from the CIM church in Chungking to Moody Bible Institute, the three of us were able to join the Chinese students on the train.

July 6th we reached Chicago. My mother, brother, sister and nephew had driven all night to meet the train, due in Chicago at 7:30 a.m. As we were four hours late, they were about to give up on me. Believe me, there were tears of joy that day! After taking Mr. and Mrs. Yeh to Moody, we came straight home. The rest of the family was waiting for us here. What a welcome! If getting to heaven is anything like my homecoming, it will be grand!

Much had changed in the eight years I was away—not the least family members. Siblings and their spouses were closer to middle age than youth. Hairlines had shifted, figures matured, and families expanded. I met nieces and nephews for the first time.

With Pop gone, the hole he left was obvious. Mother missed him so very much. I moved in with her. Oh, it was good to be home!

But I had obligations to supporters beyond my family. The Lord had done great things for me in China, and I was happy there, hard things and all. But I couldn't have triumphed without all the prayers of my faithful prayer warriors. I was filled with gratitude for all of them and wanted to visit each one. I was soon traveling, usually by bus, from church to church, group to group, and individual to individual.

During my time in the U.S. the CIM leaders in China couldn't find a single person to take over my itinerant Bible teaching ministry. Excuses were varied: some possible candidates couldn't eat Chinese food, or they couldn't eat this or that, and others said they couldn't sleep except in their own beds. In my set-up I had often slept on boards made into beds or on some straw on the floor—whatever my hosts could come up with. The Lord gave me a gift—I could sleep on anything as long as I had a blanket to keep me warm.

I longed to return to China. But for now I was stuck at home. At the awful price of invasion and cities turned to rubble in Europe and of atomic-bomb death and destruction in Japanese cities, World War II finally ended in 1945. Hope returned to Asia's occupied peoples. But I still did not have freedom to return to China. Still no one had picked up my itinerant Bible teaching role among China's believers. I could not fathom God's ways.

Now I can trace God's hand in His mysterious leading in those months. Churches, prayer groups, and individuals with whom I shared came to form a powerful prayer shield for me through the years ahead. In fact, the prayer group in Zion, Illinois, still prays for me to this day, though only two of the original members survive. That adds up to decades of faithfulness!

In God's time, as 1945 moved into 1946, with World War II history, the way did open for me to return to China. Family assured me that they would give Mother the support she needed. As hindrances melted away, my focus shifted to shopping, packing, correspondence with CIM leaders to make arrangements, renewing my passport, and making final rounds to say good-bye.

Suddenly I could see only clear paths ahead. Of course, only God could see around the corners of the future. I would trust Him—for whatever. ∾

Chapter 13

Back to China at Last!

At last, in April 1946, I was on my way back to my beloved China. As the train rumbled and swayed its way across America, bound for California, I enjoyed my traveling companions as much as the scenery. A very friendly lady sitting across from me was going to visit her oldest son, dying in a San Francisco hospital. A young man was straight from Amsterdam. An old man from the Netherlands was bound for China. He had lived his life in China as a sea-faring man. His wife and children were still in Shanghai, caught there during the war. After his ship was blown up in South China, he hadn't been able to get back to his family until now.

I was to be in California several weeks—I wasn't sure how many as the CIM travel person was still looking for a ship to take me back to China. Shipping was still adjusting toward normal after the disruption of the war.

When our train reached San Francisco, my cousin Marie, whom I had never met, was waiting for me. As I forgot to tell her what I would be wearing, I wondered how we would find each other. She said she was looking for someone that looked a bit "different." She found me "the first shot in the box," as I wrote then. I liked Marie very much. She went out of her way to give me a good time, first taking me to a park and zoo and driving me through other interesting parts of San Francisco.

Tuesday afternoon I went to see my Aunt Em, who was in the hospital recovering from a stroke. I took her a bouquet of sweet peas and a box of candy from our family. She seemed thrilled. Though she could not speak understandably, she recognized me, I thought. When I quoted John 14:1-3 very slowly for her, she followed, silently shaping her mouth to form each word. When I prayed with her, she seemed pleased.

Wednesday night I had dinner with my friends, Evangeline and Bob Tharp. The last time I had seen them they were in India, remember? Now here they were in California! They were waiting to sail for China too. Evangeline's cousin, a sailor, was also there. He was from Holland, Michigan. When I showed Evangeline my family picture, she passed it on to her cousin. He looked at it and said, "That's John Custer! He preached for us a few times."

"My brother," I acknowledged. The cousin attended Pastor Beerthuis' church in Holland, Immanuel Baptist.

No one proved to be better friends during my weeks in California than Mr. and Mrs. Zimmerman of the Immanuel Mission to Seamen. I stayed in their lovely cottage in Mt. Hermon, open for missionaries to use freely. The first weekend found twelve of us staying there.

Mr. Zimmerman and his son put Christian literature in all the cabins or bunks of every ship that came into port. Altogether they and native workers in many foreign ports gave out Gospel literature in a hundred and twenty different languages—a wonderful work.

In fact, the Zimmermans were wonderful *people*. Mr. Zimmerman was *the man* to help us with the problems of shipping. He knew his way in and out of all the shipping companies and ships.

Early in May I received a telegram from the North American

Director of the Mission with this message: "Sarah Marquis Agency offers only one passage from San Francisco May 29th on *General Meigs*. Have accepted for you. Tickets being sent." The *S. S. Meigs* had been taken over by the government and reserved for government officials and Japanese prisoners of war. I didn't know which class they considered me—Japanese or official! I surely wished that at least one other missionary would be aboard. On the other hand I was so eager to get back to China I didn't care how I went as long as I could get there.

We had great fun in our "camp" life in the cottage. Sometimes we didn't have enough sheets to go around when new guests came. The weather was so cold and damp that sheets didn't dry in just one day. In that case, we took the sheets off the bed, shook them, turned them bottom side up and put them back on. One such night when a group of people came, Helen of the Oriental Boat Mission and I were left to sleep between some old quilts.

The end of May found me still in Mount Hermon, but I had been keeping very busy. I went to the city to check on sailing dates and found out that I would not be leaving for several days. I planned to come back to Mount Hermon. Instead, when I got to the Zimmermans' home, she asked me if I would stay over and speak for a radio service on Tuesday night. The pastor who had this broadcast was sick in bed. Next morning she asked if I would speak to a group of women at noon, and before that was over I was asked to take the prayer meeting that night. Thursday morning I went over to Oakland and spoke to the CIM prayer group there.

Friday morning just as I was going to call my cousin Marie, I received a special-delivery letter from the CIM Home Director. One of our workers was due on Sunday on the *Marine Lynx,* coming from New Zealand. The director wanted me to find out about the ship, help the lady with baggage, and try to get a clergy pass for her train travel. We started calling the shipping companies to find who had the ship and where we could find it. We learned it had docked at eight o'clock that morning! Mr. Zimmerman and I grabbed our coats and beat it for the docks while Mrs. Zimmerman called the shipping company, had them page Mrs. Letherland to tell her to sit tight until friends came.

Because of his work, Mr. Zimmerman not only knew all of the men and the docks, he had a pass to get in. I got in with him. We found our lady sitting on her luggage waiting for things to come up from the hold. We waited with her until one o'clock, then had lunch and after that got her a clergy pass and tickets for Los Angeles and Oklahoma. She was to leave the next morning. We did not get back to the house until nearly supper time.

Saturday morning we found Mrs. Letherland sick in bed, and unable to travel. We cancelled her reservation. About seven o'clock we got a telegram, "Tolivers, Fosters due to arrive from Shanghai on *General Breckenridge*." Again we sat down and called all the companies to find who owned the ship. It must have taken us at least an hour to find out that the ship was due to dock at Pier 7 at 6:30 Sunday morning. As I was spending the night with cousin Marie, Mr. Zimmerman and I arranged to meet at the pier at eight o'clock. When we got there, we found the ship just pulling in. It was a thrill to watch it. Soldiers and sailors packed the vessel and, at first, I could not see even one civilian face. Finally I spied a lady that looked like a CIMer, with other foreigners nearby. I found they were not our folks. I walked the length of the ship again and still no sight of our folks. Then I decided to go back to this first lady, and I yelled up to her, "Is there a Mrs. Toliver on the ship?" She pointed to the lady beside her. "How many of you are there?" I asked.

"Two couples with two children, also two men and a lady," she replied. "Do you know where we can stay?"

When we said we had homes for them to stay the night, they heaved a sigh of relief. Told by others that they would not be able to get either train reservations or hotel accommodations, they hadn't known what they were going to do. As it was nearly eleven o'clock that morning before they got off the ship, I took the ladies and babies to the Zimmermans' home on the train. The men stayed to get their stuff through customs. At noon Mrs. Zimmerman fed ten grown ups and two children for dinner.

126

Afterwards Mr. Zimmerman took the folks around to the different homes where they were to stay. What would we have done without this couple?

Saturday night when I was at Marie's, who should call but her brother Hughie. He had not been home for a year. Marie asked him what condition he was in and told him that if he were drunk, he could not come. He came anyway. How thankful I was that none of my brothers were drinkers! Alcoholism certainly does mess up lives. Hughie had divorced his wife, also a drinker. Marie said Hughie's wife would walk down the street looking as if she hadn't washed or combed her hair for a week and so drunk she couldn't walk straight. How sad!

My sailing date was frustratingly uncertain. When I called the shipping company Monday, the passenger agent said all baggage must be on the dock before 4 o'clock on Wednesday morning, May 18th and we were to board the *General Meigs* at one o'clock that afternoon at Pier 42. I was really excited!!

That was not to be, however. We got new orders that we would most likely be sailing on the 29th, which happened to be the anniversary of when I boarded ship in India to come home two years before

The headlines in the morning paper that Saturday read: "ORIENT CRUISE SET FOR EX-TROOPSHIP. The twenty-thousand ton liner, *General M. C. Meigs,* first wartime troop transport to be reconverted, will be turned over to the American President Lines today. The six-hundred-and-twenty-two-foot vessel will leave San Francisco according to schedule next Thursday with three hundred and fifty first-class passengers bound for the Orient via Vancouver, B.C."

That was my ship!!! Other folk were going out on ordinary troop ships with anywhere from eighteen to thirty-eight in a cabin. Here I was traveling on this luxury liner carrying government officials. Grateful, I prayed that my testimony would count for Him among those "high-ups." My furlough would come to a perfect climax if I could win some of those folk for the Lord Jesus.

Saturday morning I went over to the city with Mr. Zimmerman, and there was the *General Meigs* cruising around the bay—a big white ship with blue and white stacks. It stood out beautifully against the mass of gray warships in the harbor.

My luggage was to go on board Tuesday, and we were to board ship Thursday at one o'clock. I was so excited I hardly knew what I was doing. Thursday noon Mr. and Mrs. Zimmerman and their son took me to the ship. I got my hand luggage aboard, had a cabin assigned and, since the ship was not pulling out until four o'clock, we went out and had our lunch. When I was getting on the ship mid-afternoon, the Zimmermans bought me a lovely begonia corsage.

This being the first ship returned to the company since the war, we left in great style. We even had colored streamers to throw out to friends on the docks to see us off. It was a thrill to travel in peace time again—no life belts to carry around, lights all on, portholes uncovered, and grand food.

The inside of the ship was still like a troop ship, however. Eighteen of us shared our cabin, including a baby about a year old and a little girl about six. Though most of the ladies smoked, on the whole my cabin mates were a good group.

The first night on the ship, I went to bed right after seven o'clock. I was just nicely tucked in when the steward came with a dozen beautiful American Beauty roses for me with a tag attached quoting Jesus' promise, "Lo, I am with you always." The flowers and verse were from a Dr. and Mrs. Webber, folks I stayed with when I took part in a missionary conference in Detroit. Surprised, I wondered how they knew I was sailing on the *Meigs*. How tickled I was that I, a lowly missionary from Michigan, was the only one who got flowers in that cabin full of officials' wives!

Though the ship rolled and tossed a little the first night as it left San Francisco and sailed northward, it really wasn't bad̄nothing like I had experienced earlier on my way home.

One day while we were having a boat drill, we saw a whale jump right up out of the water several times. One of the ship's officers said it was about five miles out and was very large.

On Saturday June 15th we landed at Vancouver about ten o'clock at night. Sunday morning fellow CIMers Hubert Fisher and Winnie Rand came down to see me. It was grand to have that little break. While in Vancouver we picked up a large group of Japanese repatriates with tons and tons of their luggage. Altogether we had 1,600 Japanese aboard.

From Vancouver to Japan was very cold and foggy. The foghorn blew every two minutes for several days and nights. The captain said he had never seen such a heavy, unrelenting fog. For a couple of days the waves were rather high, and the ship pitched and tossed. Though the waterline was normally twenty-eight feet below deck level, waves were crashing only nine feet below. Some on board were seasick, thankfully not including me.

The ship was bustling with people. The room known as the Social Hall was the only place passengers could go to sit down. People packed the Social Hall from early morning until midnight or later. Government officials, both American and Chinese, seemed to do little more than smoke, drink, and gamble. The room was so thick with smoke that a person could hardly breathe. Though those who did the smoking and drinking didn't seem to mind, I couldn't stand to be in the room more than a few minutes at a time.

Consequently I spent most of my time out on deck. It was so cold I had to wear my wool suit and coat and then wrap myself in two wool blankets. I had planned to get a lot of letters written, but my outdoor perch was too cold for that.

We arrived at Yokohama on the night of June 27th. A few of the passengers disembarked. The next morning at six we moved out a few miles and dropped anchor. All the Japanese repatriates and their luggage were then shifted from ship onto launches and taken ashore, a process that took about twelve hours.

Though a few days earlier the seas from Japan to China had been very rough, for our trip the sea was calm and the air, warm.

We landed in Shanghai on July 1st. As customs officers came onto the ship at ten o'clock with the pilot, we had all of our hand luggage through customs before we even got off the ship. We had to get the rest of our baggage the next day. I had my watches, camera, films, etc., all in my case but was not charged for anything—not even for my typewriter. I opened only one case. I guess they didn't open much of the heavy luggage, as they charged very little. We had a good man as transport manager.

Rain began just a few minutes after we reached CIM Shanghai mission home. Within a few days the compound and streets were so flooded that I wasn't able to leave immediately.

It was marvelous to be in the home, especially to think that a year before the Japanese were living in it, and our folks were in concentration camps! The home was in quite good condition. Most of the furniture had been restored.

In a visit with the director of the mission there in Shanghai I was told I would be working with Bertha Silversides again in Shensi. I was to leave in a few days and would travel with two other people. We were not only taking our luggage, but escorting things for several other people—in all 43 heavy pieces, including my big wardrobe trunk, and thirteen pieces of hand baggage. I was always amazed to see a little Chinese man pick up that big trunk of mine and carry it on his shoulders.

On July 10th we got to Hsuchow early in the morning. Because we were accompanying so much stuff, we couldn't make the transfer in the half hour between trains. We could do nothing but wait until the next day to continue on. When we could not find an inn, we decided to go to the Presbyterian Mission and were kindly taken in. Imagine my surprise when I was met by Margaret Sells—a girl who had come out to China with me the first time.

On July 11th we traveled to Kaifeng. While on the train we heard that the train that left Shanghai the day after ours had been derailed, also that Hsuchow was surrounded by communists. We seemed to be traveling just ahead of trouble. We spent the night in the mission station at Kaifeng. Being Swiss, our missionaries in Kaifeng were able to live there all during the Japanese occupation. They had a tough time, though—especially when American planes bombed the city.

July 12th we were supposed to get to Chengchow but didn't make it until the folllowing day because the floods had washed out bridges. Just as we were crossing the old Yellow River, we learned that this would be perhaps the last train through here as the line would be broken for a couple of weeks for road repair. So again, "our angel" was getting us through just in time.

I wish you could have seen us. Traveling third class, we were in a boxcar. For food we ate Army rations and Chinese breads. My big trunk made a good table. I put my dufflebag on another trunk, and that made a very comfortable seat. For sleeping we shoved some of the trunks together and slept on them. It was really lots of fun!

We left Chengchow early the morning of July 14th. But midday the train came to a stop and stayed put for nine hours in the heat. A train coming in the opposite direction had gotten stuck in a tunnel ahead. As one car was hauling gasoline, people panicked. In their fright they jumped off. A number of people were killed, and many were injured. Our engine had to extract the other train from the tunnel.

We pulled into Loyang at two o'clock in the morning. Not wanting to disturb the missionaries there at that hour, we put our hand luggage on the station platform and slept on top of it until about six o'clock and then found our way to the mission home.

In Loyang we waited six days for the express train on Friday night. Our tickets were supposed to be numbered to assure us of enough space. But in reality it proved to be a train packed beyond proper capacity. As we could find space only in the dining car, we had to sit up all night. Still we were thankful to be on our way.

Saturday night we crossed the gap, a very deep valley across which the Chinese were building a bridge. Our train was one of the first to go right through to the bridge. All we had to do was get off one train, run down the side of one mountain and up the opposite side to where there was another train waiting for us. The only problem was the heat. A blazing sun left us soaked in sweat. So as soon as we were settled in the waiting train, we called for tea and proceeded to drink eight pots full!

We reached Shanchow just after midnight. About two o'clock Sunday morning we gratefully stretched out our tired bodies on nice wooden beds in a lovely clean inn. However, about five o'clock, just three hours later, millions of flies arrived, and that was the end of our peaceful slumbers. We got up, had coffee and breakfast and then went to church.

Sunday evening our train was to leave Shanchow at nine o'clock. Though we arrived at the station at six to be sure to have a seat, the train was already full. After an hour's struggle, we managed to get our luggage aboard and sat on it in the aisles. Not until the ticket collector came through and found several folk without tickets did we get seats for the night-long journey.

Monday morning we dashed off right after breakfast for the bus station, though we were very much aware that we might have to wait several days for a bus. I was pleasantly surprised to find I could head south to Shensi Province the very next day.

When I got to the bus station Tuesday morning, my luggage was already on the bus bound for Nancheng. I found a Mr. Bartell going on the same bus as far as Shuangshipu—about half way. So I had good company that far. As darkness fell, the bus pulled to a stop at Paocheng—ten miles short of Nancheng—and could go no further because it had no lights. After a night in an inn I went on the next morning by horse cart, a fancy little buggy affair.

I walked into the Nancheng mission station about ten o'clock

Thursday morning. Totally surprised, Amy Moore met me with, "What are you doing here?" I discovered that letters had been sent to me at Shanghai and Sian to tell me my designation had been changed to Fengsiang. I got neither of those letters.

Bertha was away at meetings and would not be back until the middle of August. It was decided that I should stay put until she came back. After a little visit with her, I was to go back north.

While I waited for Bertha, I circulated in dear old South Shensi. It was just like coming home! Everyone gave me an enthusiastic welcome. Everywhere I stopped along the way, I heard the same story: "The field is white unto harvest, and there are no workers."

Shortly after arriving in Nancheng, I witnessed with joy the baptism of 54 new Christians. Nineteen of the people came from a recently opened outstation in the area.

The field to which I had been designated was a little farther north, in the central part of Shensi. I was told that hundreds of new believers were waiting to be taught. How encouraging to see how the Lord was blessing the work in all of the CIM stations! False teachers, however, were sitting on new believers' doorsteps waiting to lead them astray. With that unnerving challenge, I could not help but be ready to go.

Mid-August I borrowed a wreck of a bicycle and rode to Chengku, Shensi, to wait for Bertha, who made that her base. I used to cycle this in two and a half hours; this time the distance took four. First of all, because I waited for some things to take along, I was delayed until eleven and was forced to set off in the heat of day. Then along the way, as I was coasting down a hill, I suddenly faced passing a truck and a wheelbarrow at the same time. Judging the road too narrow for all of us side by side, I decided I'd better get off the bike. Only then did I discover the brakes didn't work. I had no option but to jump off and make as graceful a fall as possible! To top off my woes, the seat on the bike was so loose it rubbed my legs raw. I was so tired and sore that I walked the last mile or so. Was I ever glad to get to Chengku!

Some things had changed considerably since I was last here. I was surprised to find the missionaries using American butter, jam, cheese, etc. I learned that the prices were not as high as when I had left. I found American-made print fabrics in the stores as well.

While waiting for Bertha, I helped out with meetings. I took the service on Sunday and on Tuesday went to the old-people's home. On Thursday I took a women's Bible class. I was thrilled to be back in the work—and, thankfully, I hadn't forgotten my Chinese.

I returned to Nancheng toward the end of August. I was getting eager to get to my final designation and settled into the work again. Not that I couldn't find enough to do right there in Nancheng!

In mid-September I was all ready to leave for Fengsiang when a letter came telling me to go instead to Yanghsien, in South Shensi. As great a surprise as the change was to me, I was happy to stay in the south. I was to share the load of itinerant Bible teaching with Bertha and live with Helen Dalton in Yanghsien.

The trip to Yanghsien was another adventure. The bus trip to Chengku and the weekend there were uneventful enough, and I had opportunity to talk with Bertha. But rain over the weekend turned the roads for my ongoing journey into ribbons of miry mud. Monday morning I hired a mountain chair. My carriers bravely slopped through the mire. Though I was sure I would get dumped into the mud or a flooded rice field before I reached the journey's end, they landed me safely. But besides navigating the roads, we had to cross five big rivers and four rain-deepened streams. The first river we crossed by boat. The water was so swift the men could hardly control the boat. As we crossed, a passenger informed us that this boat had tipped over the day before with a load of people! Job's comforter!! The rest of the rivers had water that came up to the waists of the carriers. When one man went in to his armpits while piggybacking me across, I thought I would surely get dunked, but I arrived on the other side dry!

By the time I arrived in Yanghsien, Helen had been there alone about three weeks. She had very little by way of supplies. She was living on dry Chinese bread and honey, plus some wheat cereal she had made. Only two sticks of charcoal remained for firing. Noticing some bread pans and a Chinese oven, I asked why she did not make some bread. Helen said she didn't know how! I sensed she was depressed. The aloneness had gotten to her. I was glad I had come.

I loved the home there in Yanghsien. It had garden beds in front and in back for flowers and/or vegetables. A Chinese teacher, Mr. Lu, and his wife and baby would be living with us. He spoke English very well and was a fine Christian. My luggage was to have come down river by boat from Nancheng, but the heavy rains had held up the boat's coming. I had little clothing, practically no household supplies, and my bedding consisted of an old quilt and a straw tick. Things were temporarily a bit Spartan, to say the least.

The church building was old and run down. I sensed little spiritual verve among church leaders. The student work, however, looked as if it would offer great opportunities.

In October Helen and I attended a conference in Chengku. As Helen was too tall and large-framed to be piggybacked across rivers, she traveled to conference in a sedan chair. I walked with Mrs. Chang (the evangelist's wife), their three children, her brother, and another man. Mr. Chang had gone to another city a couple months earlier to help in the church there. Soldiers came and tried to force him out. It seems they stood behind him, leveled a gun on his shoulder and fired it. The poor fellow got such a shock he lost his mind. I felt so sorry for Mrs. Chang and her three lovely children. The little girl, "Love," was just a darling, well behaved, and a beautiful child. She and her little brother John, only a few months old, rode in baskets on the ends of a carrying pole. Peter, who was twelve years old, walked. I was happy to be able to walk with Mrs. Chang, as I was able to comfort her just a little as we traveled the 15 or 16 miles to Chengku.

Again all of us except Helen had to be carried piggyback across the same nine rivers and streams I had crossed the month before. Actually I thought it was great fun. I wished only that I could have my picture taken that way some time. About five miles out of Yanghsien the rain began to pelt down. Because the little girl and baby were getting wet, we took shelter in a farmhouse for a half-hour until the rain stopped.

The conference was a great time. God's Word lifted and challenged us, and fellowship with others refreshed us. I was especially glad for Helen. Those days did her good. And it was the time churches worked out schedules for short-term Bible schools for Bertha and me to teach in the region.

After conference an opportunity opened for me at the first school in the area to teach English. What a thrill it was! I used my flannelgraph and gave the Genesis lesson on creation. The students enjoyed it so much that they came back the next morning and asked if I would give them another hour's lesson. These were college students. I was glad they didn't know that I had not even finished high school! There were a hundred students in the class. The next week we decided to hold the class from 4:00-5:00 p.m. so that all the students could attend—about 400 of them. What an opportunity it was to tell the good old Gospel story! It just thrilled me. All those young people sat there and listened with their eyes and ears nearly popping out of their heads.

Xin Ji was one of the first churches scheduled for a short-term Bible school. To get to Xin Ji, Mrs. Tuan (pronounced *duan*), my new Chinese fellow worker, started out riding on a rickshaw and I on a borrowed bike. What used to be just three miles took us nearly three hours as we had to detour around the huge airfield the American Air Force had built when they were there. When we got back to the main road, it was so rough the rickshaw man refused to go any further. He tied the luggage onto my bike, and we pushed it and walked the rest of the way—12 more miles. By the time we reached the familiar sights of Xin Ji, my feet were sore, and I had walked a hole in my socks. Not expecting to walk, I hadn't worn my walking socks—heavy cotton socks with thick Chinese cloth sewn on the bottoms. Since settling in Yanghsien, we had walked from 5 to 15 miles every day except Saturday and Sunday. No problem with lack of exercise!

Three weeks before we came we wrote to remind the church we were coming. As they did not get the letter, they were not expecting us. When we walked in, Granny Men met me with, "This is just like the Lord's coming. They kept telling me you were coming, but you never came. Now all of a sudden, here you are! I have seen you; now I can die!"

Though it was cold November and she was 97 years old, dear Granny Men insisted on being baptized by immersion. Her relatives tried to persuade her to be baptized by sprinkling, but she would have none of that. The day before the baptismal service she walked the mile or so to her daughter's house, rested there a night, and then the next day walked the mile to the river where the baptisms were to take place. There that dear, spunky saint was baptized in freezing cold water. Weeks later she claimed she had felt better ever since! What a testimony!

The church provided us with a very comfortable set up—a nice room in the church half of Granny Men's house. It was furnished with table, chairs, cupboards, two Chinese beds and straw for mattresses—everything we could wish for, including a little mud stove in one corner, where we cooked our food and made our tea. I certainly enjoyed my sleeping bag I brought from the U.S. (I told Helen I didn't expect to wash it this whole term, and I expected by the time I went home it would have enough bedbugs and lice so all I would have to do was crawl into it, and they would walk me to the ship!!)

The only hardship, if you could call it that, was the periodic barking of dogs throughout the night. Granny Men's farm home had no wall around the yard as most farmers did to muffle the sounds. During those bright moonlight nights people seemed to be going by at all hours. One reason was that men who were calling up soldiers would go to homes in the night and drag out the young men. Because of this, young fellows were not staying at home at night but running from one place to another. Roaming wild animals also kept the dogs barking. One morning someone spotted two big wolves in the field beside our house.

It was like old times to be back with the Xin Ji folk again. There were quite a number of new folk—eleven had been baptized over the year. One man who came regularly lived 8 to 10 miles from the church. As his wife was nearly blind, she didn't usually come. But our first Sunday morning she was up before dawn, and her family led her along to service. She thought the Bible classes were that week. Since it was so hard for her to walk, we kept her with us until the next week. Classes started the following Sunday and went for eight days.

After our two weeks in Xin Ji we went back to Nancheng for a couple of days and then on to our next place. Xin Ji church wanted us a month, but we just couldn't give them that much time, or some churches would be left without any help.

In mail waiting for me in Nancheng was a letter from CIM leaders at headquarters in Shanghai. Having heard about my losing a trunk, they sent me a check of $200.00 Chinese currency. That was about $50 U.S. I was impressed. "The CIM," I wrote to my family, "is sure a grand mission."

I traveled to Mienhsien in December. We had excellent meetings there. It was a real joy to meet a number of new Christians and to witness their fresh love for the Lord Jesus and for His Word. One morning two of the ladies were coming to church for Bible class, and as they were crossing the river on a very narrow bridge, one of them slipped and fell into the river. It had snowed that morning and was freezing cold. When she got to us, she was shaking from head to foot. If it had been me, I am afraid I would have turned around and gone home. But she wasn't about to miss a meeting, soaking wet or not!

The first half of our trip home by truck was frightful. The truck was loaded up about three feet above the cab with huge boxes, oil drums, and tires. We perched ourselves on top of all that. I really felt like I was half way to Heaven. It was a comforting feeling to know that God was higher than we were and that we were safe in His care. Tree branches kept hitting us in the face, and we ducked others! In one place the telephone wires crossed the road and only missed us by a few inches. Happily we had a very careful driver. Just the same, I was glad to get off. To disembark, we had to slide off the boxes onto the top of the cab, and then take sort of a toboggan ride down the windshield and over the hood down onto the ground—good old ground!

We traveled the last half of the journey by horse cart. Ours was a very frisky horse—he went galloping along over the stony road with abandon. Needless to say, our breakfast was well settled by the time we reached Nancheng.

While we were in Mienhsien, the Reds came quite near to Yanghsien. Alarmed, Helen sent all of our valuable things to Chengku. Bertha had been out in the country, and Ruth Saunders was alone in Chengku. Not wanting Ruth to stay alone, Superintendent Percy Moore asked Faith Leuwenberg and me to stay in Chengku until after Christmas.

So ended a year that had begun with saying good-bye to kin and friends in Michigan and concluded with the joys of itinerant Bible teaching and fellowship with my wider Christian family in China, half a world away. ∞

Chapter 14

Mountain Travels

The year 1947 promised to be a year of extensive traveling as I continued to go from church to church teaching Bible classes.

Snow and rain limited attendance at a youth conference we held in Nancheng in January. Yet one could never tell what work God was doing in the hearts of the young people. Success was not always measured by numbers.

One night in Nancheng after the meeting Ruth Saunders and I came in and made ourselves a cup of tea before going to bed. My sister Grace had tucked a tea bag into a letter. Ooh, did that ever taste good! If anyone wanted to do me a favor, he or she just had to stick a tea bag in letters. At home in Yanghsien I would get up in the morning, stir up and feed the fire that was buried in the ashes, and by six o'clock I had a cup of tea! I would take Helen a cup at six thirty before she got up. Ah, missionary life was grand!

While in the country I would get up at 5:30 each morning to dress, be quiet before the Lord, then study until breakfast time. As soon as I finished eating, the folks came around and wanted help with reading. Bible classes filled most of the midday, followed by time out for the evening meal. After dinner the folks came back again for more teaching until dark. After darkness had closed in and we had sung for an hour, bed was calling.

At end of winter, while spring was still only a promise, hundreds of people gathered in Nancheng for an all-church conference. As most of them ate and slept at the conference site, you can imagine what it was like. This was the first time I had been to a conference like this.

To attend the conference, one man and his wife cycled all the way from Sisiang, with the man balancing their five-year-old girl on the back of his bike. They reached Chengku after traveling from six in the morning until three in the afternoon. Resting in Chengku over the weekend, they came on to Nancheng the next morning. For people like this family, a conference needed to be worthwhile. It was.

It did, however, have its sidetracking moments. Every morning about eleven o'clock, in the middle of the message, a huge rat would parade across the beam just above the speaker's head. The audience looked up for just a minute, some smiled or pointed, and the rat went merrily on his way. One night Mr. Rat had the nerve to come and eat my candle right in front of my nose while I was sleeping!

When the weather warmed up pleasantly mid-conference, the folks decided to move outside for meetings. That wasn't such a good idea for me, however, as I was using flannelgraph. The sun curled the figures up, and the wind blew them away. Instead of the spies going up to Canaan, they landed in the cabbage patch! Being outside wasn't a good idea for the people either. They got sleepy! While Mrs. Tuan was preaching, two of the deacons fell asleep. "You men go on home," a lady shouted, "until you are slept out and come back to church tomorrow!"

Sunday the church was packed full. The gatekeeper's wife was sitting right at the front beside the pulpit. When someone wanted to get into her room at the back, she just pitched her keys across the platform over Mrs. Tuan's head while she was teaching!

Just before the service on Sunday we were told a lady wanted to accept the Lord as her Savior. When we gave her an opportunity after the service, about fifteen others followed her forward and also knelt down to pray. What a service!

One very special attendee was girl about 13 years old. The second or third day when I went to help her after the classes, she said, "I haven't the Holy Spirit for my teacher today, and I just can't remember anything. I am going home to pray."

The next day while we were alone, the young lass told me that when she was very little, her father died. As her mother could not support her, she was given away and in her new home treated as a slave. One morning, she told me, she was out before dawn to take the cow to pasture when a wolf came. Very frightened, she called for help, but no one came. She kept hiding behind the cow, and the cow butted at the wolf and kicked at it until finally it left. Another day she was alone in the kitchen when the straw caught fire. The fire burned all around her, but the flames did not harm her. Though alone and trapped in a corner, she said she was not at all frightened. It seemed as if God was there to protect her. I was sure God was going to use that girl in His service.

In April Mrs. Tuan and I traveled extensively through the mountains. We had a great time. The scenery was beautiful. The mountains were covered with wild peach and pear blossoms, wild lilac, and other bushes with sprays of pretty yellow flowers. Along the river the iris were blooming. How I regretted that I had not taken my camera with colored film!

We went up by mountain chair and had very good carriers. It was a lovely trip. In some places the road was only a few inches wide. You looked up to high solid-rock mountains and down into a chasm, perhaps a couple hundred feet straight down, with a rocky river bed at the bottom. If the carriers' feet had slipped for just one step, the fall would have been fatal.

Coming home, we had men who had never carried before. Though we wanted to walk, the church insisted that we ride. The trip was dreadful. The first day we went twenty miles, and I am sure I walked eighteen of them. We went only a few steps when my front man slipped into a stream and left me standing ankle deep in the water. They took three days to get us home.

Mrs. Tuan and I often laughed at ourselves until our sides ached. The first home in which we stayed on this trip was a wealthy one. The people had a cow pen, a horse pen, and three pig pens. For a toilet we had a choice of one of the pigpens. The first one had four medium-sized pigs, the second a big mother pig with a dozen little ones, and the third one held two huge pigs. We were advised to go in this last one as it was a little more peaceful than the others! You couldn't even get squatted down before one pig would be in front and the other behind you to see who would get there first.

Poor Mrs. Tuan was scared to death of the pigs. One morning she called me and said, "I have to go, and there is a horse in one of the pigpens. The cow is tied up in front of the other, so I can't get in, and I don't dare go in the one with the little pigs." Another morning she came in and said, "If you have to go, go now in the pen with the little ones as they are all sleeping, and the mother is outside the pen. So I went and was no more than in the pen and squatting when the old mother pig came grunting in, and all the little pigs swarmed around me. Returning to the room, I laughed so hard I could hardly tell Mrs. Tuan what had happened.

The second place we stayed in was better because we used the cow pen and there was only a cow and a calf. They never paid any attention to us.

The meetings were held from Sunday to Friday. Then on Saturday we walked 14 miles to the next place and had eight days of meetings there, beginning on Sunday. In the two places we had a total of sixty meetings, which we really enjoyed. In both locations the church kept us going from early morning until about 9:30 at night, with time out for meals at nine and again at five. After supper we played games with the people for an hour, then had the evening meeting.

Coming home, we spent three travel nights in various inns. In one, our bedroom was behind the kitchen and was piled with wood and charcoal. In one corner was a little fence where the chickens spent the night—all but an old hen settled in a basket in another corner. At 2:30 a.m. the rooster began his duties and gave his first call for the morning. At that all the ducks came waddling out from under my bed. Mr. Rooster gave a call every hour from then on! At daylight the old hen hopped out of the basket, and fourteen little peeping chicks followed. Next the cook came in and crawled around under the bed to see if the ducks had laid any eggs for our breakfast—he found two! Certainly this was more interesting than sleeping in a bedroom with just an unmovable chair and dresser!

Since the Christians were scattered over an area of about 15 miles, one church planned for us to spend one week in two different places. Without a church building at East River, the church held services in the home of the very wealthy Huangs. The mother was a keen Christian, having been educated in a church school. The father professed to accept Christ while we were there. We prayed for him that he would grow in grace. As Mr. Huang employed several workmen who could not attend the meetings in the daytime, we held special services for them at night.

We finished meetings at East River on a Friday night, and the next day we walked to Peace Market, beginning classes there on Sunday. At this place a medicine seller, Mr. Kang, was in charge of the church work. He had built a large room onto his home for services. In this home, before they put breakfast on the table, the family gathered around to sing a hymn and read a chapter from the Bible. The father followed with a few comments. Next they memorized a verse or two, finishing with prayer. After that they brought in the rice bowls.

They really kept us busy in Peace Market. Classes went on from about ten in the morning until four or five in the afternoon. After our second and final meal of the day we played games for an hour with them. In the evening we taught them hymns. We finished the day between 9:30 and 10:00 with Mr. Kang examining us on the day's lessons.

After the day's Bible classes we divided the group. Mrs. Tuan taught the reading class, and I taught a class in personal evangelism. In six days my students learned 23 verses in just the

144

evangelism class. Saturday afternoon we had a test to see who could say them all. Most of the folk knew them perfectly. One lad was especially good. When it came his turn he said, "Teacher, I want to say them in my own order." He sat with his Bible covering his face and quoted all the verses from Matthew to Revelation, giving chapter and verse for each one. This boy, whose name was New Life, was 16 years old. He was one of four young people who had dedicated their lives to the Lord. This lad wanted to go to Bible school when he was old enough. Our prayer was that all four of these young people would be *kept* for Him.

Our classes finished on Monday, but as it rained, we could not leave. Besides, Mrs. Tuan was ill with an attack of malaria. I decided to entertain the folks in the afternoon by having a singing contest. We could sing only choruses, and no one could choose one that had been sung before. Also the contestant had to be able to lead the chorus himself. As soon as a person couldn't choose a new one, he fell out of the game. Keeping track, I counted between 120 and 130 choruses that they sang. I was amazed that the group knew so many. I think they enjoyed it as much as I did!

It took us nine days going from Peace Market home to Yanghsien! We walked most of the way back to Sisiang—that alone took three days. Mrs. Tuan was staying in Sisiang to work for a month. I got a ticket on the "bus"—actually a truck—on Friday morning. It traveled only for an hour or two before it broke down. Other passengers and I sat on top of the truck all day. When night came and there was no prospect of locating another bus, we found an inn and settled for the night.

The next day the driver worked on the bus, and we started out again. But we did not get far. The problem, it turned out, was that water, dirt, and kerosene was mixed in the gas. Every mile or two we stopped and waited for a man on a bike to come and loan us his pump to clean out the feed pipe. Finally we got to within 10 miles of Chengku and ran out of gas. Tired of the old truck by this time, I walked to Chengku. Sunday afternoon I borrowed a bicycle and went to Nancheng to collect my mail and the things I had left there before returning to Yanghsien.

Our time for the year was nearly all booked up except for May 15 to June 15, and the month of September. We praised God for these opportunities and were looking to Him to bless and use His own Word to the strengthening of the churches.

Because Bertha Silversides was to leave for furlough soon, I would be doing all the class work with Mrs. Tuan. To be more centrally located, I planned to move to Nancheng.

I greatly enjoyed letters from home. You can't imagine how refreshing it was to come home after a month in the country with no mail, take a bath, and sit down with a pot of tea on one side and a pile of home mail on the other. Pure delight!

One weekend some women came to me at home to ask me to go calling with them. We visited the home of an older lady who had just recently become a Christian, but had not yet destroyed her idols. Though she wanted us to smash or burn them for her, church leaders told her that breaking that link with the powers of evil was her job. When we suggested that she invite her relatives as a witness to them, she said, "It's no use, they won't listen." We weren't there long, however, before about twenty people showed up and listened well.

In Yanghsien a lady came to the services quite regularly who, though over a hundred years old, still went out and preached in the market. She had a good strong voice, but was deaf. One morning the cook was taking morning prayers, and in the middle of the sermon the lady started to sing. They both raised their voices, and neither gave in. I couldn't help smiling. The same lady enjoyed the flannelgraph so much that she urged, "Show them again!" I ended up going through the lesson three times. Another day, however, in the middle of the lesson, she picked up a picture of Jesus and said, "An old woman! Och!"

"Och!" I said back to her, and she sat down and was quiet.

On the first Sunday in May, with Helen away, I had to take the Bible class at the Yanghsien church by myself for the first time.

Expecting just the ordinary run of farmers that usually came to service, I was surprised to find half of the congregation to be teachers, students, and business men. As most of them had come for the first time and likely were not Christians, I changed my whole message on the spur of the moment. Though nervous, I must have done all right as the next day some of the men were back again. What an encouragement to see one of the men back the following week! He even stayed for the Sunday school class after the Bible class was finished. We had about ninety children for Sunday school that day, and this man sat right on the front bench with all the little tots. When I taught the children a chorus with motions, he even went through the motions! How I longed for a male Chinese preacher to help the men grasp the Gospel adequately!

In May rains made the streets so muddy that we were not able to get out much. One night the rain came down in sheets. A few miles from where we lived hail fell as large as baseballs, killing people and cows and smashing roof tiles to bits. I thanked the Lord for sparing us from that storm.

In June Percy Moore and dear Dr. Hsiao paid us a surprise visit, with Dr. Hsiao riding a new bike for me. Immediately I made plans to ride it the next week to go to Nancheng, where we were to have two weeks of meetings.

I was thrilled to get the new bike. Much lighter than the bike I had before, this black-chrome beauty was easier for me to carry across rivers and push up mountains! Also because it was equipped with three-speed gears, I could ride up small hills without using too much energy. All it lacked was a little engine!

As spring moved into summer, the farmers were busy threshing their now-ripe winter wheat. Earlier they had cut the wheat in the field with little hand cutters and then carried it home. As far as you could see down the street there was a thick layer of wheat. The people were beating out the kernels with flails. The straw was picked up and the sunned wheat and chaff swept into baskets, ready to be winnowed. On windy days they would use wooden shovels to toss the wheat into the air, letting the wind carry the chaff away. The process reminded me of Bible times.

The next couple of months promised to be busy ones. I would be in Nancheng the last half of June, in Yanghsien for daily vacation Bible school in early July, finishing the month in a Bible conference and beginning August in workers' conference in Nancheng. After that I would cycle to Sisiang to help in a daily vacation Bible school. I hoped to move into Nancheng to live by August 4th. I would be living with Australians Geoff and Ilma Malins, who had just returned from furlough. They had two little children—Margaret, 4, and Ian, 18 months.

During the meetings in Nancheng in July attendance averaged over thirty. One soggy day I said to an older lady, "I didn't expect you in all this rain!"

She replied, "If I don't come, I don't get anything."

Another lady came in just sopping wet. The woman behind her pulled out her hanky and wiped her hair dry for her. Once that was done, the woman pulled off her wet dress and sat down to enjoy the meeting.

One day I walked into the reading class and found ten or twelve women all sitting around the table reading their lessons aloud in good Chinese fashion—everyone seemingly reading a little louder than her neighbor! On the table lay a little baby, fast asleep!

One of the treats in Nancheng was to listen to the radio on Sunday nights and hear a church broadcast from the States—a church in Baltimore. How I wished we could get the Old Fashion Revival Hour, but that was not to be.

People by the name of Ch'en lived in front of our place and served as gatekeepers. One of their sons, John, had been in the army and away from home for six years. While in the army he stepped on a land mine that wounded his face and leg. Since then he had been in the army hospital. One afternoon John walked in on his family, much to their surprise. He saw his little brother at the front door and called his name, smiling. But the little brother didn't recognize him and stared back, mute. Then John walked in and saw his mother. His mother looked at him for half a day and still wasn't sure he was her son! He had changed so that none of them knew him. Still, they were all excited to have him home. I likened this to the Lord's coming—all of a sudden—and how many would not recognize Him.

The gatekeeper and family had been keeping silk worms and let us watch the whole process from the worms hatching out, feeding on mulberry leaves, and spinning cocoons. Last we watched family members spin thread out of the cocoons. The only thing we didn't do was help eat the dead worms! The family told us they are very good fried!

The Bible conference in Yanghsien was one of the best I had experienced since being back in China. With 120 people registered, we had an average attendance of 80. This was not counting the Sunday service on the last day when 175 people gathered for worship. One of the most encouraging things that happened was that John, the young man who had just come home from the army, gave his testimony. He told how the Lord had used His Word during the week to speak to him. He dedicated his life to the Lord for service.

In traveling from Yanghsien to Chengku, I found the roads an awful mess from the heavy rains. As usual, the farmers had cut ditches across the roads every little way to drain water off their fields. The whole trip was one of getting on and off my bike. I waded through four swollen rivers̄not all bad as the weather was very hot, and the water felt wonderfully cool!

As planned, following my move to Nancheng, I went to Sisiang for DVBS. I took the bus because it had been very hot. I was also tired from a very busy summer and did not feel like using all my energy pushing my bike over those big mountains in the heat. The "bus" was actually a truck piled with luggage. I joined forty people sitting on top. We were packed in so tight that I couldn't even move a toe! One lady was sitting in sort of a hole in the middle with a baby on her lap. All that I could see of her was her head and feet! The poor soul was sick all the way. Her daughter-in-law was sitting on the side and boasted that she never got sick.

Before they were half way she lost her last meal too. Another passenger had a stiff leg. He could find no place for his leg except to hold it straight up in the air! I really felt sorry for him. The redeeming thing was that everybody was jolly. No one complained.

In September the mission asked my former fellow worker, Helen, to go to their hospital in Kaifeng, Honan, to help with the nursing. We all hated to see Helen leave. Helen hated to leave as well as she had been in this district for fourteen years. Mr. and Mrs. Beck were to take her place in Yanghsien.

In October we had a visit from three American Army boys—a major, a lieutenant and a corporal. With the Graves Commission, they had come to look for the bodies of men that were lost when their airplanes crashed during the war. One plane was up on a very high mountain. The plane was still there and if it had been possible to take down, the Chinese would have taken the parts that could be carried. Our visitors were chagrinned that we missionaries lived, ate and slept in Chinese homes. They had their own tents, camp beds and food. As tough as they viewed themselves, they considered a 20-mile hike in the mountains very strenuous, and they were scared stiff of a bedbug or a rat!

The three men traveled from us into Szechwan Province and into some very wild mountains. Though they were supposed to have returned to our city on the 17th, by the 24th there was still no sign of them. One lady who had just traveled up from Szechwan said there were rumors all along the way that they had been taken by bandits. We were anxiously waiting for news from them. We sent a telegram to their head office in Hankow, thinking they would send up a search party for them.

As it turned out, only the major and lieutenant were missing. Having stayed with the jeep in Kuanguyuan, the corporal was okay. Only 20 years old, the poor lad couldn't speak a word of Chinese and was scared stiff. He was even scared sleeping in our house here when a rat scurried outside his door.

We really were afraid for the two who seemed to be lost. The lieutenant, a rough fellow, not only couldn't speak or understand a word of Chinese, he had no love for the people. Earlier, when he has put up his tent, he drew a line on the ground and wouldn't allow the coolies to cross that line or to come near his tent. He was a crack shot and wouldn't think twice before using his gun. That would be the wrong thing to do with the bandits. I hoped and prayed that nothing had happened to them. The lieutenant had been married only four days before coming to China, and the major had a young wife in Shanghai. Sadly, they were not Christians either. The lieutenant boasted of the fact that he was going to hell. We had a good opportunity of talking to them before they went and hoped that if they were in danger, they would call on the Lord. I don't remember ever hearing what became of them.

The Lord had been doing great things for us in answer to prayer. However, in my visitation work I was shocked to find the number of people who once were church members and then turned back to idols. The main reason for this was lack of teaching. The reason for that tragedy, of course, was the lack of workers. I sent letters home appealing to my prayer partners to keep up their good work. Without them I could not have done the work I did.

One morning we started out at dawn to visit folk who lived ten miles up in the mountains. They were too far away to attend church each week, but usually came in whenever the church had a conference or a few days of special meetings. In the first home we visited we found an old widow lady. One look at her smiling face told us she was a Christian. She gave us a warm welcome, even preparing breakfast for us. With ten miles between breakfast and us—we were ready for a second one! We had a little service in this home. It was a thrill to teach this isolated saint. She thoroughly appreciated our visit. We enjoyed having her in our Bible classes later. "I would not worry if I starved to death here," she remarked one day. "I have my Jesus."

The last two months of 1947 were happy ones for me. I continued to work hard in Bible teaching and enjoyed my life.

The CIM Home Director for Australia visited us. His messages were a fresh inspiration to all of the missionaries. At the Thanksgiving service we dedicated children, about ten of them. Among them were two babies who were not even named yet.

We praised the Lord for bringing three young Chinese pastors—Bible school graduates—to work in our district. Yet Satan was trying his best to discourage these men. Mr. Li, Mr. Ch'en, and Mr. Yang needed special prayer that the Lord's purpose for them and for their work would be fulfilled, and not hindered by the enemy. For example, Mr. Li, the pastor of the church at Chengku had been having so much difficulty with the church leaders there that he wanted to quit his job and go into business. After one of the meetings, he went to Mr. Moore, weeping, and said he would go back to the church no matter what happened. That was a real answer to prayer.

I was thrilled at the prospects of spending much of the Christmas season with my Chinese friends at Xin Ji, where I had worked my first term. I prayed that we would have a precious time with our wonderful Lord.

Actually the Xin Ji church was having difficulty of an unusual kind. They had a worker there whom they did not invite and did not want. He sat on their doorstep and said he was living by faith and was not going to leave even if he starved. This was very hard on the church! Because this man had used up all that the church had saved for conference and for Mrs. Tuan's wages, they were able to have only one week of conference instead of two.

Christmas week was a happy time, though. A lot of us knitted either gloves or socks for the little children. I knit two pairs of socks in a week's time.

Sunday the Xin Ji church had a long program in the morning. The children were cute. They had a "tin-pot" band, using every imaginable kind of thing—cymbals, bells, and covers from pots and pans, even two chamber lids! The little ones had big silver tablespoons and hit them with nails. They played these as they sang their Christmas carols. I was surprised at how well it sounded.

For Christmas Day I was back in Nancheng and spent it with the Malins. What a joyful time! I enjoyed so much being home in my own room with the nice things that I had used to decorate it that I had to pray that the Lord would not let me set my heart on earthly things!

My prayer throughout the Christmas season was that we would have a new appreciation of our wonderful Lord and that His joy would be our Christmas joy. And it was so. ∞

Chapter 15

Uncertain Times

The beginning of 1948 found us still peaceful in Shensi. However, the newspapers back home reported that communist insurgents had killed five missionaries. This put much fear into the hearts of my loved ones. I could only write letters to them reassuring them of my safety.

Actually, we were in about as safe a place as possible. The road to the south was open, and a large airfield near us provided a potential escape route. In places of danger the American Consulate had been evacuating American citizens by air. We had plans to go to the magistrate before we went to the country again to inquire of any trouble. If something were brewing, we would not go.

I was thrilled when I was asked to look after the new lady workers when Percy and Amy Moore would leave for furlough in September. I would move to the Moores' residence in Chengku. Betty Worth from Tasmania and Ailsa Lumsden of Australia, the new workers, would be living with me, as well as Bertha. Bertha and I would take turns going to the country. Quickly I began imagining how I would arrange the house in Chengku with all the things I brought from home or had received as gifts while in China. I was also looking forward to tending the big garden out back. But that was still a few months away.

In January the two-year-old Paocheng church held its short-term Bible school. As the Christians were recent believers, we simplified the lessons, keeping them basic. Because the believers were so new, they had not yet become accustomed to coming to church every day for two weeks. The result was that, though we had forty on our roll, an average of only fifteen church folk attended each day, with strangers in the audience usually swelling the numbers significantly.

Each night we held an evangelistic meeting for about two hours. The place was always filled for this. As the church seated only about thirty and the people seemed to come in groups, whoever got there first got the seats. We never knew who would come. Sometimes the building was filled with students. One day it was packed with soldiers. Another night I found all the front benches filled with policemen. They looked rather fierce with their guns and ammunition belts, but they were really very polite and listened attentively.

One night in the middle of the service a policeman walked in and spoke to me in English. "What time you where this side come?" I guessed what he meant and decided to answer in Chinese. I did not want to take his face by speaking to him in English if he were not able to understand me. After I answered his question, he asked if I was Italian?! I suppose he thought that if I couldn't understand or speak English, I must be an Italian! After I told him I was an American, we bowed to each other, and he walked out. That tickled me so. However, the slight interruption in the middle of the sermon seemed to make little difference to the congregation.

Our hearts were saddened over the plight of a young girl who has been in our classes in Nancheng and who came to us in Paocheng for counsel. A gambler and a very wicked man, her husband had threatened to kill her. Since seeing us before, she had run away and had gotten into trouble. I can't describe what such young women had to go through, especially those from heathen homes.

Betty and Ailsa came out the last Sunday morning we were in Paocheng. The two enjoyed worship and dinner with us. We cycled home together in the afternoon. I enjoyed having company on the road. Bertha and I would be home about a month this time.

Classes in Huangkuanling in the spring, in spite of numerous interruptions, were good. We taught from seven in the morning until seven at night. Two girls in our reading class learned over five hundred characters in the two weeks! One deacon had been taken as a soldier but, because his eyes were bad, he was released and came for the last two days. In that time he learned all the work of the two weeks—28 topics for Luke, thirty Bible verses, and all the choruses! Two men who came during the rain had to cross rivers with water up to their waist. Though their clothes were soaked to the chest, they came and sat all day in church.

In the middle of the week of classes we got quite a scare. We were in bed one night when church people called us and told us to get dressed and prepare for bandits. We said we did not have anything to lose except clothes and bedding. Church folk made a hiding place for us, however, and we went back to bed to wait. I slept, not too soundly, and nothing happened. Though we slept for a few nights with our clothes on, just in case, no bandits appeared.

Out of seventy-five students enrolled in the class, an average of 33 attended each day. The farmers were getting busy in their fields, yet the time was a good one for classes. The days were long. They came about eight o'clock to the church, and by noon meetings were all over. Farmers went home to work, and business men to tend to business. In the evening the city folk came back for a hymn sing until dark.

We had been in Huangkuanling for two weeks when we had another scare. The last Sunday morning I was supposed to have the big service. The folks had already gathered when the deacon walked in and said two telephone calls had come for me the night before. One had come at midnight, telling us to come in at once. *Oh-oh, trouble,* I thought. I wanted to wait and take the service, but church folk said that if I did, I would not get home before dark.

Unable to hire mountain chairs, we walked 40 *li* to the halfway place and got a ride there. Arriving home just at supper time, we found forty missionaries who had fled before advancing communist regiments.

Five women had crowded into my room. To get to my bed, I had to climb over camp beds jammed together! In the remaining bits of space the ladies were all re-packing. In the muddle I managed to do my own packing. The first thing I did was to share my clothes, bedding, dishes, etc., with folks who had lost everything. Mr. and Mrs. Fisher, for instance, had their things packed and on a cart, when soldiers confiscated the cart. All they could salvage was what they could carry in their hands. They walked about fifteen miles through the mud to the next city.

The government was bringing in soldiers by air. Planes had been flying overhead all day long. Though we hoped this response would save the situation, I had my doubts that we would be there very long. Though some people had moved on, we still had twenty folks in our house. Everyone pitched in to help. My job was to make suppers. Then in the midst of all this excitement, Ilma Malins gave birth to a new son!

At one point it looked as though we might all be moving on in the next day or two. We had sent off all our luggage with those who had already gone and were just waiting to see how the situation would go. We were ready to go at short notice if necessary.

For the first couple of weeks I was busy keeping the cookie jars and cake tins filled and preparing suppers for the crowd of people that were staying with us. I enjoyed having them all. The 43 missionaries that stayed with us during that time represented Canada, Scotland, England, Holland, Poland, Norway, Sweden, Australia, New Zealand, Tasmania and America. Sometimes we had to speak Chinese to the Norwegian children to make them understand. People talking their own languages between themselves created a real babble! However, our guests all eventually moved on. Some returned to their own stations, and others moved to safer territory.

We all had to do some moving around for safety reasons. By May I was in my beloved South Shensi. Each time I wrote letters home, I wondered where I would be writing from next. The situation to the north of us was much better, but there was heavy fighting to the east. As long as the fighting didn't come any nearer, I was sure we would be okay. If warring armies started moving in our direction, we would move out ahead of them.

While in South Shensi I visited families in their homes. How I enjoyed being out among the people again! One dear lady had been a Christian for about ten years. At first her husband beat her every time she went to church. He ripped up every Bible or book she bought—and she bought several. She continued to trust the Lord and, although her husband was not yet a Christian, he had come to the point of helping her paste up two gospel posters in their home. He also let her have prayers each evening with the children and allowed them to go to church. What a joy to see the perseverance of that dear Christian lady!

In another home we visited a fine Christian family with two children. The girl, twelve years old, had a wonderfully bright testimony. She had been accepted into the church the previous year. We found the father and mother both sick in bed and quite discouraged. As none of the church folk knew they were sick, we felt the Lord definitely led us to that home. The mother had been rolling and tossing on her bed for three days and nights in agony from a huge carbuncle on her face. It broke one night, she felt some better the next day. Even so, still the size of a baseball, it almost made me ill to look at it

As spring moved closer to summer, ministry in Nancheng continued without a pause. I planned to continue visitation work until the middle of June. Then we planned to hold two-week Bible schools for Christians in Yanghsien and back in Chengku.

Speaking of Yanghsien, a messenger came in from there one

night about this time to say that a fellow worker, Jack Beck, had fallen off his bike. He had run into a ditch and injured both legs. One swelled up, suggesting either a torn ligament or a broken bone. The other he skinned from the knee to the ankle. As new worker Betty was a nurse, she left the next morning in a pouring rain to give a hand. For three days Jack ran a temperature of 104.6 before it dropped to 102. Those with him were really quite worried.

The next week Percy Moore and a Chinese doctor brought Jack to our house. Since my room was the quietest, I moved out and fixed it up for the patient. Carriers toted Jack the fourteen miles to Chengku on a camp bed and then loaded the bed into the jeep to bring him to Nancheng. For him the jeep ride was worse than being carried. Jack had lost all his strength. After Jack arrived, the doctor opened the leg to drain off the water and pus that had by this time gathered on the knee.

On the civil war front, everything was peaceful again. It looked as if we would be able to stay on for a time—unless, of course, government or communist soldiers launched another attack. At this point we were going merrily on as if nothing had happened.

I stayed especially busy during that time as I kept house for the Malins family so that Ilma Malins, who was studying for her last exam, could get some language study done. It was a challenge for Ilma to study while looking after their three children, including the newborn. Keeping house was a big job for me as well as there was a continual stream of houseguests besides our patient, who continued convalescing in our home. Jack was improving some, but still required a great deal of care and special food.

I did manage to go calling at the home of a young couple who used to live in Chengku. They had moved to a place about six miles from Nancheng. Mrs. Tuan and Ailsa went along with me—it was quite a hike in the summer heat. This couple was working in a school for refugee children¯350 children in grades one to four and over two hundred children in the fifth and sixth grades. Given a tour of the school, I was very impressed to see that everything was neat and tidy. The smallest children had little double-deck beds. Each bed had a little white sheet for a spread and a little white quilt neatly rolled up at the head. The children were well behaved and very polite.

"Any chance that missionaries would be allowed to teach Bible stories to the children?" I asked.

"Depends on who the teachers would be," we were told.

Should the way open, it would be a grand opportunity. However, at the time no one could take on the responsibility. The Moores were about to go on furlough, new workers Betty and Ailsa hadn't enough language yet, and Mrs. Malins had her children to care for. Mr. Malins was busy with the student work in Nancheng. I would have loved to do it myself. In fact, I wondered if maybe Bertha and I could eventually manage it between the two of us.

By June I was able to do more visiting. I took Betty with me. First we visited a Mrs. Su, an older lady and the only Christian in her courtyard. Though she had believed for a few years, she was still hopelessly ignorant of the Bible. She knew she was saved, however, and was rejoicing in the peace that she had in knowing she would someday see the Lord.

Mrs. Su took us to the next home, where two little children were very ill with measles. The oldest boy, about five, was the most seriously ill. The father wept like a child, saying the boy's illness was because of his sin. We talked with the family, had prayer with them, and then moved on to the next home.

In the third home we found only one old man—his wife was out shopping. He was supposedly a Christian of many years' standing.

"Why don't you attend church?" we asked him.

"I'm angry at Dr. Hsiao," he answered. (Dr. Hsiao was one of our leading Christians.) "I went to him to have him treat my eyes, paid my money, and he let one of his helpers do it," he explained.

He wasn't through. "And once I saw one of the missionaries get angry with her househelper," he continued. "It's not right for a

Christian to be angry. Besides, I can't even spit or blow my nose when I want to without someone coming and telling me not to do that in church!" (He wasn't used to using a handkerchief.)

"We'll all have to reckon our own accounts with the Lord," I told him. "If the Lord asks you why you never worshipped Him with other Christians, you would be ashamed to say, 'Because I saw so-and-so sin' or 'Because so-and-so offended me.'" After a lot of talking, we had prayer with him, and he promised to come to our classes.

Next we visited the home of a couple who, though members of our church, were dreadfully mixed up with a cult-like group. The wife told us that at one of this group's conferences, "A lady, an unbeliever, was moved by the spirit to be nailed to the cross. She went to the front of the church and lay down on the floor with her arms outstretched, and with eyes closed, cried out, 'Nailed, nailed, nailed! Hurts, hurts, hurts! [I'm] filled by the Holy Spirit.'" This went on for four hours, the lady told us. People in the group claimed to see the Lord or marvelous lights, evil spirits, etc. This poor couple, especially the wife, was so mixed up with these teachings and practices that they didn't know what was right and what was wrong.

On our way home we saw all the Youth Army out helping the farmers plant their rice. That was really quite a sight to see soldiers working! Though they worked when they were at the front, when in camp, they often had little to do.

Last we visited the home of Christians where a newborn had recently died. The poor young mother had had four babies in four years. Only one of the four was living, simply because the family didn't know how to look after their babies when they were born.

I enjoyed going out with new workers. By this time I had begun to take everything for granted and had forgotten how unfamiliar things struck me when I had seen them for the first time.

Betty and I went to see one dear elderly lady who was a refugee from Honan. She lived in a refugee camp, in a little bamboo mud hut. In a space the size of many home-side yards were crammed twenty or thirty similar homes. Built one against the other, the huts were perhaps only seven or eight feet across. When we walked into the clearing in the center of this cluster of homes, we found that the women had been gleaning wheat. They were now sitting on the ground in the heat, beating out their precious wheat a handful at a time with sticks. The lady we went to see was sitting in the middle stripped to the waist, wearing only a huge straw hat and a pair of black trousers. When we came in, her neighbors laughed at her. One said, "You have long dresses and short ones, and yet your friends come and find you naked!" She didn't care one bit—she was a very jolly soul and made a joke of it.

The folks all gathered, and we had a good preach. One pleasant young lady showed serious interest. She said she would have believed long ago, but she had one hope: to go home and see her parents again. She was afraid her parents wouldn't approve. We tried to show her that life was too uncertain to reject the Lord for that reason. She promised to come to the classes. I prayed that she would come and better understand the way of salvation and accept the Lord.

The last two weeks of June, when it was the district's oldest church's turn for Bible classes, were extremely hot. We were kept busy from morning until night. We were somewhat disappointed in the number of attendees. The leaders seemed to think that the classes were for only illiterate people, and none of the leaders came. But people who did come received a blessing. Twenty-eight lessons from Luke formed the backbone of the week's study. By the close, some of the men and women in my personal-evangelism class could quote from memory thirty or forty verses.

A number of wounded soldiers attended these classes. One of them heard the Gospel for the first time in the personal-evangelism class. One day he came to me and said, "I have never confessed my sins to the Lord, and I know I am a sinner. I have never prayed and don't know how. Will you help me?" After I had talked with him, he prayed, "Lord, you know I left home as a child and have never worshipped any gods. I have committed all the sins there are in the army! Forgive me and help me to live for You."

Another young married woman, a new Christian, came to ask for prayer. Her husband said he could not have her on the streets going to church every day. If she attended again, he threatened to "break her legs" (common expression for a severe beating). The woman wept and prayed all night. The next morning she got up early to wash the clothes. As she was putting the soiled clothes into the water, her husband said, "I thought you were going to church?" After that she came every day.

Meanwhile Jack Beck was still suffering from his accident. He was taken by jeep to Paoki and then from there by train to Sian. They made a special frame for his leg. In the jeep he sat in a deck chair with his braced leg hanging from the ceiling of the jeep! In Sian x-rays showed his leg to be infected. The doctor said he must go home at once for a new treatment available there; otherwise Jack would probably always have a stiff leg.

I spent the whole month of July in Yanghsien teaching classes. When we arrived, our first meal was thick dough strings made out of very dark flour, cooked in bean milk and served with raw string beans and hot peppers in vinegar. This was the sort of meal we had almost every day, along with cooked dried beans and fried green tomatoes. I wasn't sure if the diet or a bug was the culprit, but my tummy was upset the first few days. I asked a medicine seller to try to get some Sulfa-guanidine for me. The trouble was I did not know the Chinese name, and the medicine seller did not know the English! He came around at midnight with some little pills wrapped up in a bit of Chinese paper and said that was what I needed. I took the pills and, thankfully, they did the trick!

People from two churches attended the meetings in Yanghsien, where the Becks had been. Even after they left, the church carried on the Sunday school. Tiny children packed one room, and older children filled another. It was a thrill to see the deacons—one an old man with white hair and a flowing white beard—going through the crowd of youngsters and listening to one after another say the day's memory verse. What a grand sight to see the church leaders take such an interest in children!

The trip home from Yanghsien was another adventure. As it had rained the day before, we trudged through endless mud. By the time I got half way my feet were so muddy I did not even bother to take my shoes off to wade the rivers! I reckoned my shoes were soaked anyway and that was an easy way to get them washed.

With the Moores leaving for furlough in September, Mr. and Mrs. Fisher, workers from the north, were to take the Moores' place temporarily. When we arrived home, we found Mrs. Fisher ill in bed, and it looked as if she would be ill for some time. Poor Mrs. Malins looked very thin and tired. She was feeding the Fishers, Betty and Ailsa, and other guests besides her own family. As soon as I got a smidge of rest myself and finished my washing and ironing, I gave her a hand.

After the Moores left, Betty, Ailsa, and I moved into their home in Chengku. Betty and Ailsa were already speaking Chinese remarkably well, considering they had been in China only a year. No sooner had we settled happily into our new home, however, than we learned that Betty would be with us for only six months. A nurse, she had always felt called to work with people suffering with leprosy. The mission asked her to go to the leprosy section of the mission's hospital in Kweichow Province, once she had some initial months of experience. I loved Betty and hated to think of her going.

Life as part of the Chengku church was full. On Saturday evenings eight to ten schoolboys gathered for a Bible class. God was working in this small group. Early in our time there we noticed a boy with tears rolling down his cheeks as he listened. The pastor talked with him after the meeting.

But Saturday evening was only the start of weekend ministry. On Sunday morning at 9 o'clock students packed the church for the English service. Betty and Ailsa were in charge of that. Mr.

Chang, the English teacher at the First Middle School, interpreted for them. We wanted to make sure the students got the message as well as the English.

Immediately after the student service we had Sunday school for everyone. The worship service followed. New folks came virtually every week. Mr. Li, our Chinese pastor, was very fine.

After worship, when everyone had gone, the church leaders and workers met to pray for the work of the week. That time, I believe, tapped God's power for this thriving ministry.

At 4 o'clock, after dinner and a wee rest, Sunday school teachers gathered for preparation class.

At 5:30 we went to Mrs. Su's home for a cottage meeting. Mrs. Su was a deaconess in the church, and Mr. Su was a teacher in the middle school. They invited their school teacher friends and their wives and children. Ailsa took along a little hand organ, and I took my flannelgraph. We had most interesting meetings. The trouble was so many folks came we had to sit in the courtyard, rain or shine. If the wind blew too hard, I couldn't use my flannelgraph, but then I searched out another Bible picture to take its place. If we could manage to arrive a little early, Mrs. Su liked to take us calling in the homes of her friends.

As Monday we had no meetings, it was a good day for study.

Tuesday morning we trooped to Mr. and Mrs. Lo's home out in the country for a meeting. As the class there did not start until 11 o'clock, we could visit in a home or two on our way. In September and October the farmers were busy harvesting rice, and numbers were smaller. More people joined us when the busy season passed. Two ladies there told us in one of our first meetings that they had never heard the Gospel before.

Tuesday night was Bible class; I started with Acts with the folks and thoroughly enjoyed it.

Wednesday morning we joined the pastor in visiting the prison. Mr. Li preached to the men, and we went to the women. The women were confined in a rather dark room with beds along one wall and spinning wheels along the other, with just walking space between. The women spun thread for a living. The ten ladies were of every imaginable type, old and young, educated and illiterate, neat and untidy. Only one had heard the Name of Jesus, and another, a Catholic, knew of the "holy mother." We would sing a chorus or two and then give them a Bible story. The women listened most intently.

Wednesday night was the church prayer meeting.

Thursday morning we participated in a women's meeting at the church. In the evening we went to a Mrs. Chang's home for a cottage meeting. As the people in her courtyard were afraid of us and our religion, only one or two besides Mrs. Chang and her mother ventured to come. Yet the first week we helped one person make peace with God.

Friday was taken up with visiting and study. I spent a half hour teaching the pastor's wife to read, and then the Pastor came for an English lesson. Betty and Ailsa would sometimes come along for help with their study in the afternoon.

Friday night was Bible reading.

So the week went. Oh, besides the meetings I've introduced you to, in our home we had daily Chinese prayers before breakfast and English prayers after.

Bertha joined us in Chengku in late 1948 to take over the class work. I hated to give it up. I enjoyed Bible teaching from church to church and was looking forward to continuing to work with Bertha. Sure, however, that the Lord had led, I was happy also in visitation and student work.

Though conditions were still peaceful in the Chengku area, we were unsure of the future. Still, we knew the Lord was able to keep us there if that were His will.

Though we were getting nicely settled into the work before winter settled in, we were living without our major baggage.

Since we moved to Chengku, we had been using an old G.I. curtain for a tablecloth. The only knife we had was a big butcher's cleaver. We cut our bread, carved our meat, and cut whatever else we needed to with this one knife. Finally one Saturday I had been out visiting all afternoon and had just come home about suppertime, when Geoff and Ilma Malins arrived with the jeep loaded with our stuff. We soon hauled out some dishes and pots and pans (I had had only one pan to do all the cooking in).

Then besides our luggage Geoff walked in with two *huge* parcels from my family in Michigan. What excitement! Betty had made a fancy dessert for our Sunday dinner. It is made like macaroons except you make it all in one with a hollow in the top to be filled with fruit. We had had only persimmons. Betty was just fixing the persimmons when I pulled from one of the parcels a can of fruit cocktail. Perfect for our dessert!

The parcels solved another problem. Butchers had been on strike for several weeks, cutting off our supply of meat. In the packages, just in time to meet our need, were various kinds of meat, fish, chicken and cheese. We got such a surprise when we opened a can of wieners and found them packed in tomato sauce! I had to go upstairs and show the girls. They could not get over all the wonderful ideas we had in the States—they said they never saw anything like that in Australia.

When we spread out the contents of both parcels on our table, the lot looked like a big family's order at a grocery store. In Chinese dollars, there lay *billions* of dollars worth of stuff!

That was the beginning of the excitement. Then Thursday, just as we were going to sit down to dinner, Bertha walked in with our new superintendent Fred Smith and Geoff. I managed to stretch our dinner for three to make enough for six! Then I made a nice tea in the afternoon, with a white cake and chocolate frosting. The girls declared they had never seen such a white cake! As we could get only whole-wheat flour in China, everything came out brown. This cake, made with flour from the parcels, not only looked snow white, but was beautifully light. We all declared we had not tasted anything as good since we left home!

Opening my just-arrived trunk, I found envelopes, but no writing paper. Then Thursday along comes another parcel from home with stationery in it! Though strawberry jam had leaked on it, I simply cut the edges off.

While the weather was still mild, Betty, Ailsa, and I went visiting with one of the local Christian ladies. What a good time we had! Though neither the lady's school-teacher friend nor another lady on whom we first called were at home, we decided to visit a lady who lives right near us. She welcomed us enthusiastically. After we had been there a while, she said, "What are we sitting here talking for? Let's go and see Mrs. U!"

I had been trying to find Mrs. U ever since I came to Chengku. She had attended our classes, but no one seemed to know where she lived. Excited at our arrival, Mrs. U called in all her neighbors. Once they were settled, she said to us, "Preach to us! We want to believe."

After we had gone over the way for people to be reconciled to God, one man asked, "If I want to believe with my whole family, what do I do?" What a joy to answer *that* question!

As this group of people invited us back, on the following Friday I asked the pastor to return with me. He couldn't get over the openness of this group. When we left, they said, "Our whole courtyard wants to believe"—five families, I think. They seemed deep-down happy in deciding to follow Christ. "This is a grand work," I wrote at the time. "The longer I am here, the more I like it!"

The year 1948, however, did not end as peacefully as it had started. I knew my family was concerned about our safety. I wondered what they were hearing on the news. Everyone in Chengku thought we would have to leave before too long, while we hoped to stay at least for a few more weeks or even months.

We had no way to know what would happen next. Our team was ready to move quickly if we had to. Our plan was that the girls, including me, would all cycle out, and the rest would go by jeep. At least they would go one stage by jeep and then come back to pick up the bicyclers. From there we would go on another stage. We were instructed to be prepared for a telephone call on a public phone, followed by the jeep in about an hour to pick us up.

Can you imagine our leaving our homes, work, church and everything with just an hour's notice? But we would not stay if it got dangerous or if our presence put local Christians in jeopardy. We simply had to find our peace in the Lord. ෨

Chapter 16

Big Changes

We started the New Year, 1949, with daily vacation Bible school. Over a hundred children registered with an average of 60 to 70 attending every day. As the walls in the room where we met didn't go up to the roof, we had more than enough fresh air. Though we papered the windows to keep out some of the winds, it was still very cold. We had the children do all sorts of exercises just to keep warm. As the older girls all were tending their little brothers or sisters, they had to do their handwork with one hand and carry the baby in the other arm—or put the baby on their back to perch precariously while they bent over a bench to paint a picture.

At the end of the week, just as we were having our supper on Friday night, a message came for Betty to return to Nancheng in preparation to moving to the Kweichow leprosarium. As soon as DVBS was finished Saturday noon, I cycled to Nancheng with her.

Oh, how I hated to see Betty go! I had learned to love her like a sister. She was a lot of fun, and we had had many good times together. Betty was an excellent nurse; I didn't know of anything she couldn't do.

Since everyone would be celebrating the Chinese New Year for the next two weeks, all the shops would be closed, and business places would go on vacation for two weeks. That would leave the people sitting around in their homes with nothing to do‾a good time to go and hold meetings. Usually people welcomed us.

One of our stops was to see a Mr. Su. He had been out of a job for some time. In fact, he and his family literally faced starvation at times. Recently the Lord had led him to go into a small business. From a table on the street he had begun hawking combs, tooth brushes, belts, face soap, etc. The idea was suggested to them on a Wednesday. Thursday they began business and sold three dollars' worth of stuff. Friday they sold five dollars' worth and Saturday twelve. Sunday we had our congregational meeting. Mr. Su spoke to one of the deacons who was a photographer and who did business on Sunday. Mr. Su was exhorting him to keep the Lord's Day. He said, "The Lord gave me a double portion yesterday, and I believe if I keep the Lord's Day, He will always bless that."

Mr. Su went on to say how many of his friends wanted to go in with him or supply him with money. He refused. "First I tithe all of my money," he explained. "They would not approve of that. Furthermore, because I visit for the church on Saturday afternoons, I won't work then. And if the church has a conference, I will not do business." I believed the Lord was going to use Mr. Su's testimony to speak to many in the church. Already one man had given up doing business on Sunday and selling cigarettes. As cigarettes and wine bring in the biggest profits of all, Christians are tempted to sell those products.

In March at a conference in Nancheng fifty-seven people professed to accept Christ as their Savior. Afterwards the lady deacons and I went out every day to call on the women among the new converts. Pastor Li and the deacons visited the men. We had some very interesting times.

The conference seemed to be a blessing to the deacons as well, as evidenced by their new willingness to take responsibility in the church. With no electric lights in the church, few people came to the evening meetings. Because of that, the deacons decided to change prayer meeting from evening to five-thirty in the morning—and they had a good turnout.

Seven people were baptized in those days. Pastor Wang examined the candidates. The questions went something like this:

"Are you saved?"

"Yes."

"How do you know you are saved?"

"I asked the Lord to forgive my sins, and He did."

"Do you come to church regularly?"

"I was here year before last—it is too far to come."

"How did you hear the Gospel?"

"My brother came and told me."

"Have you ever come to a conference?

"This is the first one."

"Are you willing to invite the preachers to your home, give them some good food, and let them preach the Gospel there so that others will be saved and you can have a church in your home?"

"I'd welcome them."

"Can you pray?"

"Yes."

"Kneel down here and show us!"

When one dear old lady knelt down and prayed a few sentences, Mr. Wang broke in and said, "That's enough." Then he asked more questions about the Lord's life, death, resurrection, ascension, second coming, etc. The lady answered them all, though she couldn't read a word. It showed us how the Lord was able to enlighten those who want to know Him.

Pastor Wang was a real character. His text for one series was, "The Lord is my shepherd, I shall not want." As he had been an actor before he was saved, he acted out everything he said. One night, speaking on, "I shall not want food and drink," Pastor Wang mimicked the sheep that was away from the Shepherd: "Thirsty—*baaa!* Hungry—*baaa!* Danger—*baaa!* Lost—*baaa!*" "But when the Shepherd is close by," the pastor went on, "there isn't a sound. Most Christians are *'baaa*ing' most of the time because they don't recognize the Shepherd's leading them—they always have something to complain about."

Right around this time we received news that some of the Scandinavian missionaries who left Sian a few months previous were coming back. The American Consul had advised them to go back and stay put until they were ordered out. For us things were still as peaceful as ever.

In the early months of 1949 mailing a letter suddenly cost about a thousand dollars (Chinese). As we could buy only fifty-dollar stamps, I couldn't always get enough stamps at one time to mail all of my letters. Even the post office couldn't keep up with itself!

When four of the families where we had cottage meetings moved, the work seemed to come to a standstill. At a congregational meeting, however, church leaders suggested they start holding family meetings in their own homes and promptly appointed a meeting for every night of the week!

The prayer meeting that had been changed from Wednesday night to five o'clock Wednesday morning continued to go on strong. The turnout was the best I had seen to any prayer meeting since I came to China. The church leaders all came as well.

The devil was definitely not pleased with the spiritual progress that had been made. He was trying hard to discourage Mr. Chang, one of the deacons. Mr. Chang had paid a lot of money down on a house he wanted to buy. The owner decided he didn't want to sell to Mr. Chang and refused to move out. He threatened to sell it to another buyer. Chang went to court to try to settle the matter. We feared it might cause a lot of trouble.

I wish you could have seen our garden that spring! The narcissus, daffodils, snowdrops and violets all blossomed at the same time, not to mention the peach and cherry trees. In addition our Judas tree was decked with pretty pink flowers from trunk right out to branch tips. In another month we would have beans and peas out of the garden. How I loved spring!

We had a great time visiting in March. The first day we could not find the folks we were looking for. They were not at the addresses they had given us. The next day it was just the opposite. Every place we went we had a welcome. We went to a doctor's home. The oldest of his two wives was not wanted because she did not bear him any children. The poor soul had a miserable life. When we showed her the way of salvation, she seemed most interested, as if she really wanted to believe. She took us over to an elderly neighbor who before the war was a very wealthy woman. Her family had to evacuate when the Japanese came. Her husband and sons died, leaving her all alone. She was forced into working at odd jobs for a living. We had the privilege of showing her the way of salvation and taught her a prayer. She was so pleased. She came along to women's meeting the next Thursday.

Another day we visited a man who had accepted the Lord during the conference. His wife and mother had never heard the Gospel. The old mother was very bitter. They too at one time had been exceedingly wealthy, but now? When we walked in, the old lady was sorting over some weeds that she had collected for their vegetable. Though she did not seem to be touched by the Gospel, the daughter-in-law came along to the women's meeting.

We saw a lot of hardships those days. The First Middle School, with over a thousand students, was all out of food and money. They had applied to the local government for help as teachers and students alike were near starving.

It had been a very, very dry spring. The spring rains did not come, and it looked as if there might be a famine by summer time.

At the end of March I went to Nancheng to get a cracked tooth fixed. The dentist wanted to cap it with gold. Ailsa was sure I would come home with a "broad glittering gold grin." Actually I had a white tooth put in. The Chinese told me it was made of china.

As Ailsa was home alone, I did not want to leave her any longer than necessary. For that reason I decided to head right home even if I had to walk most of the way. I had ridden my bicycle there, but had had a strong head wind. I decided to stay on the bike for five *li* and then walk for a while. But when I made the first five *li*, I decided to see if I could make it ten. Once I did that, I pushed on to the halfway mark. I had to walk up all the hills and grades, but for most of the way I managed to pedal myself along. It was a total of seventy *li*, thirty-one kilometers, to the city and almost another mile home. Was I glad to get home and sit down! My verse that morning, "As thy days so shall thy strength be," surely proved true for me that day.

Our numbers in the Thursday meetings kept about the same in spite of the fact that folks were leaving us each week. We were drawing new people. I did hate to see our friends go, but surely would not have wanted to keep them from the Lord's will. Many of them were going back to where there were no churches, some of them hoping to start work in their own villages.

By the end of April I could not write letters because the post office had no stamps. Even if there had been stamps available, it would have taken so many that the envelope would have been too heavy.

We had lots of guests—eight missionaries with six children for a time—all living in our house. As I did all the cooking, I was really kept busy. Fortunately, I have always enjoyed cooking.

We were delighted to have some good music. Mr. Malins brought his phonograph, and we played our new records. Mr. Malins had George Beverly Shea and George Edstrom records, and I had some featuring Helen Barth and the Moody Choir. We played them over and over. They seemed to suit the times.

Spring was bringing big changes in China. We were wondering what sort of news the folks back home were reading in their papers. No change in government had occurred near us, but we were expecting a changeover very soon. We knew we were safe in the Lord's keeping. He is never bound by outward circumstances. We just praised the Lord for the wonderful opportunities we had for preaching the Gospel those days when men's hearts were failing them for fear. Things were pretty grim for many of our Chinese friends. Only the Lord Jesus could meet their needs.

We had asked for five new workers for our district. The new workers were all in Shanghai studying. If they got out of Shanghai before the changeover to communist rule, they would be able to reach us soon. Otherwise they would be held up in Shanghai at least for a while. Since I was to look after the new ladies in my home, my work would be cut out for me. Our team was glad to have them and planned to give them a warm welcome.

By May things had gone absolutely crazy. Inside of a week prices went up five to ten times. Vendors wouldn't even look at a million-dollar note. All bargaining was done in rice and salt. It took about a peck of rice to buy a pound of meat. A half a peck bought a pound of vegetables. Hundreds of people in the city were faced with starvation. Even the government-supported First Middle School couldn't get their money through. Several thousand students were stranded there without food.

Prices all trebled again. It made me dizzy just to try and work out my accounts. One day I bought some charcoal. The price was 22 million dollars for a hundred pounds! We got a bargain on eggs one day at $180,000 *apiece!* Don't ask me what that was in U.S. money. I lost track of that. New currency had come in, but the old had not been collected, leaving things in more of a muddle than ever. We still couldn't buy stamps, and in Nancheng they were sending out letters with the backs of the envelopes not only covered with stamps but with five layers of stamps!

Each time support money from my family came I was reminded of their faithfulness. I was so thankful to them and to the Lord for all He had done for me through my loved ones. Very few missionaries had their families' love and interest as I did. I prayed that the Lord would bless each member of my family abundantly.

Around the middle of May I received two letters from Mom and one from my sister-in-law Dorothy—also two parcels. The one from my brother Ben and wife Alice contained a new dress! I wish you could have seen us. I had it on within two minutes of opening the parcel. The exclamations were something like this: "But look how long!" "The color is just perfect for China. It is pretty and yet not too gay." "Just feel how nice and soft the material is!" Besides the dress the box contained some foodstuff, always more than appreciated in those times.

I didn't know who the other parcel was from—the name was torn off. It had a two-pound can of coffee, a pound of tea, a can of cocoa, and a huge can containing a whole roast chicken. I could hardly wait to open that, but decided to keep it for Bertha's birthday, a month away. There were also small cans of fruit, milk, etc. Bertha received a parcel, too, and so did Ailsa. We just praised the Lord for bringing this to us just when we were expecting to be cut off at any time.

A city nearby changed hands. Almost any time Nancheng's turn could come. Hordes of people were coming down from the north. A crowd of government officials descended on us one afternoon and left the next morning. We braced ourselves for a flood of missionary refugees.

At one of our cottage meetings I had the joy of watching a man take down his idols. He had believed for some time, but it seemed that his father and wife refused to have the gods removed. Finally both consented and even seemed quite responsive to the Gospel. The believing member of the family pulled down the ancestral scrolls and rolled them up. Then he pulled down all the door gods. But when the pastor suggested he burn them, he said, "I will give them to my relatives; they are still good." After we showed him how foolish this was, he proceeded to burn them. What a great fire! The kitchen god he washed off the wall.

As a result of our cottage meetings, the church was beginning to fill up on Sundays. It kept us busy after the meeting to meet all the newcomers and to introduce them to the church leaders.

In June we received a letter from headquarters in Shanghai dated May 30, 1949, from General Director Frank Houghton. In it he described the communist takeover in Shanghai. The letter was titled *"Occasional Letter No. 1."* and marked, "Private. Not for publication." It read as follows:

> Although it is not certain whether this communication can reach you...I do not want to leave you without some record of the events of last week. If we are cut off from you for a further period, a good deal of what I recall today may have been forgotten, and I certainly want you to join with us in thanksgiving to God for His many mercies.
>
> A week ago fighting was still proceeding fiercely on the Shanghai perimeter, with the Nationalist troops professing determination to continue the struggle. Our nights were somewhat disturbed by heavy firing, but it was fairly distant, and life proceeded normally in the city itself. One of our problems was that Dr. and Mrs. Fish were here, hoping to proceed on leave of absence, and it seemed more and more doubtful whether many more foreign planes would land here before the changeover. Thus it was an immense relief when they got away on the afternoon of Tuesday, May 24. Although we did not know it at the time, this proved to be the very last foreign plane which touched down here. That same morning the Lutheran plane, "St. Paul," had left for Chungking, and Mr. and Mrs. Douglas Robertson were on board. On the previous afternoon Mr. Robertson had suggested that, if he was to draw the plans for the projected new hospital building in Lanchow, [they] ought to make the journey while the way was still open....
>
> That afternoon, May 24, the Nationalist troops were very much in evidence.... But the news was not allowed to

leak out that the incoming forces had defeated them. As the evening wore on, however, the sound of rifle and machine gun fire increased in intensity. It was obvious that... fighting was going on in our neighborhood. By the mercy of God, however, the retreating soldiers did not attempt to enter our compound. By the next morning we had the news that the changeover had taken place and that the whole city on this side of the Soochow Creek was in the hands of the incoming [communist] forces.

You are well aware that during the last few months there was a good deal of talk about the possibility of an interim period between the departure of the Nationalists and the arrival of the communists, and that during this period disorder and anarchy might be expected. In answer to your prayers and ours, nothing of the sort occurred. As far as this part of Shanghai is concerned, the communists took over swiftly and quietly, and since then they have behaved with admirable discipline. We have heard of no cases of foreigners or foreign property being molested in any way.

[Two days after the changeover] on Lammermuir Day... [commemorating the sailing of the S.S. Lammermuir with the first China Inland Mission workers on board in 1866] we felt there was no reason why the language students from the other two households should not join us for our sessions of prayer. The women students came over from Wycliffe in the pick-up, and we had sessions of prayer from 10 to 12 and 2 to 3:30, the Communion service following from 4 to 5, so that all could get home well before dark. Even this precaution was not absolutely necessary, for the curfew has been lifted, and apparently there was no serious risk in walking the streets after dark. At the same time, we are advising the language students to exercise particular caution, especially as they do not know the country and the people, and might cause difficulty...without any intention of doing so.

We found that it was possible to send cables to the home countries, and therefore on Thursday afternoon I sent you the following message: "Tranquilly joyfully celebrating Lammermuir." That day we were delighted to have a telegram from Mr. Mellow in Peiping. Since then we have had word from Mr. Faulkner in Nancheng, who reported that seventeen missionaries were gathered there; from Mr. George Steed at Suanchang, who says that all the Anhwei workers are safe and well; and from Kuling. It was, of course, a particular joy to hear from my brother in a telegram...that the turnover took place peacefully on the 17th and that all were well.

This information was transmitted to you by cable, and I trust you received it. At first we were permitted to send telegrams even to the parts of China which have not yet come under the new authority, and so on Friday the 27th I sent the following message to various places in this part of China, and also to Lanchow, Chungking and Kunming: "Ephesians three twenty fulfilled." We all felt that the Lord had worked beyond our asking or expectation.

I mentioned that fighting on this side of the Soochow Creek ceased almost completely on Wednesday the 25th, but it continued north of the creek for another couple of days. Our friends in the IVF house and in the Kiangway Bible Seminary had some difficult moments, but the whole area is now clear, and they all came through without loss or injury.

Sunday May 29th was a peaceful day, and Christians throughout the city met for worship without any difficulty. We were delighted to see Pastor Yang from Nanking and Miss Warin from the Holy Light School at Soochow.

So far we have no direct word from Hangchow, but Miss Warin had a letter from Miss Kathleen Heath...reporting that the Bible college classes were continuing as usual and that they were all well. Pastor Yang brought good news of Mr. and Mrs. Glazier and Mr. and Mrs. Guinness, and he says that in Nanking there is no hindrance whatsoever to Christian activities. As far as the Holy Light School is concerned, careful inquiries are being made by the authorities, but we trust that it will be possible to complete the term quietly and also to hold the special summer conference for present and past students....

Miss Warin had no difficulty at all in coming here by train. The railway between here and Nanking is open. It now remains to be seen whether there will be any boat or plane to take her to Hongkong in time for her booking for England on June 9th. Yesterday it was reported that foreign mail will be accepted by the post office since it is hoped that a foreign vessel will call here within a few days...

The gold *yuan* currency, which had become almost worthless, can be exchanged for People's Bank notes at the rate of 100,000 to 1, but the exchange for People's Bank notes and the silver dollar or the American dollar is not yet fixed. We are praying that the authorities may be given great wisdom in dealing with the chaotic financial situation.

...It is obvious that the communist forces are making further advances in Chekiang, Kiangsi, and Shensi. According to the reports published in the Chinese papers today, they are already well beyond Ningpo in Chekiang and are advancing upon Kian in Kiangsi and Paoki in Shensi. A telegram from Chuhsien, Chekiang, reports that Miss Reynolds and Miss Barham, together with the normal Chuhsien workers, were all well on May 28.

I have attempted to give you some of the facts with very little comment. We do not know what the future holds, but we are confident that we are here by the will of God and, as I have suggested, the events of the past week provide very great cause for thanksgiving.

In June the post office came up with a new system, making mailing letters possible again. No price appeared on stamps. They were marked only Ordinary Mail or Air Mail. You paid the price at the date it was issued, and it held its value. Before the change one lady received a letter with 500 stamps tied to the envelope with a string!

I went to Sisiang for a few days and had a warm visit with my dear friend Mrs. Wu, who used to work with us at Xin Ji. Blind now, the dear old soul was spending her days carrying her grandchildren around. As her daughter-in-law was not being too kind to her, life was more than a bit miserable.

As one of our little Sunday school girls had often invited us to go to visit her mother, I went calling on the household one day. The child was a bright little thing. She could say all the memory verses for the whole year. Her mother told me: "She is a real little Christian. She misses her breakfast in order to go to Sunday school every Sunday. She reads her Bible, and wants me to read it, but I don't even have time to read the newspaper. I tell her I think she should go to Bible school and be a preacher when she grows up." How is that for a testimony from a non-Christian mother?! When the mother came to our women's meeting, I prayed that I would have the joy of seeing this whole family become Christians. These educated people from Peking claimed they didn't have time to go to church.

By the end of June we were cut off from Shanghai. But we praised the Lord that we were not cut off from Heaven! Our luggage came back from Szechwan. It had been gone for a whole year. I was glad to get some clothes and some of the other things back but realized I might lose them all again. Thankfully, I had long since given up putting value on my *things*.

I received word from home that my mother was having trouble with her legs and was in a lot of pain. How I wished that I could be home to look after her—or at least send her part of our flower garden to cheer her up!

In July I pulled my typewriter out to start writing letters again. As it had been a few weeks since I had used it, it had grown moldy fur all around the edges.

That month we had a vacation Bible school with 173 children enrolled, with well over a hundred children attending every day. All but one of the five Chinese teachers were refugees living at our place. I could not have had the school without their help. After Ailsa led the singing, Pastor Li gave a lesson for all the children̄ usually a chalk talk. After that we took roll call and welcomed the new children.

Each class began with a big sheet of white paper and a tree trunk painted on it. We glued a leaf on the tree for every child who came, ending up with some nice looking trees. The second week we gave fruit cutouts for everyone who brought a friend. One class had pears, another peaches, another apples, oranges, etc.

After all these activities the kids went out for a drink of tea and a spot of exercise. Then we divided them for classes and handwork. The big kids painted and colored. We gave the little ones Christmas cards, which they made into books.

Besides all the children's meetings we continued our regular schedule: two women' meetings, four cottage meetings, and the Tuesday night Bible class. We did not have much time to play. But whenever I had a few spare minutes, I would walk around my garden. It gave me much joy. Sometimes I would get the hoe and do some digging. Midsummer red and pink roses, peonies, iris, daisies and marigolds were in blossom. Chrysanthemums, dahlias, gladiolas, and wall flowers were growing like weeds. I think all my looking at them helped them grow.

Our peach tree was loaded with peaches that year. It was against the wall right on the street. One night the cook reported that soldiers were on the other side of the wall knocking off the peaches with a bamboo stick. I ran out on the street and was there before they saw me coming. I looked square at the man with the pole and said, "What is your name and where do you live?" It scared the wits out of the whole gang, and they took to their heels, leaving their pole behind. I calmly threw the pole into our yard and came inside. A while later an officer came to make apologies for his men and asked for the pole back! How we laughed!

But the story didn't end there. Sunday morning a cute little girl came into Sunday school. She looked shyly at me and then came over and put her arms up for me to take her. After I had set her on my lap, she said, "When the men were stealing your peaches last night, I didn't take any, not even one!"

I said, "That is good."

After Sunday school she went into church, and, bless me, if she didn't come out holding the hand of her father¯the culprit who was knocking the peaches down! Though I invited him to stay to church, he went home with his child. He had evidently been to Sunday school, however!

By August it had been three months since I had received a home letter.

Late in the summer the weather was so hot that I discarded my faithful friend, the rat¯a special piece that I wrapped my long hair around to make a bun. It rubbed my neck so that prickly heat became sores on the back of my neck. Instead of my usual hairdo, I did my hair in braids and fastened them on top of my head. In spite of rubber bands, ribbons, hairpins, bobby pins and combs, it still kept coming down. Once when Mrs. Su and I were about to visit a wealthy, refined lady, the braids came sliding down. The two of us just stood and laughed. I laughed so hard I could hardly get all the paraphernalia out of my hair to redo it.

One September night a thief came into our compound, entering the window of a room where three students were sleeping. He went in, collected a huge bundle of clothes, and emptied out a suitcase. He even took things off of one girl's bed while she slept. Just as he was leaving, one of the girls heard a noise and called, "Who's there?" The man got a fright and ran. The lady next to the girls' room heard him run and called, "Thief, thief!"

In no time everyone was up and on the man's trail. Each one had a candle in one hand and a weapon in the other: fire tongs, pole with hooks on each end for carrying water buckets, bamboo poles, hoe, shovel, sticks, etc. The man went through the church windows into the church yard. About this time, seeing he was being followed, he dropped his bundle of clothes and ran for his life. The students all went in a long file following his easy-to-follow trail as in his haste he had dropped a piece of cloth outside the church and a hanky at the window. When they reached where the bundle was, someone hollered, "Here he is!" Then everyone shouted, "Hit him, hit him!" With all their various weapons they were beating this bundle of clothes! We really couldn't help but laugh.

We discovered later that the thief had come over into our yard, swiped two of the cook's shirts and a sheet he had left on the line, and then had hidden in our out-house until everyone had gone to bed.

One Sunday in early October a granny walked into a meeting soaking wet. She had no socks, and her shoes were oozing mud. I said to her, "You should not have come in all this rain."

The dear lady looked at me quizically and replied, "But I am starved, and what is a little wet when I can come and sit down to a spiritual feast?" She really appreciated every little bit of help we could give her. To her delight, we sat down then and there and taught her a Bible verse.

Heavy rains and floods hindered autumn ministry. But out of those rough times came some wonderful stories of deliverance. Among those living in the flooded area was Mrs. Liu, baptized the previous spring. The water began to rise very suddenly at midnight. As it was very dark, the family did not dare to leave their home then, but waited for dawn. When they left the house, the water was up to Mrs. Liu's neck. She had her two-month-old baby tied to her shoulders and took another child by the hand.

The father took the other two children. They dragged the children through the water, just managing to keep their heads above the surface until they reached the mountains two or three miles away. They stayed there until the water receded and then came to us. Local Christians rallied around and outfitted them in clothes and bedding. They did not save anything. You couldn't even see where their home had been except for a little willow tree left standing.

A family of eight people living in Nancheng saw the floods coming and climbed up onto the thatched roof of their house, hauling up also their pig, dog, cat, and chicken. The floods swept away their home, and they came floating down to our place, over twenty miles! A man with a boat saw them and rescued them. They gave the boatman the pig in appreciation of his services.

When three bright, clear days followed the flooding rains, we were ever so thankful to see the sun. Everywhere we went women were washing. After six weeks of rain, clothes were dirty, bedding and other things had become moldy. Our garden wall had collapsed, the house leaked, and the garden needed working. We had our work cut out for us.

"Coming on the first plane," announced a wire from Faith Leeuwenberg in Chungking. From my home church, the Open Bible Church in Grand Rapids, Michigan, she had just come back from furlough. Can you imagine my excitement? We scurried to clean house, plan special meals, and make arrangements to meet her. I was eager to see her as we had been cut off from correspondence since May. I longed to get all the family news.

When Ailsa became ill with suspected appendicitis, she was sent to Nancheng to see a doctor. The doctor said that she had studied too hard and needed a rest. Actually Ailsa put in only the required amount of hours, but the weather was very hot. It didn't help that the soldiers had put up a siren that went off all hours of the day and night. Apparently they used it to get the soldiers out of bed in the morning and to call them back at night. Just the sound of the siren upset Ailsa so much that she could not sleep at night. I didn't even hear it.

China was declared fully under communist control on December 12th. Our hearts were filled with praise to the Lord for His keeping in the changeover. The city changed hands without a single gunshot. The old army and government officials moved out over the weekend, and the new ones came in on a Wednesday morning. As conditions had deteriorated to a dreadful state, everyone was relieved to have them come. We had soldiers in to see us several times, but they were very polite and friendly.

And the mails *finally* started coming. Mailed items from as far back as March were at long last delivered to us. The Smiths got seventy-one letters from their children in one batch! Bertha had a pile of mail, too. I did not fare as prosperously. I hoped the others, which had been sent to Chengtu, would come later.

So far our work had gone on as usual, apart from daily visits of soldiers. We were promised freedom to preach and, so far, had been given it. We were truly very grateful to the Lord.

The single lady workers had planned to come for a few days after Christmas Day. But Mr. Smith advised them to travel only in their own county. As the Sisiang road was not open for buses yet, the ladies from there wouldn't be able to come either. My fellow workers and I just had to celebrate by ourselves this year.

These were more than unsettled times. ❧

Chapter 17

New Regime–Same God

The cloud of uncertainty cast its shadow over the way ahead as we moved into the new year. What would 1950 bring? Nobody knew.

Yet we had the same God. Our eyes were fixed on Him, not on the uncertainties. We took note of the realities and, shoulder to shoulder with the Chinese church, rolled up our sleeves to tackle what seemed most important to do—including a vacation Bible school for the children right at the start.

Two good decisions were made at our congregational meeting about the same time. First, the church decided to rent a building for a street chapel on the main street for daily preaching. Second, they decided that we would go out in teams at Chinese New Year's time into the country. We already had an invitation to two places. We hoped that eventually Sunday services would develop and lead to new churches in several places.

The latest plans afoot at this time were to open a Bible school in Chengku. The best part, I thought, was that the Chinese planned it all. The idea was for the students to work half time and study half time. Under the new regime *everybody* had to work and produce something. The school was to have weaving machines and stocking machines. We hoped to start with about twenty students: two classes—one for advanced and one for beginners.

We already had quite a number of students who had had a year at Bible school, but had to come home because of disturbed conditions. Everyone was very excited about the possibilities.

In February I received a nice pile of home mail. Among the letters were two from Mom and two from sister-in-law Dorothy. They were January letters. December letters were still missing except a Christmas card from my sister-in-law Alice. A lot of news was missing. Mom wrote that my youngest sister Grace had been sick and would write to me about it herself. No letter came from her, however. Dorothy wrote, "Dean (another sister) had nothing to do in her new house." *Where is she*? I wondered. "Ben (brother) bought a big house, and they have moved," Dorothy continued. I was afraid that all these moves meant that people were not getting my letters either. Furthermore I wondered if suddenly I were to go home, I wouldn't be able to find anyone except my mom!

We started going out every day in groups of two or three. One Saturday Bertha and I joined a lady who was a new Christian and another who had been a Christian quite a long time. We called on a woman who had recently come to believe in Christ through prayer. She had fallen the summer before and knocked her hip out of joint. Without good doctors or a hospital where we were, it was a miracle that she was able to walk at all. But as she was not able to walk to church, we had cottage meetings in her home.

A Mrs. Meng had come to one of our meetings and heard the Gospel for the first time. She seemed ready to accept the Lord. When we took her up on her invitation to visit her home, did we ever have a good time! She greeted us eagerly and had a little table and four chairs out in the village square, right at the crossroads. As she had already invited the people of the village, they were all there ready to hear the Gospel. We had a big crowd and good attention right to the end. After the preaching we gave away gospels and tracts.

Afterwards Mrs. Meng invited us to her home. As we talked, she told how she stood every day at the place where her idols used to be and prayed to God. She thought that was the only place she could pray! She was most interested when we told her that God would hear her wherever she was. The women who went with me were so thrilled over this woman that they were all talking to her at once, giving her advice on how to pray, how to love her husband in spite of his treatment to her, etc. The ladies who went with me had never done this sort of work before. I really enjoyed their enthusiasm.

By April it was evident that we were going to have difficulties with the communist authorities. Initially we were forbidden to teach Bible in the Bible school. To try to run a Bible school without Bible studies was crazy. The students were not even interested in other subjects. We were losing the confidence of the students and just did not know what to do. We just committed it to the Lord. It was His work, and if He wanted the school, He would have to work for us. When the authorities rescinded the ban on Bible teaching, our hearts filled with praise to the Lord.

Our next problem was that the authorities wanted to use our premises for billeting soldiers. They had warned us earlier and told us to get ready for them. We really hadn't any empty space, so again we were reminded that the buildings were the Lord's to do with as He desired.

As we weren't getting any news from the outside world, we knew absolutely nothing of what was going on. I was relieved that my family left all politics out of their letters. With censorship a reality, it was not good for us to get political comment.

March in China is a windy month and is kite-flying time. Folks were on the city wall flying kites all day long—grown-ups as well as children. These folk really knew how to make kites—some of them real beauties. If things were peaceful when time came for me to go home, I hoped to buy at least one of those huge kites. The kids at home would love to see them.

New problems came up in the Bible school. The principal came to tell me that the students had hired a cook. They were supposed to be doing their own cooking. Only about ten of them, including the principal and his family, ate together. They had been out of money so could not afford to buy vegetables, let alone hire a cook. I was treasurer for the school. What a headache! The school was supposed to be a local church project. In other words, the Church Association of South Shensi should have been supporting it. They supported the principal, but it appeared he was expecting help from the mission also. I definitely needed prayer that the local church would support the school so that it would not matter if we missionaries were there or not.

The Smiths and some of the Chinese leaders were supposed to come and visit us. After waiting for them a week, we discovered that the Smiths, at least, were not able to get a pass. Apparently the only foreigners getting passes for travel were those who were homeward bound. I was disappointed, as they needed to make some important decisions regarding the school. I did not feel adequate to make those decisions myself.

Once we got through the first term at the school and got some exams completed, we felt as though we had really accomplished something. But then two new students arrived right at mid-term time, just adding to the variety of our already varied standards of students. Some students couldn't read; others were middle-school graduates. Some students had been believers for many years while others were Christians of only a few months. Now we would have students who came at the beginning of the term and those who entered halfway through! We wondered what the Lord would do with this not altogether promising group.

In June we received a letter from CIM leaders warning of the possibility that we would all have to go home, though not necessarily at once. They had not decided when or how we would leave, or in what order they would send us. I sent a cable home for prayer. I expected my family would hear the news, and I prayed it would not upset them. We felt perfectly safe in the Lord's keeping. The problem was that the new communist government felt that we missionaries were less than essential, to say the least, in their scheme for the future.

At this same time I received a letter from my Mom saying she couldn't walk anymore and would not be able to live alone much longer. Before this news I felt that I could not leave China unless the Lord sent me out. Now I was wondering if this was the Lord's way of taking me home just when Mom needed me. I could do nothing but rest in the Lord's knowing of His plans for me. Made before the foundation of the world, His plans are never out one day. Everything works according to a perfect schedule. Isn't it wonderful that we don't have to plan our own lives?

Bertha had a birthday in June. Knowing we might have to leave, she did not want us to give her things she would find difficult to get rid of. We had been buying a supply of Chinese commentaries and books that we felt would be helpful to the folks there if we had to leave. We decided to give Bertha a book shower. We hid the books all around her bedroom. We had our afternoon tea at her desk. The birthday cake was in the middle of the table, with streamers of colored paper coming out on all sides. These streamers led to her gifts. She had to go and find them all. We sure had some good laughs. We had some fake books¯dictionaries to improve her language skills, an atlas to improve her knowledge of China, a book on British husbandry with a poem purportedly from a bachelor in the mission saying he heard Bertha was looking for a husband, so was applying for the job! When she went to bed that night, she found a nice leather Bible wrapped up in her pajamas.

Bertha also received a parcel of good foodstuffs from her mother just before her birthday, though it had been meant for Christmas six months before. In the package was a fruitcake, a box of chocolates, some salmon, and powder for orange drinks— wonderful treats!

About this time a man came one night to inquire about the way of salvation. We nicknamed him Nicodemus. After we had talked to him for two hours, he asked, "Can I be a believer in my heart and not be baptized?"

"Salvation does not depend on baptism," I told him, "but if you are truly saved, you will be so happy you will *want* to be baptized."

We did not see him for a long time after that. He went through some very trying circumstances. Then he came back and said, "The work of the Holy Spirit is wonderful. One can't see Him or understand Him. I have found real comfort and peace in the Lord. I feel I *must* be baptized."

By August all of the church representatives cooperated with planning in making arrangements for the Bible school's coming year. They needed to decide whether or not they wanted the school to continue and how they wanted it run. Before the school opened we were not sure that there would be enough students to make it worth while or how many teachers we would need.

Actually the new term went much better than the previous one. A better spirit prevailed among the students. They worked hard and put their best effort into their work.

Late summer sunsets were absolutely glorious. One evening the clouds in the west looked very black against the bright, but dimming skies. Unexpectedly lovely white clouds slipped out from behind them. As the sun slipped below the darkening hills, it turned them all into a fiery red. One of the students remarked, "That is probably like the cloud the Lord used to lead the children of Israel through the wilderness."

Our garden by now was a jolly wilderness. The beans and tomatoes were propped up with all sorts of stakes—about ten feet high. The beans completely covered the stakes. The vines were so thick you could hardly get through the mass of leaves to find the meaty beans. Tomato plants were about four feet high, and the corn about seven feet. Our highest hollyhock was 22 feet when I measured it last, and it continued to grow. We had a row of six-foot sunflowers at the back of the garden. Dahlias were as tall, or taller, than I and were loaded with flowers. In among all the tall things were pumpkins with massive vines growing everywhere. We certainly were "producing" that year, as the new government was urging everyone to do.

In our spare time we canned the produce from our garden. We

canned peaches and plums and made jam. Speaking of jam, a jar of my precious apricot jam fermented. It blew the cover off and splattered jam all over the ceiling. For those who are building new homes or redecorating, I can suggest something really new—fermented apricot ceilings, or walls too, if you like a bright yellow color. I suggest furnishings of brown or pale shades of green. Then when the jam gets dry and moldy, you can still use the same furnishing because they will match the green jam.

At the end of summer we had just started our prayer meeting on Saturday night at our fall conference, when government representatives arrived to inform us that we could not proceed with our conference until we notified the provincial government.

After special prayer meetings on Sunday we went on Monday to the authorities and explained to them the purpose of the conference. We also told them it was not a new thing, but had been held every year for the past ten years. After that they allowed us to go ahead and finish the conference. The Lord had answered our prayers. The conference kept us extremely busy.

We were all excited when I received four big parcels my family had sent me via Faith. What fun we had as I opened them! The fun, however, didn't last long. I had to scramble to put the things away when that same afternoon solders came around to inspect our premises. In the parcels were things like sweaters from my mother, new dresses, warm winter boots, a flannelgraph background, two aprons, bedroom slippers, cotton stockings, stationery, flannel pajamas, face soap, phonograph records and, last but not least, a box of chocolates.

We didn't know how much longer we would be able to stay in China. No one knew for sure. Our future was unknown to all of us, but known perfectly to the Lord. As much as I loved China, I wanted to go home for my mom's sake, but I just had to await the Lord's guidance. I knew that when it was the Lord's time, He would take me home.

One Saturday night a big residential fire roared so close we could see its glow. Fortunately the wind blew the fire away from us and from the city. Though we were spared, the fire destroyed eight or nine homes right on the other side of the wall against which our home was built.

In October I did some really hard study for the next term in Bible school. I would be teaching Acts and needed sixty lessons. In one week I did 28 lessons, writing them all out in Chinese character.

That fall we were feeling rather discouraged over our cottage meetings. We just were not getting any invitations. We didn't know if the folks were just too busy making a living or if they were afraid to have the missionaries in their homes. Changes had created a lot of uncertainties.

Winter arrived with a cold blast in November.

One mid-morning I received a call to inform us that one of our best students from last term was very ill. The caller said the girl was dying, and the father wanted the missionaries to come and have a little service with her. Though the family had been giving her penicillin, when she seemed better, they stopped. Immediately she became worse again. This girl was the only Christian in her home. She had no mother and was the only daughter. Most of the time the poor thing had no one to care for her in her illness except her father and an aunt, who came briefly a couple of times a day.

When this girl's mother had died years before, she heard terrible noises of evil spirits. One night the girl declared she heard them again and was afraid. After we went and read to her and prayed with her, the girl said her heart was at peace. If the Lord spared her, she wanted to serve Him, she said, and if He chose to take her, she was ready to go. We prayed earnestly that the Lord would work a miracle and heal her—that His name would be glorified and her family and others might be saved.

Problems cropped up at the Bible school. The principal got angry with some of the students. As a result, two of them left, and another was about to leave. A fourth was disgruntled. The father of one of the girls who left came and met with one of the deacons and talked to the principal. They asked me to talk to the girls to try to persuade them to come back. I was able to persuade only one of them to stay on.

Happily a new principal with a good reputation arrived to take over the school. There were some real possibilities for the school with the right leader. The churches wanted it and were willing to support it. A good spirit returned among the students. One little fellow always started his prayer with, "Thank you, Lord, for watching over us through the night." He had only recently started praying and was so nervous he could hardly get his words out.

In spite of very few resources we managed to come up with all sorts of ideas for Christmas decorations for the church. For example, for tree decorations I opened walnuts, took the meats out for our cookies and put a string in the shell and stuck them together again. Then I covered them with silver, gold, blue and red shiny papers out of old Christmas cards.

When I looked over the past year, I saw the bumps, but was amazed at what the Lord had done in a year of uncertainty. ❧

Chapter 18

Time of Waiting

We knew that eventually the communists would not allow the students to attend Bible school. But their infiltration into the school was so subtle that we didn't notice right away. Though the principal of the school claimed to be a Christian, he proved to be the one to undermine my classes. Right after the communist takeover he told his brother and his neighbors, "Now you do not go to Miss Chung (my Chinese name) or the missionary Bible classes anymore." So everyone stopped coming. Nobody would come near us. Eventually the man confessed his duplicity, but I did not learn about it until years later.

The communists had a three-pronged strategy called the "three-self" order. Churches had to be self-propagating, self-supporting, and self-governing. Because of CIM's philosophy, the churches actually met all these requirements. I was certain that it was the Lord who gave CIM a vision for the indigenous church way back in 1933. As demonstrated in Xin Ji during my first term in China, their plan for the churches was that after ten years local congregations would be totally self-supported and self-governed. By the time of the communist takeover every one of the churches had taken over the complete support of their pastors. They were completely self-governing and self-supporting. We acted only as their consultants, helpers, etc.

Shortly after the communists took over, we had a conference in Sian. Every church had to send representatives. Well, the communists sent an official from the Religious Affairs Bureau in Peking to question the people of the church. They preached to them the three-self strategy, then told them, "You must be self-propagating."

The church leaders listened quietly and respectfully to this man and then replied, "We've been doing that for years."

"What do the missionaries do?" asked the official.

"What we ask them to do," the leaders replied. "They teach, help us organize conferences, help with the Bible school—they just do what we ask them to do."

Then they were questioned about the church being self-governed. The same thing happened. In typical Chinese fashion, the church leaders listened politely and let this official harangue them for an hour or two and when he was finished, they said, "We've been in control of our churches for years."

"Well, when you have a meeting, who chairs the meeting?" the interrogator asked.

"We do," replied the leaders.

"Well then, what do the missionaries do?"

"They come only when we invite them, when we need advice or help," said the leader.

The official asked, "Well, who runs your church?"

"We do," replied the church leaders.

When the subject moved to self-support, this official from Peking really got the shock of his life because he thought he would have the church people stumped there. When he finished, it turned out that his official Religious Affairs Bureau was the only one supported with foreign funds!

When the conference was over, the government sent papers to every member of the church. Everybody had to sign this paper saying: "My church will be self-supporting, self-governing, and self-propagating."

Well, the innocent farmers in this province thought, *that's what we are, so what?* So they all signed the papers—every member. A few months later government leaders came along to the church leaders. "You signed a paper that says you are self-supporting," they said accusingly. "We saw the missionary sitting in your church, and she put money in the offering plate." Church leaders had to come to us and ask us, "Please don't put any money in the offering plate." We immediately warned our missionaries not to even touch the plate, but to let the Chinese pass it right around in front of them.

The last straw came when the church leaders, in response to the pressures, had to come to us and ask us not to come to church anymore. The government accused us of "governing" the church by our attendance. So there was nothing left for us to do. In the present climate we felt ourselves a hindrance, not a help. We felt it wise to ask permission to leave. We also found it prudent *never* to blame the communists for anything.

So in February of 1951 my co-workers and I went to Nancheng to wait for exit permits. We would end up waiting many long weeks.

While we waited in Nancheng for the exit passes, the people of the area were ordered to gather, and we were summoned to join them for an accusation meeting. Communist interrogators came prepared with a list of questions for us, designed to show us guilty of imperialism. Bertha was accused of having a "bad attitude." But most of the people's answers only exonerated us. One person said of me, "She's all right. I saw her carrying a child on her shoulders."

On the day of the accusation meeting I wrote the following

poem:

> There is JOY in believing when all around
> Trials oppress one, and troubles abound.
> There is JOY in believing, and nothing to fear
> With Almighty God, our God, always near.
>
> There is PEACE in believing though no way out,
> No one to help us, and Satan's about
> To try us, and tempt us, our life he would take,
> The Almighty God, our God, He'll not forsake.
>
> There is HOPE in believing, e'en though distressed,
> Faith would fail, and we feel oppressed.
> There is HOPE in believing, and this we must.
> The Almighty God, our God, in HIM is our trust.

Waiting day after day with nothing to do was tiresome. A letter from Shanghai told of folk leaving from all over China. Most of them had to wait about six weeks for their pass. Since we had already been waiting for six weeks, my hopes were up.

Once we got to Hong Kong, we knew we would still have to wait for shipping. The mission wrote to say shipping to the U.S. was cheaper via England. That would mean several weeks on the sea. I did not mind, although by this time I was eager to get home to my mother and family.

The ninth week of waiting the Annual District Conference was held in Nancheng. Though we couldn't attend, our friends from the country churches all came to see us. They shared with us how wonderfully the Lord was working. In one mountain village where the Gospel was recently preached, 21 families turned to the Lord. One man offered his home for a meeting place. Sadly they had no one to lead the services. Some of the Bible school students had been used of the Lord during this time. One boy had a wonderful testimony in his own village, where quite a number of people took down their idols and turned to the Lord.

The end of March came, and we were *still* waiting. We didn't know exactly what caused the hold-up—nobody seemed to know. One thing that helped our situation considerably was that our househelp had left, giving us something to do. Bertha and I shared household chores and the cooking.

By this time the Bible school had moved from Chengku to Nancheng.. Some of the students had to go back to their homes again to get letters of introduction from their local governments. Twelve students enrolled. New ones came, and old ones left, but each term twelve students settled in to study. It reminded me of the twelve disciples.

The house in which we and the students were staying had just one room that was used for living room, dining room, childrens' lessons, bathing the baby, childrens' play area, sewing room, and Mr. Malins' office work area. Bertha and I stuck to our bedroom!

In late March I advised my family not to get their hopes up too high for my homecoming, that it might be quite a while yet. "If it is the Lord's will for us to stay, then we will be happy to stay," I penned. "Don't worry—pray on!"

Early April the mayor promised faithfully to let us know within a week if we could leave or not. The week passed, however, and still no sign or word came from him. We certainly knew the meaning of waiting by this time.

The Malins' and my exit passes finally came through mid-April. The fact that Bertha's did not come took the edge off our relief, however. Still we scrambled excitedly to pack and to find places on a truck to travel to where we could board a train bound for Sian, on to Hankow, then south to the Chinese border with then British-controlled Hong Kong.

When my Australian co-workers and their small children and I stiffly emerged on the China side of the border after days of travel, we faced the grilling and searches of border guards. After more than 50 years, I forget most of the details of that ordeal. I smile, though, to remember the face of the guard going through my one and only suitcase when he discovered a piece of shrapnel among the contents. "Why do you have this?" he asked, puzzled.

"That's a piece of a Japanese bomb that landed in our back yard," I told him. "I wanted to show it to my family. I wanted them to know how God protected me and others when that bomb exploded so close to us."

Only when I walked across the border to the outside world did I realize the extent of the tension that had built up within me. What relief! Yet I left a big chunk of my heart in China, where dear, dear friends, both Chinese and Western, remained. I would always be thankful for the years I had spent in my adopted country.

Happily I wasn't delayed in Hong Kong for long. By May 10th I was aboard the *S. S. Bougainville*, headed for the U.S. A fellow passenger wrote a poem that describes our trip home. Unhappily, I have forgotten who the author was. As I have no other written record of the voyage across the Pacific, I will let the poem tell the story. The author begins the voyage in Manila, then swings by Hong Kong before heading to the U.S.

THE VOYAGE OF THE BOUGAINVILLE

The year 'twas nineteen fifty one, in the temperate month of May,
That the Norse ship Bougainville sailed forth out of Manila Bay.
A vessel of 9,000 tons; she was built in Amsterdam.
The Klaveness Line her owners were, and a cargo fleet they ran.

Now, in command was Captain Sund, a Norseman fair was he,
And all his officers and men from Norway they would be,
|And also two stewardesses, who were elegant, tall and fair,
As well as "Sparks," a Canadian lass, who spent her life "on the air."

And further there were Chinese eight (they always strive and toil);
And the men who spent their working hours 'midst engines, heat and oil.
For horse-power 7,000-odd the old "Chief" could control;
At fifteen knots, and more at times, he'd speed her towards her goal.

Thus so much for the vessel, her captain and her crew.
There're many other minor points and I'll mention just a few.
The smoke stack's black with band of red; her sides a whitish gray;
The superstructure's gleaming white—the whole effect's quite gay.

Abeam the funnel's crimson band, two large white K's are seen.
The derricks, samson posts and masts are all a yellowish cream.
The main deck is black as a Stygian night, the bridge deck's polished teak.
A pleasanter range of colors, t'would be difficult to seek.

Now after some days of sailing the Waglan Light is seen,
Which indicates close danger by its bright rotating beam.
Here caution must be exercised, or the ship may meet its doom.
So nor' nor west, then swing to port, and slowly through Lye Mun.

The mountains green on either side rear upwards towards the sky.
Past Shaukiwan and Taikoo Dock, North Point and then Wanchai;
A harbor vast comes into view, which many vessels throng.
Most beautiful of Eastern ports, that crowning jewel—Hong Kong.

From Shamshuipo and Yaumati, Kowloon to Connaught Pier,
Full many a score of ferry boats converging courses steer.
Whilst to the buoys, aligned in rows, great ocean vessels tie,
And at the wharves on Kowloon side, Leviathans may lie.

Thus was the Bougainville one night; it was the tenth of May;
Around her like a brood of chicks, huge junks and lighters lay.
Hoarse shouts came forth from hold and winch, as over swung the slings
From Junk to deck, and down to hold̄ how many curious things!

At last the boats no cargoes hold and the Chinese give a cheer.
Then back to their rolling sampans, and to other joys, I fear.

The ship now lies deserted—in the dark shadows lurk.
And everyone has retired to sleep, to prepare for tomorrow's work.

But the crew have not yet finished, for the ship must sail tonight,
And Captain Sund stands on the bridge, the pilot to his right.
The "mate" he's in the f'castle, the "chief" he's down below;
The pilot's skiff alongside rides, preparing for a tow.

The shackle pin is loosened and the mooring chains swing clear.
The "chief" and his mechanics sense that sailing time draws near.
The engine telegraph rings out, and points to "slow ahead."
Its distant echo sounds below—to the motors oil is fed.

Pulsating to a rhythm strange the pistons rise and fall.
The screw is gently turning and the movement's felt by all.
To port there glows a red light, to starboard it is green,
Whilst on the masts both fore and aft white specks of light are seen.

The Bougainville to eastward swings, obedient to the wheel.
The wind blows cold, deck lights are dimmed, as through the night we steal.
Victoria Peak and myriad lights, at last are hid from view
By man, a hill and mountain high, outlined in darkest hue.

And now Lye Mun shows straight ahead, the pilot takes his leave.
Past flashing lights and unknown isles a winding course we weave.
The warning beam from Waglan, to starboard close at hand,
Its farewell greeting flashes—'tis our last sight of land.

The night is dark but crisp and clear; the stars peer from the sky.
The waves their foaming crests uncurl—the wind's a low-toned sigh.
The telegraph some time ago has changed to "full ahead,"
And Captain Sund has set the course, and the "Chief" has gone to bed.

At revolutions one one three the speed is knots fifteen,

Beneath the prow white bow waves leap with phosphorescent gleam.
Whilst on the bridge amidships, a phantom helmsman stands—
He's neither made of flesh nor bones, no head, no arms, no hands!

What is this unseen specter that needs not food or light,
That does an everlasting watch throughout each day and night?
Shades of the "Ancient Mariner' about me tend to fall,
I greatly fear this spectral thing will beckon me and call!

No phantom, but 'tis wondrous how the auto-gyro steers.
Once on a course, and if not stopped, 'twould steer for countless years!
For "this" in fact replaces full quartermasters four.
In future years the answer'll be, "Alas, they are no more."

Day after day towards the east we sail on a long Great Circle Route.
Up north to parallel forty-six; so don your heaviest suit.
The meridian west is one seven nought, as checked by the stars in heaven.
Four thousand miles and twelve we've done—to go, two seven four seven.

Eleven days of sailing fast, and ne'er an isle in sight
And other eight more still to do, e'er we catch any glimpse of a height.
But now our course lies southwards, to San Pedro we must run;
And day by day we welcome more that bright life-giving sun.

So far the voyage has progressed, with varying pleasant days
The passengers disport themselves in many harmless ways.
The festive boards are weighted down; full justice we all do
To meat and fish and salad dish and many another too.

And finally, the Bougainville draws near to U.S.A.
And all packing must be finished by the 28th of May.
So praise be to our Maker; to the officers and crew
For safely bringing us so far—to all we say, "Thank you."

S. S. Bougainville, May, 1951

Within days I was gazing at American countryside whizzing past, the wheels of the train marking the rail seams with a mind-numbing *clackity, clack, clack*, as I made my way to the Midwest and my Michigan family. I was headed *home*. The security of love and welcome awaited me.

But what about those I'd left behind? How would remaining fellow workers fare as they sought a way out of an increasingly hostile China? And how well would Chinese brothers and sisters in Christ weather the pressures of an aggressively atheistic government for years to come? *O Lord, they are Yours. Shepherd them through the storms ahead!* Those may not be the actual words I prayed. I don't remember. But they represent the cry of my heart as the fifteen-year China segment of this vagabond's life came to a close. ೞ

Chapter 19

Another Call—
Battle for Sungei Ruan

After arriving home in Michigan, I spent the next few years caring for my invalid mother. At first we stayed at her home in Allendale. Later we moved to Grand Rapids to be closer to her doctor. Eventually my mother required more care than I was able to provide alone. Then we moved in with my youngest sister Grace and her husband Mart.

Living with Grace and Mart allowed me to travel more freely and to accept invitations to speak about China in churches, youth groups, Christian colleges, etc. I really enjoyed telling of my experiences in China. My purpose was to encourage young people into the mission, now concentrating on the unreached in the countries on China's periphery. I also hoped to motivate people to support those who go, not only financially, but especially through a commitment to pray.

I knew from my own experiences that I would never have made it through without the intercession of my faithful prayer partners back home. One particular incident stands out. An elderly lady whom I did not know personally had been praying for me for years while I was in China. Told that she was in the hospital, probably near death, I went to visit her and thank her for her prayers. I found her ill but alert and talkative. We chatted for some time, and then I asked her if she could remember any particular time she had been led to pray for me. We discovered that two of the times she responded to the Holy Spirit's prompting to pray were the very times that the bombings occurred. That is why we were so protected. I should have shown her my piece of shrapnel!

While I was in Hong Kong on my way out of China, Bishop Houghton, the director of CIM, spoke at a prayer meeting I attended. Having visited Malaysia (in those days called Malaya), he was overwhelmed with the need and opportunity there. "We have *got* to go to Malaya," he said impassionedly. "[Because of the communist threat, the British colonial] government has taken all of the Chinese from their farms and put them into new villages. There are 500 villages of Chinese in Malaya [Malaysia today] that have never heard the Gospel."

The mission couldn't send families with children because conditions in the country were too unsafe. With too few single men available, leaders were asking the single women to go. Well, I fought it. I did *not* want to go. I didn't ever want to see another communist again. Besides, I had to take care of my mother.

The Lord did not let me off the hook, however. His response took aim at my heart. "If I loved the Chinese in Malaya enough to die for them," He said, "is it too much for you to go and tell them?"

"No, Lord, it is not too much," I answered, ashamed. "I'll go."

But the Lord's immediate task for me was the care of my mother and the openings He was giving me to speak in the U.S. Midwest. My prayer—and I shared this with people wherever I went—was that God would make it clear when the way was open for me to go to Malaya.

Four years went by with no green light from the Lord. Then in 1955 I came home from Zion, Illinois, bubbling with joy and encouragement. A group of young wives and mothers there had committed themselves to meet weekly to pray for me and for other missionaries. I could hardly wait to share my news with

The Zion prayer group years later. Though numbers dwindled as, one by one, members went to Glory or retired in warmer climes, this group prayed for me and for people to whom God sent me for five decades.

Grace and Mart, with whom Mother and I lived.

But Grace had news for me. While I was away, the doctor had called the family together to tell us that our mother must go into a nursing home. She needed medicine, shots, and other medical services that the family couldn't provide. I took that to mean that the Lord was freeing me to go to Malaya. I had my green light.

But how was I going to get enough support to allow me to go out on the field again? As usual, God had the answer. I had gone to the Lansing Bible Church in Lansing, Michigan, to speak. The pastor asked me if I had all my support. "No," I told him truthfully.

"Well, how much do you have?" he wanted to know.

I told him, "Some churches give as much as they can, but I don't know how big their 'can' is!"

I returned home on a Monday, and on Tuesday I received a letter from the Lansing Bible Church. They had decided to give toward my support. I wrote back to my mission director right away to let him know, and before long I was scrambling to get ready to go to Malaysia.

At the end of July I sailed from Montreal, Quebec. The voyage from Canada to England was beautiful, smooth, and cool. As we passed north of Newfoundland, we were among icebergs. It was quite cold, but oh, such a welcome change from summer's heat!

On August 12th we arrived in England and took the train to London, where we had a four-day layover. Staying in the China Inland Mission Home there, I felt like I was on holy ground as I thought of all the spiritual battles that had been fought and won within those walls. I was reminded of the great work that God had accomplished through one man, Hudson Taylor, who founded the mission. What if he had failed to go to China? What if I failed in God's purpose for me?

Our voyage from England to Singapore was a most fascinating one. Every few days we would see land. We traveled along the coast of Spain and Portugal and glimpsed the Rock of Gibraltar. We plied the turquoise waters of the Mediterranean, passing Malta at night, and made forays ashore at Port Said, Aden [today Adan, Yemen], Bombay in India, Colombo [now Sri Lanka] and Penang, a city and island off the northwest coast of Malaya. Between Port Said and Aden, we enjoyed a hot but calm trip through the Suez Canal and the Red Sea.

After we left Port Said, it took several hours to pass through the Suez Canal into the Red Sea. What a magnificent piece of construction the canal is! At one spot we were tied up with eight other huge ships waiting for four other ships from the opposite direction to pass us. It didn't seem quite right to be aboard a ship with a motor road and trains running right alongside of us.

How often we were reminded of Moses and the children of Israel as we passed through the Red Sea! We must have passed the place where they crossed. When you see the width of the sea and the waves rolling, you marvel at the power of God. It was too hazy to see Mount Sinai, but we could see the mountain range in the foreground. As we traveled for hours along the desert, we saw nothing but sand. Temperatures were sometimes over a hundred degrees. We couldn't blame the children of Israel for murmuring. We complained because we didn't have ice water!

In the Red Sea one of the crewmembers fell overboard. The crew stopped the ship and turned it around. Two lifeboats went out, and one man jumped into the shark-infested water and pulled the man in. The victim was brought back to the ship, but was dead. I could not help but think of the price that was paid, and the energy spent for one life—and how little we do for one soul!

On this part of the voyage I traveled with Miss Cork and Fern Blair, also of the Overseas Missionary Fellowship (OMF), the new name for the China Inland Mission. We were all in separate cabins. Someone suggested that we try to get in together after we were aboard ship. We decided that since we had prayed and asked the Lord to put us where He wanted us, we would accept our placements as from Him.

One of my cabinmates was a young English lady who was traveling to Hong Kong to marry a Chinese man, Mr. Li, who was also traveling on this ship. He was a pro-communist and hoped some day to take his wife to Shanghai. She had no idea what she was getting into. The first Sunday night I had a good opportunity to show her the way of salvation. Another night I talked until after eleven o'clock with the two of them. Shirley said she wanted to believe, but I feared she was so involved it would be difficult for her. Another day I had a Sikh come and ask if he could talk with me about my religion. He really came with a seeking heart. His difficulty was that he wanted to reason everything out and not accept it by faith.

When we reached Singapore, my home-church friend Faith Leeuwenburg and several others were on the dock to meet us. Faith met me with a lovely bouquet of orchids in a beautiful brass bowl. How good to see her again!

On Friday we arrived by train at Kuala Lumpur, Malaya. This was to be my home for the next three months. I began my language study soon after arriving. After only one lesson with the teacher, learning Cantonese looked like a pretty grim job. I was counting on my prayer partners, especially since Mr. Su, my teacher, was not a Christian. Oh, how I struggled with Cantonese! I just could not hear the different tones. All of a sudden one day I heard the difference and could say one of the tones to suit Professor Su. A week later I learned that people who received my circular letter were concentrating their prayer on my learning the language. The eventual result: I got through my first exam successfully—a start!

The Lord reminded me again that He said of Himself, "All power is given unto me," and that in Him that power was at my disposal. I wanted to be conscious of His power in my life and ministry.

During this language study time I was asked to take over Mrs. Moore's Sunday school class of twenty-three English-speaking Chinese and Indian girls. About fifteen years of age, all but five had accepted the Lord. Again, I believe my friends were praying faithfully, for God continued to work in these girls' lives. Though a few of the girls dropped out, more new ones took their place. Soon twenty or more were coming on Sunday morning. Four girls soon expressed their desire in writing to be saved. Another one was not sure of her salvation and wanted to be sure. I praised the Lord for these girls.

After my initial three months of language study and orientation in Kuala Lumpur, I was excited to be sent to Sungei Ruan, (pronounced *Sung-eye Roo-an),* known to the missionaries as "The Ruins." It had been described to me as "the beauty spot of Malaya," "hidden in the mountains," and "right in the jungle." It sounded wonderful to me.

Dorothy Hirst had opened the work in Sungei Ruan eight months previously, but had to go home early because of illness. Quite a number of young people were coming around, showing interest in the Gospel, but so far none had been baptized, and there were no church members. I implored my prayer partners to please pray with us that a whole family would accept the Lord. One good family would make a foundation for a church.

My fellow worker June Lindfield and I were reminded frequently of the strong power of ancestral worship and spirit worship in this land. Humanly speaking, it seemed well nigh impossible for these folk to take a stand for Christ. I was greatly encouraged, however, by reading of Paul's response to the idol worship in Ephesus. Though the whole city bowed to the Goddess Diana, he spoke of his prayer that church members might "receive that inner illumination of the spirit which will make [them] realize… how tremendous is the power available to us who believe in God" (Phillips' translation). So I went to Sungei Ruan, expecting to be covered in prayer. We would give our very best, and I believed that God would manifest His power.

Satan had such a strong hold on the people of Sungei Ruan, however, that the work would prove to be a hard-pressed struggle.

Sungei Ruan was built on a hill. From our home at the top of the hill we looked over the homes of the three thousand people of the village, built all around us. To combat communist recruitment and intimidation, the British colonial powers had uprooted these people from their farms and forcibly relocated them in what were called "new villages." In each of these villages—including Sungei Ruan̄ a barbed-wire perimeter fence created a barrier between the townspeople and the communist bands roaming the jungle beyond. We claimed the mountain inside Sungei Ruan's fence for the Lord. "Caleb said, 'Give me this mountain, a mountain of giants,' and it was given him because he wholly followed the Lord," says the Scripture.

I believed that God gave us part of that mountain during the evangelistic meetings we held in March. At the meetings the Lord touched many hearts through the teachings of two OMF men, Ewan Lumsden and David Beard. We thrilled to watch 150 to 200 people, mostly men, listening intently to the message of salvation. At one of the first street meetings Mr. Goh professed to accept the Lord. When Mrs. Goh came to the house with a friend, June urged them to give their lives to the Lord. Later we went to visit the Gohs in their home. Mrs. Goh said she was thinking about opening her heart to the Savior, who died for her, but her mother did not want her to. Obviously that bit of the mountain was not yet conquered.

On days when they didn't hold street meetings, Ewan and David called in homes or had meetings in other parts of the village. At one of the Saturday night meetings was a young man, Mr. Lau, a part of a family that included several young people to whom Miss Hirst had witnessed. It looked as if God was working in that home. Mr. Hui, their teacher, did not attend many meetings, but did come and give his testimony one night. The following day he received a telegram from his mother: "Father dying—come home at once." The father did not die, but I was sure it was all in God's plan to speak to the people and to show Mr. Hui his responsibility to witness to his own family.

Two Sundays after the meetings our little room was filled with fourteen men and four women. We had a very good time with the group and were encouraged. The next Sunday, however, only the Chinese-Sakai young people came. Obviously we were in the midst of a battle. The devil was fighting to hold his own.

A new fellow worker would soon be coming to live with us, Ethel Hoff, from Louisiana. I hoped that from the very first day together our hearts would be knit together in the love of Christ.

We had so hoped and prayed that by Christmas time we could have our first Christmas service in a new church there (people, not a building). A few months previous it looked quite hopeful. Now we were in the midst of another counterattack from the enemy. For two Sundays not a soul came to our service. I was so glad my joy was in the Lord Himself, and not in my circumstances, otherwise sometimes I might have lost my joy!

We did have much to praise the Lord for. Our Sunday school usually had about twenty children each week. Language study was moving ahead. We had some good contacts in visitation, especially young people and children, who knew Mandarin. For all this we heartily praised the Lord.

I called 1956 "The Battle for Sungei Ruan." In March the Gospel Van came for two weeks of meetings. A host of friends around the world stood with us in prayer. Our prayer partners were interceding for us from as far away as California, Canada, and England. As a good number of village people were brave enough to take books, we believed that God was working. However, for two months after the evangelistic campaign no one came to service. We had reason to believe that someone was in the business of intimidation, but behind it all we recognized the work of the enemy, Satan.

We held two separate daily vacation Bible schools during that year. In the first one about twenty-five children came. We were conscious of the enemy's presence when some of the bigger boys tried to make a disturbance. Later, in August of that year, during the second DVBS we started with fifty children and finished with eighty-eight. The Lord blessed, and we saw a number of children profess to accept the Lord. However, shortly after the second DVBS, just when we should have been busy with the follow-up work, June, who had been feeling better, became ill again. As she was the only one who could speak Cantonese, her illness seemed to be an attempt of the enemy to hinder the Lord's work.

We were still praying that one family would be saved. Each time we thought a family was lining up on the Lord's side, it seemed the enemy would snatch them away.

But real victories did come. One evening three girls, ages about eight to twelve years old, came to our home and announced that they wanted to be Christians. We had the joy of leading them to the Lord. These same girls brought some of their friends along to DVBS, and they were the ones who professed to be saved. One of the girls was from the Hau family, and the next Sunday night, the whole Hau family attended church. Later the older sister came alone and said she wanted to be a Christian. When asked why, she said, "Because my sins are so many." She continued to come to services and bring her friends.

The battle continued, however. Sunday school attendance, which had been as high as 24, was down to three, mainly because the local school held English classes, dancing lessons and movies on Sunday nights. Another disappointment was the fact that the boys taking the Bible correspondence course had not done their lessons for two months or been to Thursday Bible study. Also, we had lacked a teacher for Bible study class. Whatever I taught had to be interpreted from Mandarin Chinese to the local dialect.

Even though the fighting was fierce, we continued to praise the Lord. Some battles had been lost; yet it was the Lord's battle, and victory was therefore guaranteed.

By March of 1957 I was very encouraged. The last couple of months had been the best ones since I had been in Malaya. People had been coming into our home, some for medical help and some just to visit. Ethel did clinical work. The first half of March she had eighty-five patients—not that many different patients, but some who came several nights for treatment. The clinic gave us opportunities to reach the people. We preached from posters or used a phonograph. Some evenings we visited people in their homes. One afternoon a week we held an open-air meeting for the children.

The fact that very little rain had fallen that spring was good for outdoor children's meetings, but also meant we had to go down to the village well to do our washing and sometimes carry our own water up to the house.

We believed the Lord was answering prayer for Mr. Goh. He had been coming quite regularly to the Sunday evening services. Because sometimes he was the only man, we prayed he would not be discouraged. We rejoiced when he brought a friend.

June was to leave for furlough in May. We would miss her greatly, especially because she had more Cantonese than any of the others of us.

As I thought of the work in Malaya, I was reminded of the frozen lakes back home in Michigan. Mid-winter they were very hard, without a crack in them anywhere. Then suddenly they would begin to crack, and a good strong March wind would come along to break up the ice. We were beginning to see the cracks and were looking for a strong work of the Holy Spirit to break the resistance of people's hearts.

One day right after breakfast a lady came into our place and sat for an hour. She wanted to know about the way of salvation. Before leaving, she gave me her name and house number. But a couple of days later when I went to visit the woman, I could not find her. There was no house with the number she had given me. The people in Sungei Ruan were very afraid and often gave us the wrong house number. Unable to find this lady, I went instead to two of my own neighbors and spent an hour and a half visiting with the women and answering their questions. Some of their questions were: "If we become Christians, must we be vegetarians?" "Can we eat pork?" "May the women get married?" "Do we have to be nailed to a cross?"

One day Ethel and I went to a home where a number of women were sitting out in the yard. We began to preach, and all went well until a man came and started to oppose our message, declaring in a loud voice that the missionaries were wrong and that their Chinese gods would get them to heaven as well as the missionaries' God. I did not try to argue, and the man soon left. I continued with my message, and the women seemed to listen even better than before.

On another day after teaching and singing with several children, a very sad young girl came up to me and spent over an hour pouring out her tale of woe. Her own mother had died, I learned, and the girl was living with her father and stepmother. As she and her stepmother didn't get along well, the parents had arranged for her wedding. The girl did not want the man they had chosen. All I could do was to comfort her and urge her to accept Christ as He alone could help her.

We felt the powers of darkness the week local leaders held a great heathen festival in the village. The government had given out two thousand acres of land to five hundred families. When several men were either killed or injured in clearing the land, the people blamed the bad fortune on a demon in the jungle. Everyone was ordered to go on a vegetarian diet for the week. People donated thousands of dollars, and priests came out from Kuala Lumpur in chartered buses. A great wooden idol was brought from Raub. The school was all set up for a place to worship. The first day an artisan made a paper god. At midnight the god was put on a truck and taken to the jungle. The idea was to entice the demon to come to the village. After a worship ceremony out in the jungle they brought the god back.

Fire walking was a part of that week. Several loads of wood were put in a pile and set afire at three o'clock. About midnight the priests walked through the embers, evidently without getting their feet burned. Then the relatives of those who had been injured in the jungle had to walk through the fire. Many of these ̄ twenty-two in all ̄ had badly burned feet.

I understood so little of the various dialects that I was not sure if I got the meaning correct. As near as I could understand, the fire was a spirit bridge, and they were taking the demon across. After the last one had gone through, the paper god was burned in the fire. Then practically the whole community turned out to kill chickens and ducks, to worship their gods and to have a great feast. According to their beliefs they had to send the demon away well filled and satisfied.

How our hearts ached for these people! I could not blame them, as they knew nothing else. I only blamed us for not giving them the Gospel. If we had done half as much for the Lord as they did for the demon, these people would have heard the Gospel long ago.

Discouragements kept nipping at our heels. Just when it looked as if we might see some advance in our work, the enemy would come with a counterattack. For instance, when we saw Mr. Goh after not seeing him for a few weeks, he asked if we would have Sunday morning worship services, as he would like to bring his friends. Of course we were thrilled. Three Sundays in a row a couple of people showed up at each service, but Mr. Goh never appeared, nor did he come by to give any explanations. When I went to visit his home, he was not there.

Next our serving girl, who was a Christian, asked if she could be baptized. But when she went home and told her mother, her mother stormed over to our home and accused me of taking her daughter away from their gods. I assured her that her daughter was saved and going to Heaven whether she was baptized or not. When I tried to explain the way of salvation to the lady, her only reply was, "Hell is the only place for an illiterate old lady like me to go." After that she forbade her daughter to come to church or to work for us. Once again I called on my praying friends to pray for this mother that she would come to know the Lord.

One day I was startled to discover a big Chinese man standing in the doorway. His eyes were bloodshot, and he talked in a slow voice. "Is there a telephone here?" he asked.

Everyone knows there isn't a single phone in the village, I thought. *The man is drunk.* "No. I'm sorry," I answered.

"Are you a Catholic?" was his next question.

When I explained that we were Protestants, he said, "I saw a cross on the picture in front of the door and thought you were Catholic." We had a very vivid poster of a man bound by Satan, a dragon, and another with the same man through the power of the shed blood of our Lord standing on the dragon.

Our visitor turned out to be a Singapore businessman who wanted to open a gas station in Sungei Ruan. He was a keen Catholic. He knew and quoted the Bible, and had an open mind. We talked for over an hour. The next day he came back for another session. When he left he said, "Surely God has brought me here to show me the truth. I must go back to my priest and see what he says." How we prayed that he and his family would be truly saved and not come to hinder our work!

In 1958 we began to see strong evidence that God was answering the prayers of my praying friends

In March we spent a lot of time visiting and inviting folk to a special meeting. Mrs. Ong arrived with a carload of folk from

Raub. On the way she stopped at the school and invited the principal and teachers, who all came. It was a good meeting, and the Lord used it for His glory. The following week some of the teachers were back. One of them asked, "Would we dare put God to the test and see if He would save us?" One of the young ladies raised her hand and said, "I will!"

The next Sunday we had fourteen at the service. The teachers were back, including the language teacher, Mrs. Hui, who brought some friends. When the invitation was given at the close of the meeting, Mrs. Hui raised her hand. As I had no opportunity to speak with her there, I went to visit her in her home the next day. When I asked her why she had raised her hand, she replied, "Until now I believed in my mind that Jesus died—now I have invited Him into my heart as my Savior." After that Mrs. Hui went out with us to the children's street meetings. Before handing out the special children's tracts we brought with us, Mrs. Hui read them to the children and explained them.

The Lord especially blessed our Saturday night Bible club. About thirty-five children were attending each week, and the numbers were still growing. When I would finish my story, the children often cried, "Tell some more! Tell some more!" I prayed that the children would not just be entertained but would really come to know the Lord as their own personal Savior.

Fifty people—one or more from *every* church attended the first believers' conference for the state of Pahang, held in Temerloh. The messages were all interpreted so that everyone could understand. The newest Christian was our Miss Su, a school teacher who had accepted the Lord just a month before. Nine others either accepted the Lord or were backsliders who came back to the Lord during the conference. A good number also dedicated their lives to the Lord. A committee of one representative from each church was formed to plan the next conference. This we believed was a wonderful answer to prayer. I wish you could have walked into the dining room with us during meal time and heard the bedlam—Cantonese, Hokkien,

Mandarin and English all being spoken at the same time. Talk about speaking in tongues!

Mr. and Mrs. Hui moved away from the village just after she accepted the Lord. She planned to go with me to conference, but was too ill to go. I felt sure this was a direct attack of the enemy. I asked prayer partners for continued prayer for them.

The day after the Temerloh conference Mr. and Mrs. Yap, with four young people, came and had supper with us. Then we went out for a street meeting, which lasted for two hours. They all gave their testimonies or messages, and each one was interpreted so that all the dialects used in this village were spoken some time during the meeting. It was a thrill to see the villagers gather and listen to their own people talk about the Lord. One Hokkien lady professed to accept the Lord. Our new problem was to know how to lead her on with the Lord as none of us spoke that dialect.

Mr. Lok, a Christian school teacher from Singapore, heard about the need in Sungei Ruan and offered to come and help us for four weeks. We watched the Lord use Mr. Lok with amazement. Without even a loud speaker and seldom even using a picture or poster, he stood and preached the Word for almost an hour each night for three nights. Some three hundred people gathered around and listened. At the close he asked any who wanted to believe in the Lord to come and take a gospel. The first night eight stepped forward; the second night eight more, and one lady came up to the house with us. While we were talking with her, three young men walked in. The last night twenty-one people took gospels and came up to the house afterward. Others stood outside and listened while Mr. Lok talked with them until ten o'clock.

In our Saturday night Bible club four boys won prizes for attending every week for three months and reciting all the memory verses. About fifty children gathered for the special award meeting and thoroughly enjoyed Mr. Lok's message. The second week that Mr. Lok was there we began with about a dozen children. When I asked where the others were, the children replied, "People are telling us we must not believe." None of the boys who won prizes dared to come. We ended up with thirty children, however, and a roomful came to sing before the evening service the last night.

Both the Temerloh conference and Mr. Lok's visit had been a tremendous help to my grasp of Cantonese. It was wonderful to hear Chinese preaching and praying in this dialect. I learned more than I had in all my study of the past year. So our hearts were filled with praise to the Lord for all that He had done.

Hokkien-speaking Mrs. Huang, one of Sungai Ruan's early believers.

As 1958 drew to a close, I praised the Lord for all the blessings of the past year. I was especially grateful for having had Emily Stewart come as a fellow worker. She had already had one term in Malaya and could speak the language fluently. What encouragement to have her take on a big share of the work! With her help the Sunday school continued to grow. In fact we were so crowded that we had to move to the community hall. We prayed that by this move we would be able to reach more children and perhaps some adults. The Bible club continued to go well too. When we held a special meeting, almost all of the boys attended. Since the boys had memorized many Scripture verses, we prayed that they would not only make decisions to accept the Lord, but would also dedicate their lives to Him.

A very friendly spirit grew among the people of the village. We made many friends through clinic contacts. Many showed interest in our message. However, interest in the Gospel was not enough. We longed to see a real work of the Holy Spirit in their hearts and lives. A good number of people had professed to accept the Lord, but not one strong spiritual leader had emerged from among them. We felt sure that if one strong leader would emerge, many others would be ready to follow.

The village was growing with some fifty new homes the past year and another 120 to be built the next year. A new road was

Emily Stewart and I in Malaya days.

coming through also. With all these new folk coming in, we were asking the Lord to send more Asian Christians to help in the work.

With all the encouragements in Sungei Ruan, still not one of the people who professed faith came regularly to Sunday services. We had yet to see one Christian who had a strong testimony and who was bearing fruit. We could not look to ourselves for the answer for this stalemate. Our eyes were unto the Lord of the Harvest. "So then neither is he that plants anything; neither he that waters; but God that gives the increase."

Once again disappointment knocked at the door early in 1959. After moving into the community hall for the Sunday school, we started off with a bang with seventy-five children present. But then the numbers steadily dwindled down to twenty or twenty-five. Also, we were concerned that we were not reaching the adults as we had hoped. We were not ready to give up just because it was difficult. We simply asked for prayer for guidance.

Another big obstacle came in the form of a new theater in the village. One Friday the girls came in early and said, "We want our meeting early so that we can go and see the movies." Deciding it was better to have them early than not at all, we complied. In addition to the movie theatre, youth clubs were being formed, drawing young people into activities every night. As I prayed about these tremendous obstacles to our work, the Lord spoke to my heart from Numbers 13 and 14. The spies came back from Canaan with the report that there were *giants* in the land. "We were in our own eyes as grasshoppers," they confessed, "and so were we in their sight." Caleb's attitude was, yes, there are giants and we are as grasshoppers, but, "If God delight in us, then He will...." We thought of ourselves as "little grasshoppers," but so long as God was delighted, He would work for us.

By June of 1959 we were facing many changes. One day, or instance, we went down the street and found that a family of Malays had moved into the room of the community hall that we used for our Sunday school. We had been praying for the Lord's will as to whether we should continue at the hall or return to the house for our meetings.

We considered holding a street meeting on the main street, but it seemed such a futile effort for two ladies with inadequate language. But one day the Lord spoke to me from the verse, "I have much people in this city; be not afraid, only preach…" I decided we must have the street meeting to introduce the people to their Lord. To prepare, I developed a set of twelve lessons on "How and Why Christ Came," using pictures of the life of Christ, posters and Scripture verses. We would also take the phonograph and use Gospel Recordings in various dialects. We truly went in fear and trembling, but the Lord stood by us each time we went out. Though the crowds were not large, some listened attentively.

One new lady started coming to our services. She was a mother of three children and expecting another. She had lived in the village only a few months. She had heard the Gospel in her hometown. I wondered if this was an answer to our prayer that new families coming to the village might be Christians.

Not too far from Sungei Ruan a new village by the name of Tras was just being built. With police permission, we jump-started witness in the village with an evangelistic campaign. Rainy weather kept some people away from the meetings, and others were still too busy building their houses and getting settled. The people were friendly, however, and invited us back.

For that week in Tras the house we used for meetings had to serve as living space for the team as well. The technician had to sleep in the room at the front where we held services. The other guests used bedrooms, and I slept on a camp bed in the kitchen at night. My head was right by the stove, which was most convenient for lighting the fire in the morning. With all the team members being very thoughtful and helpful, the week was a really happy one. We were conscious that the Lord was in our midst.

God was obviously answering the prayers I had requested for several individuals. Ip Sai Mooi, our former house-helper and a backslidden Christian, attended some of the meetings. Leung Mei-I, our present house-helper, was at some of the meetings and one day prayed, "Lord be merciful to me a sinner..." Mr. and Mrs. Laai, who had Catholic backgrounds, also became believers, and Mr. Laai enrolled in a correspondence course.

The meetings greatly helped Mrs. Huang, a Hokkien Christian. But she was a tremendous help to us as well. She gave her testimony in many of the homes we visited. Unhappily, because of her testimony, she was persecuted more than ever in her own home. Her older daughter even threatened to pack up and go back to China!

Though we experienced many ups and downs, our hearts were filled with praise to the Lord for all He had done. New believers came every night to study the Word. What a thrill!

My last conference before my 1960 furlough, the Pahang Believers Conference, was a real blessing for me. Between 85 to 100 attended the services. Fifty lived on the premises. Fifteen to twenty women slept in a room—some on tables and some on the floor. People fellowshiped in Hokkien, Cantonese, Mandarin and English. The messages were excellent—all of them interpreted so that everyone could understand. After the Sunday evening service the men went to their room to pray, and the women came to our room. The weeping and confessing of sins was such that we could not stop the torrent. The majority of those seeking God's mercy were young people from non-Christian homes.

Though I arrived in the U.S. mid-May rested and ready for work, I first spent time in Michigan with my family, getting caught up on the changes in everyone's lives over the years I was away. Once that was done, I traveled around Michigan, Illinois, Ohio and other states reporting on my work, telling stories, teaching, encouraging others to consider missionary work. I frequently dressed in my Chinese clothes, showed slides, and used other objects that I had brought back with me to enhance the stories and make them real. I was always eagerly accepted and was frequently invited to speak at churches, especially for young people's groups, and at schools. I sometimes prepared Chinese meals for the hosts of the homes where I was a guest and for special groups.

I was grateful for the privilege of attending CIM prayer conferences. At these and as I traveled from place to place, I made every effort to form prayer groups. In my opinion, the greatest need for missionaries on the field always has been for solid prayer support. After all, look what the Lord had done with me these past few years! Nothing of worth would have been accomplished without the faithful prayers of my prayer partners. ❧

Chapter 20

Itinerant Bible Teacher in Malaya

By mid-April 1961 I was back in Malaya. This new term I would make my home in the OMF center in the capital city of Kuala Lumpur. From there I planned to travel to various churches, conducting short-term Bible schools, much like I did in China. I would teach in Mandarin Chinese or English, and someone would interpret into whatever dialect of Chinese was spoken locally.

In my first weeks back in Malaya I heard that some of the boys from the former Bible club had been in to the clinic at Sungei Ruan. They wanted to assure me that they really believed on the Lord but, because of parental opposition, could not attend Christian meetings. My heart went out to them.

In June I visited Sungei Ruan myself. The visit was pure joy for me! I received a royal welcome and had the pleasure of seeing several of my old friends. It was like going home! I was tempted to just stay right there.

However, I needed to begin the Bible-class ministry. I would be going off to a different province every week the first stint. No two of the churches I faced in those months had the same needs. One, for instance, was a young church that had built its own church building, but was currently without pastor or missionary help. Because some of the people were illiterate, I would attempt to teach them to read. At another church I had opportunities to work with children and young people. I endured long bus journeys between churches, but hoped that I would be a blessing both to the churches and to individuals that I would meet along the way.

The devil put up a real battle in those meetings. In one church two elders and their wives were ill part of the time, and one night the roar of rain on the tin roof was so loud that I could not make myself heard. We had to resort to writing the outlines and Scripture references on the board and letting students look them up for themselves. Another night the lights went out just as we were about to start. And another night a man professed to accept the Lord, came regularly for a week, and then landed in the hospital after a family brawl.

How would you like to have a feast every day of chicken, duck, pork, shrimp, fish balls and rice? Wonderful!—except that we had that almost every day, sometimes twice a day, during our two weeks of Bible classes at the lovely village church in Sungei Way. As delicious as those meals were, I could hardly look chicken or shrimp in the face after that! Toward the end of the second week I began to look forward to going home to a simple cup of coffee and a piece of bread!

OMF opened the ministry in Sungei Way in 1952. When the congregation had appointed their own church leaders and had built their own church facilities, missionaries moved on.

The hardest village in my itinerary was Kuala Kubu. Two young lady missionaries, Barbara Hovda and Joyce Mitchell, were not only doing a job that men ought to be doing, but they were carrying the load of about six missionaries! They were maintaining the work in four different centers, doing all the travel by bus, and putting in long days—all because of too few workers.

Kuala Kubu was steeped in demon worship. Young men gloated over the power that demons had to work miracles for them. Secret Society members not only tore the poster off our house and burned it, but sat outside our front door, frightening people away. Though we had contact with over twenty young people, they did not dare to come to classes.

What a joy to be in a well-organized church! Teaching at Muar Presbyterian Church reminded me of China. It made me homesick for my old stamping ground! The first night over a hundred people attended. The next night people not only filled over sixty extra chairs, but each night after that some folk had to stand. A church filled with young people, with wonderful singing. The last night a good number gave in their names to declare their desire to believe on the Lord and to get further help. Among these were several children from Christian homes and two young men from the Chinese high school.

I felt it was a privilege to live in various missionaries' homes— whether that of a lone missionary, a pair of single ladies, or married couples with children. I also enjoyed weeks of staying in Chinese homes.

Once I had the rare opportunity to live in a home in which the head of the home was a gentleman who had raised families with three wives. Wife No. 1 was a Christian, and she was my hostess. Wife No. 2 had died, but left two sons, one of which had two wives. Wife No. 3 had a married son with seven children. Other relatives lived in the home too no one seemed to know just how many. Life in the home was a kind of organized bedlam. Lining up with the family for a wash in the morning and a bath at night was interesting, to say the least! No one went to bed before eleven o'clock, and all lights were left burning throughout the house. Some members came home between one and three in the morning, and the rubber-tappers left at five! Incense burned from early morning until late at night, with people involved in all sorts of worship over the week.

My hostess was the one lone Christian in this huge family. One day when the family was having a great feast, she apologized, "Sorry I can't give you any of this food. It has all been offered to the spirits. I don't eat it either."

It was a thrill to teach this lady to read. She was at it from six in the morning until eleven at night. After she had done a few lessons, she said, "It's the Holy Spirit who is helping me. I remember the words now." A few days later, when she started the third reader, she said, "I understand what I read now." In one week she learned 250 words. As for me, I was brain weary!

By December 1961, I was writing, "Emmanuel: God with us!" That is how I felt about the past year! The Lord Himself had been with me each step of the way—in the U.S., across the ocean, in villages where there had been strong opposition and in large churches with people waiting to meet God.

News from time to time of Mrs. Huang from Sungei Ruan lifted my heart. She continued to stand alone in her home. Though often sick, she always seemed to come out on top. I was glad to see her at the believers' conference that year. Her arm was black and blue where her still unbelieving husband had beaten her, trying to extract her conference money for gambling. She wasn't about to give it to him! In the first meeting of the conference, when the congregation was asked to choose a hymn, she was the first to choose "Oh Happy Day!" Surely God was answering the prayers of my prayer partners on her behalf.

By the following February Mrs. Huang's husband had a change of heart. Not only did he start reading the Bible, but he was also talking about it.

In the village of Kuala Kubu, though still pulsing with demon worship and still without conversions, a few signs of the Lord's working encouraged us to keep focusing prayer there too.

During my weeks at the Raub Methodist Church I was kept very busy. The Christians not only began each day with an early morning prayer meeting, but held another prayer meeting in the afternoon. Spare time I used for visiting Christians. To walk into that little church to see it nearly filled with 50 to 60 young people thrilled me. Even when it rained, they came! When the invitation was given for folks to accept the Lord as their Savior, a man by the name of Ah-Teck put his hand up. He, along with his wife, had professed to accept the Lord when we had meetings there in 1956. What went wrong? At that time Ah-Teck was a gambler and in real difficulty over money matters. After he became a Christian, he ran well for a time, but then he fell in with a gang of professing Christians from another church who were gambling. Now he was coming back to the Lord and was soon doing a Bible correspondence course and joined the Tract-of-the-Month Club. I believed he was just the type of man needed in the Chinese church and would make a good leader.

We also worked in Tanjong Sepat, a village that looked out at the sea. From the seashore a person could watch the fishermen load their boats with ice, haul in their nylon nets, and go off to sea. What a sight to see boats come back laden with fish! In the coffee plantations acres of beautiful bushes bore fragrant white blossoms and green and red berries all at the same time. Beyond the coffee plantation was a durian orchard of huge trees laden with big fruit, which never needed to be picked. When they were ripe, the fruit fell to the ground. It always fell during the night. The owner would sleep out in his orchard so that he could listen for the fruit falling. Early in the morning trucks came along and collected the fruit for the market. It was best eaten the same day. Beyond the durian orchard stretched two thousand acres of graceful oil-palm trees—a wonderful sight. Their dark berries turned a lovely red and yellow when ripe. A factory in town produced oil for margarine, soap, etc.

The missionaries in Tanjong Sepat told me not to expect very many people at our meetings in this village. Only three Christian women and one other normally attended meetings. I assured them I would be happy to come if only one came. One Chinese, wholly dedicated to the Lord, makes all the difference to the work in a village. That week I was thrilled to see husbands and families of the Christian ladies! Some never missed a night. One husband said, "I would believe, but I can't worship God and sin against Him too." God was obviously stirring up hearts.

The need in the villages at this point was not so much for more missionaries, but for a real work of the Holy Spirit in the lives of people of all races and dialects who already believed. I would have loved to see a revival sweep through the land through the existing churches. I prayed that, as a teacher of the Word, nothing in me would hinder the working of the Holy Spirit, and that I would be ready for whatever He would have me do.

Mid-year I wrote to my prayer warriors, "You surely have done a lot of praying since I wrote my last letter. How shall I give you all the answers? I can't. Only eternity will give you the full picture."

In four centers Chinese fellow workers interpreted for me. What a difference good interpreters made to the classes! Two ladies of different dialects each enjoyed interpreting so much they said they wished they could go with me all the time.

The class in Buloh Kasap, with an excellent Chinese interpreter, was greatly blessed of the Lord. The church had never had such good interest in any meetings. When we finished, some of them said, "The class isn't long enough. Next year we must have two weeks or a month." That is exactly what we were praying for.

My days in Sungei Ruan thrilled me because I met my old friends. But we were disappointed that people did not attend the classes regularly. Mr. Wu came to the house to see me. It was the first time he had been to the house since the Ellergodts moved there. I regret only that I did not make more of the opportunity. I thought he would come to classes, but he didn't. How often I would like to live an hour or a day over again!

The Benta Methodist Church was made up of Christian families mostly with the name Chan (also my Chinese name). I didn't know exactly how many families there shared that name in the village, but fifty-three young people and children in the church did. With no pastor, the folk thoroughly appreciated the teaching. Ten young adults, mostly 20 to 30 years of age, professed to accept the Lord during those days.

The three leading Christians in Tanjong Sepat in early days.

Mrs. Goh.

Chia-Chi.

Mrs. Ong.

One of the most interesting meals I had in this place was a dish of pig's ear! The person who cooked it cut it in slices and fried it in fat with a little sugar, soy, garlic and salt—very tasty, but tough!

During this time I lived in three different Chinese homes. The first one was the big heathen family that I had lived with the previous year. In the next home I just rented a room, as the missionaries did not have room for me in their small house. In the last place I lived for a few days with a Christian family. Classes with them as a family were a real joy! They treated me as one of the family. They served good strong black Malaysian coffee for breakfast and a glass of hot barley soup for afternoon tea. I had a tiny room with a low tin roof. Though the temperature in there must have been about 110°, it was such a privilege to live with them and study the Word together that I hardly minded the heat.

In Pahang State I traveled from one center to another over mountainous terrain. The whole five-week tour was grueling mainly, I think, because I had the flu for three days just before I left. I had meetings almost every day and sometimes twice a day. I came home tired, but my faithful prayer warriors prayed me through. Imagine my joy when I got home after a six-hour ride over winding mountain roads to find mission-home hostess and friend Jessie McClymont had moved me to a nice, quiet room upstairs! The room had been newly painted and washed, and I had all my things moved. I cannot tell you how much I praised the Lord for this wonderful home to come back to. The McClymonts were real saints in their ministry there.

I finished the year of 1962 with the Scripture, "Thanks be to

God, who continually leads us about, captives in Christ's triumphal procession, and everywhere uses us to reveal and spread abroad the fragrance of the knowledge of Himself" (2 Cor. 2:14).

In Genesis, chapter one, we read that each day the Lord looked upon His work for the day and saw that it was good. My prayer was that each day of the coming year the Lord would look upon His work done in and through me and would be able to say, "It was good."

The year 1963 was to be a momentous one for the area. With the British colonial government withdrawing, Peninsular Malaya joined with Singapore, Sabah, and Sarawak (the latter two in northern Borneo) to become the new nation of Malaysia. When Singapore seceded in 1965, the tension-filled political balance between the number of Chinese and the number of Malays shifted toward the Malays—with Malays making up about 44 percent of the population, Chinese about 36 percent.

We were thrilled when we arrived at the Mentakab Methodist Church to find it filled with Chinese young people—a good number with Bibles and notebooks ready for action. At the close of the meetings on the third evening I asked if any would like to accept the Lord as their personal Savior. Hands went up all over the room. Thinking they misunderstood, I told them all to put their hands down and explained again. I suggested that all those who really wanted to believe on the Lord stay after the meeting. Even after they were told that they were expected to go home and tell their families about their decision that night, thirty-two signed decision cards. Three never came back. Four were forbidden to come two nights, but they came back for the closing meetings. All except one was known to the Chinese pastor, either former or present students of their Sunday school, day school, or youth fellowship. All except two brothers came from non-Christian homes, so would face fierce persecution and opposition.

In March I taught in the Serdang Church. Mrs. Chan (known as Mrs. Wong in the children's story, *The Rat Who Lost His Tail*) came as interpreter. The Lord greatly used her. Each morning we began at the local old people's home, ministering to the lame, the blind and the halt. Mrs. Chan found an old man from the same place in China as she came from and gave him no peace until he said he would believe!

Another of the residents was a 30-year-old crippled lady, Golden Chain. Already she had been in bed for 15 years. She was in the ward with a lot of old ladies, some of them mental cases. She did not even have a proper nurse to care for her. Since she had never been to school, I suggested that she learn to read. The young woman was thrilled with the prospect. A Christian lady in the ward was appointed to teach her. The reading books were all Scripture readings. I prayed that no one would confiscate them.

In the afternoons we visited the Christians in their homes. Most of the people invited us either for a meal or for tea, which also provided an opportunity for us to talk with the relatives and friends of the families. Among those we visited was a former medium. She had been converted and was bringing a friend to church. During the visit the husband came home. He had heard the Gospel in China. Mrs. Chan did most of the talking in this home and, before we left, the couple took down all the spirit worship paraphernalia and burned it. They began in the living room and then took the papers off the bedroom doors. Next they removed the incense pots from the kitchen—even one in the pig pen. Until then their whole house and all their possessions had been bound up in spirit worship.

By May this couple was still going on with the Lord. Golden Chain still had her reading books and was well into the third reader and enjoying it.

The class at Banting was the best I had ever had. I felt the Lord's presence in this group of about 25 young people. What started as a simple class developed into a prayer meeting as well as a Bible study. It was most humbling for me to hear the people confess their sins with weeping.

In this place I lived with a Chinese family who owned a big shop.

All their goods were stockpiled in their home. I had to work my way not only through thirty pairs of shoes at the foot of the stairs to reach my room, but also up stairs half taken up with tins of cookies. All except one of the ten children lived at home. The family employed four helpers for the shop and two servants for the home. Meals had to be eaten in relays. Everyone had to take a turn in the home's single shower room, in spite of the fact that the frightful heat and humidity made showering necessary at least once every day. I greatly appreciated the board bed at night in spite of the heat and the jukebox in the room beneath going full blast singing, "Put on your dancing shoes…"!

We prayed that at least one family in each church would set the example of daily family worship. We had long asked God that whole families would be saved and that the churches would grow and be strengthened as the family unit became strengthened. The elder in the church at Cha'ah testified at the close of the classes, "I have never memorized Scripture myself. Now with the Lord's help I am going to do it with my family."

Another prayer goal was that at least ten young people would commit wholly to follow the Lord. For some time many of the workers had prayed that the Lord would call out one from each center to serve Him. Now we were asking that over and above that God would work through the classes to call out ten people who in the future would be teachers or leaders in the work.

When we had classes in Raub Methodist Church the previous year, a young man dedicated his life to the Lord. This year when we were in a village two miles from there, that same young man came out each night to interpret for me. One night when he couldn't come, the young lady to whom he was engaged offered to do it. She had never interpreted before, and when she finished, she bowed her head and said, "Thank you, Lord, for helping me." Here was a young couple, both school teachers, both with wonderful personalities and real gifts. If they were to go on to wholly follow the Lord, they could be mightily used of Him. How I coveted them for full-time service!

In the area of finances, I prayed that by 1965 all the expenses of the Bible-class ministry would be met by the local churches. That objective was reached. When one church in which I taught gave me a generous gift for the work, they said, "It will help to pay expenses in some new little church that is unable to give."

The Lord generously met our need for interpreters also. Mrs. Tan was willing to help in all of the Hokkien-speaking churches. Mrs. Chan helped in some of the Cantonese churches. She wanted to go with me to others, but could only go as the Lord opened the way for her. She had aged parents to care for. One time when I was talking to her, I suggested that she purchase a small home instead of putting out so much money in rent. Mrs. Chan said, "I don't want to be tied down with *anything*. As soon as my parents are gone, I am going to serve the Lord. I *must* be free."

When two weeks of meetings in the Kluang area were canceled, I wondered what the Lord had for me. I came home from Sikingchang, was given a cup of tea, and Mr. McClymont said, "Would you mind taking over the housekeeping as Jessie is sick in bed?" I had my answer! During my housekeeping stint I began having Bible classes with the house helpers in the mission center. As a result, two of the girls professed to accept the Lord. I also had the privilege of talking with a new office girl.

A special privilege along the way was that the Cha'ah church invited me to spend a weekend with them. At the women's meeting the ladies recited twelve verses they had memorized since I was there three months before. I talked also with the young man who had testified that, though he had never memorized Scripture before, he was going to begin to do it with his family. When I asked him how he was getting on, he said, "When I am at home, we have family worship." The missionaries told me that this family "sings lustily, without much tune, until all hours of the night!" While that month did not go according to schedule, I was very conscious of the Lord's leading each day.

When I went to Gambang, it had been just a year since my last class there. A year earlier engineer Mr. Boon said, "There is no hope for me. There is not one of the Ten Commandments I have not broken." He accepted the Lord, and in the year since had made a clean break with the world. He told me that one day a fellow engineer asked him, "What's wrong with you? I have not seen you smoking."

Mr. Boon replied, "Nothing wrong. I am a Christian now."

The man challenged, "Will you give me a month of your wages if I catch you smoking?"

Mr. Boon said, "I'll give you two months' worth, because you will not see me smoke. The Lord has delivered me!" Mr. Boon brought his wife and another young engineer to class, who both became believers and asked for baptism.

In Airport Village I lived in the home of Mr. and Mrs. Leung, the only Christian family in the village. After a slightly restless night on a hard wooden bed, my *Daily Light* challenged me with, "Endure hardness as a good soldier..." (2 Tim. 2:3). The year before, the Leung family and another young lady were the only ones to attend classes. I expected the same audience this year, but a surprise awaited me. Mr. and Mrs. Eu (pronounced You), owners of a large rubber estate, came each night. Not only so, but Mrs. Eu came in her car with ten to twelve passengers, including children, and Mr. Eu came behind on his motor bike with two more men! I wished I could have had a movie of them!

The last night when I gave an invitation, a Mr. Lam raised his hand. His daughter and another teen-age girl also accepted the Lord. I could not help them very well as they spoke another dialect. Excited at the response, Mr. Leung was determined to be the first to give Mr. Lam a tract. He rushed around that crowded little room, turning out drawers and boxes until he finally found a dirty, crumpled tract! I assured him I had tracts ready and suggested we pray first, but he *had* to give his tract first!

I wish you could have seen the joy of the believers when these three people decided to believe. I assured the Leungs that it was their fruit because they used their home, and the Eus because they brought them to the service. Everyone was rejoicing! The

238

Lord in His marvelous planning had arranged even before the classes that one of our missionaries who spoke that dialect was already planning to visit them the very next month!

In the latter part of August my interpreter and I traveled each day to Machap Bahru, where one of the Christian families wanted some extra help. In order to get to the home, we took a bus for the first stage of the journey and then, leaving the main highway, had to thumb a ride the rest of the way—our first effort at hitchhiking! How wonderfully the Lord provided so that we always got to our class on time! And what a variety of wheels we had, too—a taxi, a gravel truck with an Indian driver, a young Chinese man with an elegant car (he had heard me preach five years earlier in the Raub Methodist Church), an English rubber planter, another taxi and, last but not least, a Malay state assemblyman! Could these all be in answer to the prayers of my prayer warriors back home in the States? I wouldn't be surprised!

In November, when the church in Triang was having their dedication service for their new building, Mrs. Huang, the Hokkien lady, wanted to attend the service. My friends had been praying earnestly for her husband, who had been showing signs of softening. At this point Mr. Huang was so miserable he threatened to go to the jungle and hang himself. Mrs. Huang's discourage-ment showed on her face when she came on Sunday night, "He has been angry with me all day," she said. "Now he says he is going to hang himself." The service began with singing John 14: *Let not your heart be troubled...I will come.* Her sad face turned into one beaming with the joy of the Lord. Her special joy that night was to see her youngest daughter accept the Lord. The next week her husband let her attend the dedication service without saying a word!

Another lady, Mei-Yee, was also allowed to attend the Triang church dedication in answer to prayer. She had seven children, an unsaved husband and in-laws. The day she wanted to leave for the special service her husband said, "I will take all the children with me out to the jungle so you can go." Mei-Yee had not been outside of her village for several years. For these ladies to see a little church that had built their own little place of worship—and it was a lovely little building—was a special joy.

Unexpectedly Mrs. Tan, my fellow worker who interpreted for me when I went to Hokkien groups, took herself off to the U.S. A.! She was 63 years old and could not speak a word of English. (When she translated for me, I spoke Mandarin Chinese, not English.) She left to see her son who was a doctor with an American wife. I felt bereft.

In the coming year I planned to teach the doctrine of demons. As the people in Malaysian villages were bound by the fear of demons, I hoped this teaching would be helpful to them. I was quite sure the devil would give me a hard time, either in the preparation of these lessons or in the presenting of them. In that expectation, I asked prayer partners for extra prayer.

Early in 1964 Mrs. Huang was very burdened as her husband showed every sign of slipping toward death. Heathen relatives were already planning his funeral. Suddenly he began talking in another language—Mandarin. Mrs. Huang could not understand him, but the daughters, who used Mandarin in school, knew what he was saying. In fact, they said he spoke the language perfectly. He was so frightened after this incident that he told his wife that he wanted to believe. We prayed with him, and he began reading the Bible as he had done for a time earlier. He continued to improve physically and after a few days was able to walk down the street. Twice his gambling friends tempted him—twice he gambled, and both times he was much worse physically when he came home! Chinese New Year's Day the Huang home was free of heathen worship. We were invited there for a meal and worshiped God with the family. Mr. Huang joined in happily. The Lord sometimes works in mysterious, yet wonderful ways.

The Catholics baptized Golden Chain, the paralyzed girl in the old people's home. Happily her faith was solidly planted in God's Word. In the year since she started her reading program she had finished all the reading books that we gave her. She memorized twenty-five Bible verses in the week that I visited her and was subsequently enrolled in the Navigators' Scripture memory course.

We held two classes a day in Serdang in 1964. The church there had made real strides since I had held classes there the previous year. The believers decided they were going to build a church building and were really enthused about it. The lady who had been a spirit medium for over forty years had become very ill. Her family, thinking she was dying, called a misssionary at midnight to come and pray for her. The Lord answered prayer for the lady's healing and, as a thank offering, she gave a hundred dollars toward the new church building. At Chinese New Year time she ordered a new cupboard for the new church. Her enthusiasm quickly became contagious.

OMFers Mr. and Mrs. Brooks with their three children worked in a little Presbyterian church in Bukit Pasir. The family lived in the back of the small church building in two small rooms, plus a kitchen a few feet square and a passageway in which they squeezed a folding table at mealtime. Not a word of complaint came from these workers. But when the leaders of the big-city mother church came out one night to see what was happening at my class, they found eighty people packed in. Children were sitting on the platform and down the aisles of the church. The result: "This place is not large enough," said the visitors. Plans were soon afoot for adding to the church, including an extra room for the missionaries.

Once while one of the newer believers in that church was at a service, her husband came after her. He was so angry that he knocked her down right in front of the pulpit!

My interpreter, Mrs. Tan, who had gone to the United States to visit a son, returned after three months. With no one to talk Chinese to in all that time and nearly freezing in the cold climate, she was more than glad to get back to comfortable Malaysia, climate-wise and language-wise. I was more than happy to have her back!

In April I spent a fascinating two weeks in Banting. You will remember that I was teaching the doctrine of demons and had asked for special prayer. As I expected, the enemy put up a fight. We set the dates for the classes a year before to make sure classes would be during the school holidays so that students could come. The government suddenly changed the dates, and we missed the holidays. Then election came during the second week, and we had to cut the dates short. We had political rallies on all sides of us. The neighbor's three dogs barked during the first few messages, but got prayed down! Then one evening their chicken got on the tin roof that the church and their house shared, and the boys were up there running after it. Can you imagine the noise? Two nights the lights went out in the middle of the message. But refusing to be defeated, we kept right on preaching. In Malaysia it was always well to have your sermon thoroughly prepared!

There was a battle for souls too. But, praise God, fifteen Sunday school children professed to accept the Lord, and two girls came for the assurance of salvation.

We lived in the home of the wealthy shopkeeper with his ten children. Since one of the boys was getting married the week we were there, they were remodeling the house. The old tile roof, which had been on since 1927, was taken down and a new roof put on. With no ceiling in the house, broken tiles and dust filled the rooms—but how nice to share in the wedding preparations!

Tanjong Karang boasted one Christian family, but no church or worker. In this well-to-do family two brothers had seventeen children between them. A married sister with four children lived with them because her husband was ill and couldn't support them, and also an unmarried brother. They all slept in four bedrooms above the shop. With two beds among them, most of them slept on the floor. The floor was beautifully clean, washed every day. No one would think of walking on it with shoes. Mrs. Tan and I were given one of the two beds and shared the room with a mother and some children sleeping on the floor. The first morning, I stumbled over a boy sleeping in front of the door. After that I learned to step gingerly. We were fed royally. I put on five pounds!

When I was first invited here, I was told it was to be for Bible classes for this family. I prepared accordingly. When we arrived, we found this family had rented a shop to be used as a church building and spent a thousand dollars for repairs. Since there was no electricity in that town, we used gas lanterns. The shop was windowless, its front open to the street. The temperature must have been about 100 degrees at class time. At least two hundred people showed up. Some were packed into the shopfront, and others spilled out the front and into the street. What a marvelous opportunity! Our hearts cried out for God to supply a pastor.

One morning three of the boys of the family came to our room and said, "Teach us to read our Bibles." I had the joy of leading them and their three older sisters to the Lord. They all started doing correspondence courses. As exhausted as we were when we came home, our hearts were bursting with praise!

I received a SOS to pray for Mrs. Huang. Her husband had died, and their Buddhist relatives insisted on a non-Christian funeral. When the local missionaries heard the news, they went to call in the home and found neighbors and relatives burning incense, worshiping idols, etc. Mrs. Huang was sitting in the midst of them wailing because she thought her husband had gone to hell.

Mrs. Tan and I decided to go to Sungei Ruan to visit Mrs. Huang. The Lord wonderfully answered prayer for us that day. After traveling five hours by bus and taxi, we found Mrs. Huang at the missionaries' home just ready to eat dinner. Mrs. Tan, being a widow lady herself, was able to give comfort and advice to Mrs. Huang, encouraging her to have a memorial service with plenty of singing.

While in Cha'ah, I found they had just finished a youth retreat at which seven young men and a girl had accepted the Lord. The interesting story here was how the youth retreat came into being in the first place. Because the older people in the church had grown cold in their love for the Lord, we trained twelve- to fourteen-year-olds to be Sunday school teachers. When one of these young girls moved to Singapore and joined a church there, she maintained a real burden for Cha'ah and wrote to ask if she could bring a group of young people from Singapore for a youth retreat. It was marvelous how the Lord answered prayer! He gave them the school to use for living quarters and meetings, and speakers for the meetings. It surely was all the Lord's doing. And all because a fourteen-year-old girl allowed God to use her!

The new believers walked into the Bible classes I was teaching with Bibles and notebooks and were a real challenge to the older believers. The church leaders sort of blinked and said, "We have a church to look after now." One deacon, who had been out of fellowship with the Lord, stepped in and acted as a spiritual father to the boys. The OMF in South Malaysia had been working on a sample church constitution to give to the emerging churches. As this came off the press just before the Cha'ah classes, we were able to present it to the church at the close of the classes. How carefully God plans for His church!

The Kuantan Methodist Church people were noticeably enthusiastic in their welcome. Rev. Jacob Lim, the pastor and a young Trinity graduate, had known Mrs. Tan when he was a little boy. The family was thrilled to have her in their home because she had been such a spiritual blessing to them in the past.

Only eighteen attended church the first Sunday we were in Kuantan. The Lims prayed that the people would bring their friends and that the congregation would double. They finished the Bible-class weeks with sixty!

Pastor Lim took Mrs. Tan and me visiting several mornings. In a home the pastor called "Caesar's Household," we visited an extremely wealthy family. The man sold cars. He had three wives, all Buddhists except No. 3, who had become a Christian when her little girl died of cancer.

From there we went to a young widow lady whose husband had been a bleeder. He had a tooth pulled and bled to death, leaving her with seven small children.

The last home we visited was a Malay-type house with beautiful flowers. We walked up the steps into the living room and found that five generations of people lived in the house. The man of the house, who was about fifty years old, was a Christian, but his wife was a Buddhist, as was his ninety-year-old grandmother. The first room had a picture of Jesus and the second had the gods up on the wall with all the incense, etc. Mrs. Tan went almost directly to the grandmother and was able to lead her to the Lord. Pastor Lim kept saying, "Isn't it wonderful? So many of us have tried to talk to her but could never make her understand."

The man's seventy-year-old mother was a Christian and attended all the classes, walking to get there. Before we left I felt that I must speak to the man's wife. I began by saying, "It makes me very unhappy to see you have the True God's picture in this room and your god in that room. You can't have two gods in one house." After an exhortation I asked Mrs. Tan to read I Corinthians 10, after which Mrs. Tan said, "Let me preach now!" The lady came to the Bible class the next two nights. The last night it seemed as if the devil was trying his best to make her go to sleep and not be able to listen. Mrs. Tan and I both felt we had never prayed so hard while we were preaching. When the invitation was given, this lady came forward along with twelve others. Our hearts were thrilled!

"Would you like help taking your idols down?" Mrs. Tan asked the newly reborn lady.

"Yes," she answered sincerely. Thus that Sunday afternoon, after the service, the church folk all went over. The gods came down from the walls, the incense pots were emptied, the ancestral tablet was taken down and the "house was swept clean." When Mrs. Tan and I went back later, the wall had been newly papered and Christian posters put up. The Bibles were lying where the incense pots had been before. Christians in the family beamed their joy.

In November of 1964 I took a little vacation. I intended to skip my prayer letter and just rest, but I had had such a good time the weeks prior that I just had to share the news. The church in Temerloh had been a hard center in every way. The main street going from the town to the neighboring village went right past the OMF house in Temerloh. A constant stream of trucks, cars, and motorbikes rumbled by, leaving clouds of dust rolling into the glassless windows. The noise continued until midnight and started again at 4:00 a.m. Children playing on the front door step punctuated the roar with their shrill shouts and yells from morning till night. In addition, Temerloh was a very hot place. Because the landlord had kept one room for storing rice, the house was overrun with rats. One of those rats died during the classes, and we could not find it. The smell was worse than the noise and heat! In spite of all that, God worked. New believers from a recent evangelistic campaign all came to the classes, memorized Scripture, and some even brought other members of their families.

The little church in Jerantut brought me a real thrill. Though the small group there had been at a standstill for the last couple of years, it had recently come into new life. When the work was opened there ten or twelve years before, the OMF bought a village house. Now the church had bought it from the mission. They had remodeled it so that they had a very nice little chapel in the front and two small bedrooms and a living room at the back for the missionary ladies. The place had been painted inside and out and the chapel furnished with forty new metal chairs with green Formica backs and seats and a fifty-dollar pulpit. Next they were talking of buying an organ!

The devil had not left the work unchallenged, however. One of the leading men of the church whose wife had died some years earlier made noodles for a living. The Lord had prospered his business so much that he had five women working for him. His life and work with these women was not to the glory of the Lord and was a tremendous burden to the church.

Nevertheless, it was thrilling to watch the churches emerge. Six churches now had their own property. I considered it a privilege to have a little share in the ministry of these emerging churches.

If I were an artist, I would draw a picture of a Malaysian scene of villages clothed in fog, and steeples of churches just appearing above the mist. This past year we had been able to see the churches emerging and standing tall as visible witnesses in their communities.

The last series of a month of classes in the State of Johore was in Buloh Kasap. The noise in that place never stopped. At 2:00 a.m. a baby cried endlessly on the other side of the tin partition that separated my bedroom from the neighbor's house. Mrs. Tan says the baby was not getting enough breast milk and often cried pathetically for two hours at a stretch. I could hear the mother cooing and the father giving his advice. At 4:00 a.m. an alarm clock went off loud and long, followed by noisy preparations for breakfast. At 5:00 a.m. the rooster began crowing and chickens cackling in the neighbor's kitchen. Daytime noises included trucks, motorcycles, vendors, children playing on the doorstep. In the evening the Labor Party competed with our services. In response one night we lustily sang, "Be strong and of a good courage."

Though a number of young people came to service after service, did the memory work, and seemed under conviction, in the first few days not one of them made any decisions, possibly for fear of the people next door. I asked for prayer that God would deliver them from *all* fear—of secret societies, friends' ridicule, parents' opposition, etc. Wonderfully resistance faded, and the young people warmed to God's Word. Mrs. Tan worked with one enthusiastic group in the church while I helped others in the kitchen! As God's Word is a living seed, it must bear fruit. We sowed the seed carefully in the hope that it would bear fruit that would remain.

My term in Malaysia was drawing to a close. Tired, I was feeling very ready for furlough. By April 1965 I was really on the "count down." Almost every day I did something that reminded me it would be the last time I would be doing it that term.

During the last quarter I worked in the Methodist churches in Raub and Benta. It was difficult to explain the contrast in the two churches. At Benta whole families came out to study the Word. It was thrilling to see a father, mother and eight, ten or twelve children walking down the road together on their way to church. I thrilled even more to hear the whole family doing their memory work! In Raub there used to be a keen group of young people, but life seemed to have drained out of the group. I felt as if I were talking to a stone wall. I suspected a strong communist influence within the church, but wasn't sure.

In spite of the disappointment in Raub, this had been a very happy term for me. The Lord blessed the class work. I wondered if this door would be open another term. I heard from my home letters about the divisions in denominational churches over curriculums. If that happened in Malaysia, it could well close the door for us to the Methodist and Presbyterian churches. I was very grateful for the way we had worked hand in hand and for the opportunities I had to work with them.

Even my last weeks were filled with classes and meetings right to the very end. I had one last visit at Banting. This was the place where the previous year the roof was changed and the house was being made ready for a wedding. This year they were preparing for a new baby. With business prospering, the family now had a new tape recorder, a television, and a car. The television went loudly until midnight each night on one side of Mrs. Tan and me, and the neighbors on the other side had built a gambling den on the back of the house, where business was going on day and night. As the children were all home for school holidays and the family had visitors, living with a family of some twenty people was most interesting. One night I thought the two cats were having a game under my bed. Two days later I realized it had been a battle, and the combatants had left the prey!

In spite of the fact that I finished the last week with a cold and fatigue, I was thrilled to see what the Lord had done anyway. The Lord's verse to me at that time was, "God is my strength (physical) and power (spiritual). He maketh my way perfect" (Psalm 18).

On May 4th I wrote home: "I'm coming. The Lord willing I shall be leaving here next Wednesday, sailing from Singapore on the 19th, and arriving in New York on July 5th. It may be the Lord will come before that, in which case I shall meet you in glory, which is far better!"

I closed my last letter to prayer partners before furlough with, "This is what the Lord has been pleased to do in answer to your prayers. I am most grateful for all you have done for me this term. My prayer is that the Lord will richly reward you for each minute you have spent in His Presence on our behalf." ଔ

Chapter 21

Grace Years in Malaysia

In June of 1966 I was on my way back to Malaysia for a third term. A long delay in Oakland had us wondering why the holdup. The Lord knew what He was doing, of course. The captain of the freighter *Neder Elbe* told us that had we sailed six days earlier, we would have run right into Philippine-bound Typhoon Irma.

I had a first class cabin all to myself. It was a beautiful room with a built-in desk right across the end and two portholes to look out of. It was a perfect place to study.

One Sunday morning as I was sitting out on deck worshiping the Lord, the waves were crashing against the ship. The sun, catching the spray, made a rainbow in each wave. *The ship is like the church in the midst of the waves,* I thought. *But the Lord has a rainbow in every wave because He is in it.*

While the captain and officers of the ship were all Dutch, the crew was Chinese, making for very interesting conversations. I shared the passenger list with only two others, a Scot business man and his Chinese wife. The man, though Presbyterian, was far from the Lord. His wife was Catholic, born in Indonesia and educated in Dutch.

As the captain invited us to sit at his table each evening for dinner, I had some good opportunities to witness and was very conscious that the Lord was there to give me the answers to my table mates' questions. One evening we talked until eight o'clock. Regrettably I did not lead even one through to faith or repentance.

Though we reached Singapore the morning of May 27th, by the time I reached the OMF mission home, the dining room was alive with chatter around cups of afternoon tea. I enjoyed meeting all the headquarters staff. The next day I ate Sunday dinner at the Language Center with the Arthur Mathews and the new workers. Sunday supper I enjoyed with my Indian friend Mary Thomas and her family. At ten o'clock that night they put me on the train, and I was on my way to Kuala Lumpur.

I arrived in Kuala Lumpur on Monday morning just in time for the monthly day of prayer. Fellow workers who had gathered gave me a warm welcome home. Two co-workers led the meetings, and both had a real message from the Lord. Time was given for heart searching and intercession. What a grand way to begin a new term!

The next Sunday I had the privilege of speaking to a Boys' Brigade class and of leading a Hindu lad to the Lord.

During the following week I was in Temerloh for my first week of classes. The trip there was a fast one. With the radio blaring Indian and Malay music, the taxi driver covered the miles over winding mountain roads at top speed, giving a great blast of the horn each time he screeched around a sharp curve. A trip that should have taken two and a half to three hours took only two. I was grateful for the covering of prayer as I traveled.

I was very conscious of opposition from the enemy at Temerloh, but also of the Lord's help. Of the thirteen to fifteen people attending the classes each night, the majority were young people. Some were brand new believers when I was there 18 months before. Most of them attended every night and joyfully memorized a verse for each day.

My prayer was that through the personal-evangelism lessons the Holy Spirit would move believers to witness, especially among their families and friends. But as I taught evening after evening, some in the class also came under very real conviction on issues in their own lives. One young lady asked, "I want to be baptized, but my parents refuse to give permission. How long should I wait?" Another young lady whose parents had offered her to the temple lacked assurance of salvation. In trying to help her, we found she was still afraid of evil spirits. A third one was the only child in the family. As her father had died and her mother had remarried, she was the only one to carry on the ancestral worship. She said, "I want to be a Christian, but how can I?" We had her memorize 2 Timothy 1:7, "The Lord hath not given us the spirit of fear..." She took hold of this verse and seemed close to making a commitment of her life to Christ

Next my interpreter and I went to the village of Buloh Kasap, where there was a group of people who had been believers for some time. However, the first part of the week they showed little interest. We finished the classes with thirty, however. Two young

Enjoying durian fruit (distasteful to many people) at Dr. Ng's home.

252

ladies accepted Christ as Savior, and two young men stayed behind one evening to ask for baptism.

In Buloh Kasap I lived in a Christian home with grandparents, a son and his wife and five children. Fifteen Indian and Malay men digging ditches for the electricity board occupied the other half of the village house. The cooperation of all members in this household was amazing. Everyone had to use the same wash room! One of the treats in the home was eating durian every morning. Durian is a fruit that some folk disdain because it smells bad. But to those who like it, it is delicious. I like it!

In October I made a quick visit to see Mrs. Huang in Sungai Ruan. She loved the Lord but, with no one to read or pray with her, found life lonely.

Ten years previous, when I was in Sungai Ruan I had asked for prayer for the village clerk. Though brought up in the Presbyterian Church, he at that time was far from the Lord. When I visited him in another village this time, I found him vibrantly alive spiritually. What a change! The Lord had done His "exceeding abundantly above" all that we had asked or thought in this man's life.

Ten years ago this man had spent his time drinking and gambling and had two wives. Back then he told me, "I'll never darken a church door again." Very wealthy, some of his family apparently loved their money more than the Lord. He was an adopted child, and when his father died, he left him money, but the family refused to let him have it. That was what has turned him away from the Lord.

At Easter time this man's seventh baby from his second wife seemed to be dying. The wife worshiped all of her gods and tried all their heathen practices to no avail. In desperation the wayward Presbyterian thought, *Why not try my God?* He took the baby in his arms, went to the bedroom, and knelt down to pray. Three minutes later the baby opened his eyes! Although it was very late, they took the baby to the hospital and found both a doctor and a nurse there ready for them! Afterward the man told his wife, "I will not hinder you from worshiping your gods, but from now on I am worshiping my God." She said, "If my son comes back alive, I will also worship your God." This child is living today, and they are a happy Christian family with daily family worship. Testified the transformed man: "I never knew real joy and peace until now. I believe this was God's last chance for me."

When I visited, this man was planning to go home to see his first family after Christmas. When I had had dinner with his mother and sister not long before this, his mother had said, "We won't believe he is a Christian until he comes back and sees his family." Though he is physically weak because of his former way of living, we prayed that the Lord would use his testimony among his first family and also his friends and that he would not be sidetracked by his family's abundance of wealth and property.

In August 1966 the immigration authorities came out with a new ruling. All people in Malaysia with only a visitor's visa, which included over half of our workers, would be allowed to stay in the country only ten years from the date of their first entry. Three of our workers had already put in ten years on a visitor's pass and yet had their visas renewed. We did not know what the future would hold. If this law was put into effect, my ministry would come to an end in September 1967. However, by November none of our mission's workers had had to leave, and our visas were renewed. It looked as those who were already on the field would be able to fill out their terms. I reminded myself that I was in the Lord's hands! His way is always perfect.

I had the privilege of spending a weekend with the happy group of students at the Christian Training Center. They worked half time on a farm raising chickens and pigs. One of the prayer groups gave them a pig-feed chopper, a real time saver. The students used to spend hours chopping up banana stalks but now they could run them through the chopper in no time. They used fruits to make into jam to sell. The work gave the students good exercise; plus it meant they were well fed. They did very well in their studies and practical work. One night I went with them to a street meeting and was very impressed with the messages they gave as well as by their musical talent. Out of twelve students in the program seven would graduate soon, and new ones were due to come in.

In my classes at the Kuantan Methodist Church was a fifteen-year-old Chinese lad who had taken "Johnson" as his Christian name. He had come to the Lord in an evangelistic campaign the previous year and had since completed the Navigators Course. He was really "on fire" for the Lord. He wanted to cycle to a town 28 miles away to have a Sunday school class for friends of his. He invited the missionaries to visit his family. Although he was very poor and just a student, he had saved enough money to buy a Bible for himself and one for his father. The father and two younger sisters came to class and showed response. The mother came to service a few days later. When I was leaving the service, Johnson came with another keen young boy who had attended all the classes. They hurried to catch me before I got on the bus, as the lad wanted to dedicate his life to the Lord and wanted me to pray for him.

January 1967 I lived for a week with a Chinese pastor and his family. He and his wife had five little boys, and brother number six arrived while I was there. Though the children had no toys, they delighted me with their fun. The first thing in the morning all five would follow Daddy, still in their pajamas, and go out to feed the ducks and chickens. After breakfast the boys would go to the drain which was filled with filthy water from the monsoons and flooding. One boy would go to the end of the drain, take a cover from an old pan which just fit in the drain and gently push it up toward the house. The other boys would feel in the water for fish. One day they caught eighty-two fish. They put them in a barrel of clean water and fed them on rice. When we checked later on, we saw that the biggest fish were about ten inches long. I was amazed at how happily these children lived together. They had to share *everything*—bed, clothes, etc. The father and mother, five boys, new baby, and a grandma all shared one room while I was there.

Our work with the young people provided us with a few smiles. The pianist would begin by playing on a piano that was all out of tune. She played with one finger of her left hand and thumped out chords of her own making on the right side. The pastor, who was the song leader, was also an actor. You would think he was directing some famous orchestra. He had a stick about a yard long. He would begin with arms upraised, following with a deep bow, his eyes closed and his head almost touching the floor. The people didn't pay much attention either to the pianist or director. Having been taught to sing the "do-re-mi" system, they sang the tune correctly without any help.

Mid-message a big rat marched across the rafter in the front of the church, down to the floor, and across the platform. No one jumped out of his or her seat! This was just a friendly rat that wanted us to know he is a regular church attendee—he never missed.

The young people were so interested that they would stop me in the middle of a message to ask questions, some of them tough: "If my father dies, is it all right for me to worship at the grave?" Or, "May I eat food offered to idols? I'm the only Christian in my family." Or, "My parents won't let me be baptized. Do I obey the Lord or my parents?"

In Bentong the people were most responsive to the Gospel. A Chinese doctor who owned a rubber estate had put his estate in charge of an older man. Though very hardened to the Gospel, the old man loved the doctor's little boy, they came every night hand in hand to the classes. On Friday night the old man yielded to the Lord. How we rejoiced! Altogether 15 people professed to accept the Lord in Bentong, and almost that many promised, with the Lord's help, to try to lead one soul to the Lord in the coming year.

In June I learned that immigration had denied my visa renewal. That meant I would have to leave Malaysia by September. Even with my future so unsettled, the Lord encouraged me wonderfully. On vacation I studied the life of Elijah again. The

Lord showed me that no true child of God has the right to say where she wants to be or what she wants to do. Whether it be to go to a king, or to sit by a brook with the birds, or to live in a widow's home for a couple of years, or go to Mt. Carmel and face the enemy, for Elijah all were the Lord's leading. All that is required of us, as it was of him, is obedience to take His hand and go with Him.

I received a letter from the Director suggesting that I consider going to Indonesia. The work suggested was in a very primitive area. However, having experienced a great revival, they needed Bible teachers. Being human, I wondered, "Can I take it in my old age? What about the language? The teaching will be done in the language I am familiar with; conversation with older people would be difficult." But the Lord spoke to me each day, through one Scripture after another: "Doth not He see my way and count all my steps...? Trust in the Lord, and He shall direct thy paths.... Counsel is Mine and sound wisdom. I am understanding, I have strength... Jehovah is everlasting strength... Their strength is to sit still in quietness and confidence is their strength.... Fear thou not for I am with thee, be not dismayed for I am thy God. I will strengthen thee, yea, I will help thee, yea, I will uphold thee with the right hand of My righteousness.... I know the plans I have for you, says the Lord. Plans for welfare, to give you a future and a hope.... For I, the Lord thy God, will hold thy right hand saying, *fear not.*" With all those promises from the Lord, I was ready for wherever He would lead.

Speaking of leading, during what I thought were my last months in Malaysia the Lord led me to the Segamat Church, where we began with thirty-five people and ended with eighty-five. One family had just had real sorrow in their lives. They had taken their children swimming on a holiday in a little pool where they always went. Since their last visit, unknown to them, a bulldozer had deepened the hole. Three of their little children jumped into the hole and were drowned. I went to live with this family for a week to try to comfort them.

Later I was in a village where the principal's wife and one of the teachers were almost persuaded to put their trust in the Lord. When I called on the principal's wife, she told me, "My very good friends in Segamat just lost three children through a drowning accident. They are Christians." I was able to tell them that, not only did I know them, but also I stayed in their home for a week after the tragedy. That same night the bereaved friends came to the meeting. They also brought a teacher friend who was a very keen Christian. As all the teachers knew them, it was a wonderful contact.

In September I learned that the government had changed the law again in such a way that I could stay on in Malaysia. It had been difficult to know clearly what the will of the Lord was. One day as I was reading my Bible, the Lord reminded me of Paul's experience when he and his party attempted to go to Bythnia, but the Spirit of Jesus did not allow them to do so (Acts 16). That same morning I read from Zechariah 8:9, 11: "The Lord of Hosts says, 'Get on with the job and finish it. You have been listening long enough!'" For me it was as if the Lord said, "You have been waiting for OMF directors' letters long enough; get on with your ministry in Malaysia!"

Shortly after that I went to Tanjong Malim, a town where Methodists had an English work and where an OMF couple was seeking to plant a church among Chinese-speaking residents. There I met a young school teacher who, though a Christian, had gotten herself involved with a married man. She had become his second wife and bore him a baby. Because her husband beat and mistreated her, she was applying for a divorce. We felt the Lord had guided us to have classes that week just so we could minister to this young lady. Truly sorry for her sin, she wanted to come back to the Lord. She was about thirty years old, very refined, and a graduate of a Christian school. I must admit I coveted her for our town. I felt certain the Lord could use her among a number of girls we knew in their late teens and early twenties. I believed that her bitter experience could prove a blessing.

I ended my year with a vacation and then immediately began

work preparing lesson materials for the coming year.

In June of 1968 I had solid evidence that God had answered my bold requests from previous letters to prayer partners. "God is still on the throne, and He will remember His own," is the chorus we were singing in our classes.

In one of the village churches we had a DVBS in the morning and Bible studies at night. One morning a young man by the name of Golden Lion told the children a story. He asked them, "Would you girls like to have a dot on your forehead and wear a long piece of cloth for a dress like the Indian ladies?"

"No!" the girls shouted.

Then he asked, "Would you boys like to wear your hair long, tied in a knot on the top of your head and bind it up with a piece of cloth liked the Sikhs?"

"No!" they said.

"Well, Hudson Taylor changed his dress and his customs because he loved the Lord Jesus, and he cared for lost souls...." Golden Lion then proceeded to tell the children how Hudson Taylor took a ship for the long journey to China to spread the Gospel and eventually became the organizer of China Inland Mission. Golden Lion was a school teacher whose poor family depended on him financially. When I was home on furlough, a fellow missionary, who had known Golden Lion as a boy when he first accepted the Lord, said, "He could well be the future John Sung!"

"I want to train to serve the Lord," Golden Lion told me.

I wasn't so sure he should. He was the first Christian in his family and was their breadwinner. Would giving up his school-teaching position and hiving off to train at Bible school not seem totally irresponsible to those who were dependent on him? I expressed my doubts to the young man. Golden Lion became a prayer concern. You will hear more of him as I continue my story.

In Kuala Lipis a small group of very enthusiastic Christians, some quite severely persecuted for trusting the Lord, attended classes and brought their friends. They had many questions. On the last evening we counseled twelve folk of various ages. I was thrilled to see them all in church the next Sunday morning.

Some of the young men expected to leave town soon to look for work. They had been singing, "Parents (or friends, relatives, money) may leave me, but I still have Jesus. I'll not turn back." As I left the group that Sunday noon, they sang, "Teacher Chen (my Chinese name) may leave us, but we still have Jesus. We'll not turn back." Though this little group had bought land for a church building, the people living on the plot refused to move. I asked my friends to "pray the squatters off."

I wished my friends could have seen me in the homes I lived in while traveling. I considered it a real privilege to live in the homes of the people, who were always very kind. There were distinct contrasts, but the love was the same.

In one home the family was extremely wealthy, and I was given a private bedroom and bath. In the garden were 285 pots of gorgeous orchids, nearly all of them in bloom.

In the next home I shared a room with a Christian lady in a non-Christian home. Every morning the grandmother ardently worshiped twelve gods. For entertainment the family played a phonograph or radio very loudly—and not my type of music. For a living they raised pigs, chickens, ducks, dogs, and fish. As friendly as they were to me, they showed no interest in the Gospel.

In another home we stayed with the village pastor and his family. The pastor and his wife were both school teachers and had given up good jobs to serve the Lord. They had seven children: one had finished university, another was attending university, and all the others were in school. I slept in a bed with the older girl with two girls on the floor beside us. The family was a wonderful testimony for the Lord. In their church fifty to seventy young people attended classes.

In the village of Pontian an average of seventy people packed classes each night. The last day 125 people came and showed a real hunger for the Word of God. A businessman with his wife and son professed to accept the Lord. The wife of a Christian man and another girl who was the friend of a Christian boy also professed to accept the Lord as their Savior. They were so eager to have us return that they booked us for classes for the next year. They sent us off with a breakfast of hot meat dumplings, fruits of all kinds, flower cuttings, and a love gift of about US$45.00. I wept for joy over what the Lord had done.

In the village of Jerantut the church had finished their new building and parsonage. However, the devil was not pleased with the progress there. A former Sungei Ruan man, Mr. T, had a fight with the church leaders over money and the building. I was asked to be the "middle man." After a couple of hours the first day, Mr. and Mrs. T. attended all the classes. On Saturday evening he prayed publicly and asked the Lord to forgive him. The church committee, however, felt he should still confess to those whom he had offended. I went back for another three hours, but did not succeed in getting him to be willing to do that. Though I could do no more, I was sure the Holy Spirit could and would.

One time we stayed in the home of a hospital attendant. I had to sleep in a bed that was built for Asians. In order to stretch out in the bed I had to let my feet go through the slats at the end of the bed. In another home the bed was very comfortable, but the only way to the bathroom was through the couple's bedroom. That was a bit awkward. In a third place Mrs. Tan and I had to share a bed. We slept crosswise on it and rested our feet on a bench at the end. The bed was donated by some of the church members. As it was in the middle of the living room, when we took a little rest in the afternoon, we usually had an audience of children! The Chinese lady church worker slept on the floor without even a mattress. This was a very new village and church.

Menus varied from home to home. In the first place we stayed breakfast was served at seven o'clock and consisted of a piece of bread and a slightly cooked egg that we drank from a bowl.

Dinner was at two and supper at seven. For these two meals we were served crabs, shrimp, fish and seafood of all kinds¯not my favorite foods. In the second home the meals were brought in from a restaurant. Again, we were served a lot of seafood—usually cold. In the last place we stayed we were nearly killed with kindness. They served only pork every day, usually three times a day for eight days. Breakfast was sometimes a choice of pig's stomach soup with some spinach in it, or sweet potato and ginger soup, or a bowl of sweet gooey rice with fat pork and hard boiled eggs—or maybe *huge* meat dumplings with a hard boiled egg, a piece of liver, and plenty of fat pork. Dinner and supper were both all kinds of pork, mostly fat, liver, and kidneys along with rice, of course.

Hosts and hostesses varied too. In one place we stayed with a newly married couple, very much in love. Neither had yet accepted the Lord. They wanted to, but were afraid of his parents. I was sure the wife was ready to open her life to Christ and would if her husband would. But they were so happy that they didn't want to do anything that would cause a rift in their married life. Though both were educated and from quite well-to-do homes, I was amazed at how simply they lived. They washed dishes under a tap and left them on the floor in the sun to dry. They owned no furniture except a round table and four hard wooden chairs furnished by the hospital.

The next home in which we stayed was the home of a headmaster and his wife. Though church members, he drank, and she gambled! The third place was with a very keen Methodist Chinese church worker. In between classes I spent one night in the home of a missionary on a bed in the office!

Through all this, however, I was thrilled about the work God was doing. We did not necessarily have big crowds, but God worked mightily in the lives of individuals.

We held classes in a village called Seri Jaya—a completely new place that had recently been cut out of the jungle. Some of the folks who had been moved there came from a town where the

Methodists have their largest church in Malaysia. Twenty to forty adults attended each night, plus almost twenty school children and little ones. In the face of very good interest, the devil found ways of distracting the people. One night the man across the street was killed while felling a tree just before our service. Another night a medicine seller with a van and loudspeakers parked right across the street.

I was tiring physically, and my voice was giving out. I was beginning to feel my age.

Christmas that year the young people really worked at decorating the local church. They stretched colored streamers from every corner, inside and out, strung greeting cards across the room, and added a live casuarina tree with beautiful homemade balls they designed out of plastic. They worked all day at it and had a good time. Christmas morning we met together to praise the Lord for His presence. In the evening the young people put on a program and had a party. The following day a fellow missionary invited us for Christmas dinner with all the trimmings. A few days later I returned home to a pile of Christmas mail. What a joyous and encouraging way to end the year!

In early 1969 I visited Triang, where we encountered the apparent demon possession of a deacon's wife. Though a professing Christian, Mrs. W. was miserable and made life miserable for her whole family. The first time Mrs. Tan and I visited Mrs. W we found she had written Chinese characters over all her doors and windows to keep the evil spirits out. She had also practiced other superstitious rites in fear of the demons. Mrs. Tan and I explained to her how wrong that was in a home where Christ was supposed to be the Head. We prayed much for this family. One day Mr. W. invited Mrs. Tan and me for supper. After the meal we asked Mrs. W. if she was willing to pray and to have the writing removed.

"Yes, if you do it," she said. "I am afraid."

"We'll help you," we encouraged. "But you must take the lead."

Tremblingly Mrs. W. prayed, asking the Lord for forgiveness and deliverance. Tackling the first characters, she tried to rub them out with chalk because they could not be washed off. She also did the outside of the front door so that neighbors could see what she was doing. Then everyone gave her a hand. From that time on Mrs. W. read the Bible, and the local workers, who continued to visit her, reported that they could see a real change. My prayer for her was that she would have such a sense of the presence of the Lord that fear would find no place in her heart. I prayed also that she would be fully delivered and that she would be willing to be used of the Lord. Her experience could be a blessing, not only in the church, but also among non-believers.

Attending a Grady Wilson Campaign, I was thrilled to see the stadium almost filled. Imagine what it meant for villagers who seldom saw more than a few tens of believers to step into the stadium and see 7,000-8,000 people and listen to a 400-voice choir sing, *How Great Thou Art!* Over a thousand people were counseled that night, and a short time later over four hundred had sent in their Bible correspondence lessons. Remarked a man from a large city, "I can now see what can be done." Before long he was part of a group making plans to hold revival meetings with an Asian speaker from Hong Kong.

While traveling on the train to one of the villages, I was the only lady in the coach. On the luggage rack was a fancy foreign lady's handbag. I kept an eye on it, wondering who owned it. An old man stood up, took down the bag, opened it and produced his pipe and tobacco, sat down and had a smoke!

Mrs. Tan and I thoroughly enjoyed being a part of a youth retreat at Kedah Peak. While the young people hiked the seven miles up the narrow, winding road to the top, we old ladies made the harrowing trip by car. At the summit was the venue for our retreat, a lone government bungalow. It was a beautiful, well-furnished eight-bedroom house with a lovely garden. One could look down from the 3,200-foot peak to the sea on one side and to miles of beautiful rice fields on the other. We had a precious time of fellowship together in this lovely spot.

In May the church in Pendamaram canceled a scheduled series of Bible classes. Within a few hours two elders from the Sungei Way church came asking if they could have classes. Again we saw the Lord Himself closing and opening the doors for us. At this point Sungei Way was a very needy church, though it was one of the first churches OMF had opened.

In Tanjong Sepat I was greeted with a royal welcome. I thrilled to meet the young people as well as the older ones. The work there was very fruitful. Several young people came to know the Lord and dedicated their lives to Him that week of classes. I could hardly keep from weeping to see the Lord's marvelous working.

I was constantly amazed to see how wonderfully God paved the way for my ministry. When I arrived in one church, I found that the week before a Christian mother had died. A few days later an unsaved son was killed in a motorcycle crash. When I visited in the home, the second son was ready to put his trust in the Lord. The next Saturday night, when the invitation was given, the boy came forward bringing his younger brother with him.

In another church I found that a young couple who were leaders in the church had had a fight. The husband had not been home for several days and had turned to gambling. After the first class he was brought in by one of the other church leaders. He declared he did not want his wife and baby and was finished with the church. After quiet exhortations and prayer, husband and wife confessed their wrongs to one another and to the Lord. The husband came home every day and attended all the classes. Again, God had timed my coming.

While I was on vacation in the Cameron Highlands, riots broke out in the lowlands. Transportation back to Kuala Lumpur ceased. I wondered if and when I could go to my next classes. On the very day that I needed to go down to the city, a missionary of the Christian and Missionary Alliance had to go down on business and chartered a taxi. He offered to take me with him. We left at four o'clock in the morning and were the first taxi to come from the Highlands to Kuala Lumpur after the troubles and without incident.

As tense as the situation was, God took wonderful care of His children. Though some Christians were injured and others lost their homes, no Christian was killed in the riots. Fires burned all around the mission home, and gunfire meant ricocheting bullets in the streets during the night. Yet all OMF missionaries remained safe and, for the most part, had enough peace of mind to carry on their ministries. If the riots had come earlier, I would not have been able to go to my classes in Kuala Lumpur. If the troubles had erupted a week later, I would not have been able to go to the Kuantan area.

Mid-year the government began requiring all non-citizens to obtain work permits. We knew that could impact the Lord's work in Malaysia. Non-Malaysian pastors (those from Hong Kong, Singapore, etc.) would be affected as well as Western missionaries. Rumors continued to fly, scattered riots flared, and tensions rose among the people. Yet, except for a couple of cancellations, I was able to carry on my classes.

We had good classes in the village of Coldstream in spite of rain almost every night. One day the rain started at mid-afternoon and was still pouring as we made our way to church at night. On the way we barely made it across a wide flooded area. Aware that the rain continued throughout the whole service, we wondered how we would get home. Just outside the village the water was rushing across the road, taking with it logs and big stones. The Lord brought us through by using a lady driver who really knew how to handle a car. Further along we were caught between two floods, yet when we reached the point we most worried about, we found the water had not risen, but gone down an inch or two. We were grateful to reach home safely that night.

By October our visa status began to get sorted out, not exactly to our liking. We thought that missionaries who came before 1954, with their permanent-resident visas, would be able to remain in the country longer than the rest of us who had visitor's visas. Not so, for when people with permanent-resident visas were issued their work permit, they were for one year and stamped with, "Not to be renewed." My visa was renewed until furlough time at the end of May 1970 and marked, "Final." It appeared that I would not be allowed to return to Malaysia. However, I had been given a "final" two years before. The Lord overruled then; He could do it again.

The highlight of my last long series of classes was the missionary conference in October—the first one in history for that district. Seventy-five people from seven churches attended. I gave two messages: "The Church (Antioch) as a Witness" and "The Individual (Barnabas) as a Witness." Stella Hooi, first OMF missionary from West Malaysia, gave her testimony. Several young people dedicated their lives to the Lord.

When a series of classes was canceled because of trouble in the area, the Lord gave me a wonderful opportunity to witness in the home of a Christian lady who had invited her friends and neighbors to come listen.

During this suddenly free time I also helped in a DVBS. Fifty to sixty children chattered their way to their places each day, and six keen young people, including two seminary students, served as helpers. Some of the boys and girls came to know the Lord; I hoped that in years to come those new members of God's family would grow up to serve in their churches as a result of the DVBS. One of those boys was severely punished by his father for accepting Christ as his Savior. He had to hold a pail full of water over his head, and if any spilled, he was whipped. He did not dare to come to the classes every day, but managed to sneak in a few times.

The classes at Mentakab in early 1970 were great. At an evangelistic campaign the previous year several young people had come to the Lord. Some of them had done all of the Bible correspondence courses since then. These eager-beavers would come early to the classes and a few minutes before the meeting would say, "Excuse me, please. I must go and get some of my friends." Every night the little church was filled.

I taught the book of Nehemiah because I thought it would be the best teaching for those new believers. After the second day the young people came to me and said, "You must give something more evangelistic. We are bringing our friends, and we expect you to lead them to the Lord." Though I continued with Nehemiah, I also worked in teaching on the way of salvation. The last night when I gave the invitation, six people raised their hands. I asked them to remain after the service so that I could pray with them. Over forty people remained behind to ask questions. They kept us missionaries busy until eleven o'clock.

During the week of classes one young lady remarked, "The devil's attacks are fierce, but the Holy Spirit is much stronger." Referring to the Bible correspondence courses, she said, "The devil says, 'You are too busy; you have no time, and the courses are too hard.' The Holy Spirit says, 'The Lord has done so much for you; surely you want to know Him better.'"

When the pastor asked this same lass if she would like to be baptized, she said, "Not yet." That night the devil kept her awake with, "You don't want to be baptized; your father won't give permission. You will never get married, etc." At three o'clock, still not able to sleep, she got up and told the Lord she was willing to be baptized. "But You will have to help me get permission from my father," she added. The next morning she went in fear and trembling to her father, and when she asked him for permission, he said, "Baptism! What's that? How much does it cost? Do you have to go to Singapore or Kuala Lumpur for that?" When he found it was free, he said, "Go ahead." God was truly at work.

In Serdang was a young lady from the Christian Training Center. The only believer in her home, she took a lot of persecution. Previously when I had exhorted the grandmother to put her trust in the Lord, her reply was, "I don't want to go to Heaven. My husband and all my ancestors are in hell, and I want to go there with them." This year I found Granny wonderfully converted, as well as the girl's sister and three brothers. The mother is trying her best to keep the youngest boy and girl from becoming Christians. She says, "I don't mind the girls being Christians; they leave the home anyway. But if the boys go to church, who will worship our ancestors and me when I die?"

I was so very grateful for my prayer team scattered around the world. Three weeks before I would finish my class work for the term I wrote to them: "You, my praying friends, have prayed and watered the seed that was sown, and God has given the increase. Let us praise Him together!"

I could almost write a book about my last trip to Jerantut, in Pahang. I knew before I went that the church was full of problems in fact there had been a split in the church. I dreaded going, as I felt more than inadequate to help in those very difficult circumstances. The first day the Lord gave me a promise: "The mountains shall melt like wax at the presence of the Lord." That was all I needed.

How did God intervene? He sent a new Christian principal to the local school. As he was a godly man, he proved to be just the right man for such a time. He and I visited every home, sometimes working until midnight, listening to all their complaints, and exhorting and praying with them. Finally on the Friday night we urged all of them to come to the Bible class. Then at a little tea party afterwards, we welcomed all of them back into the church. While all had promised to forgive, I knew that only the Holy Spirit could heal the wounds. The process was underway.

I left Jerantut at six-thirty on Sunday morning and traveled to Bentong. I had written to the church not to expect me to preach at their Sunday morning service as I might well be delayed waiting for buses and taxis. When I arrived at 11:30 a.m., however, I found a church full of people who had been singing for an hour waiting for me to come. I had time for nothing except a cold drink.

During the service in Bentong a student had a nervous breakdown. He was a clever boy who had studied too hard for his final exams. After the meeting he came into the home and became very agitated. He crushed his glasses in his hand, threw a glass of water on the floor, and threatened to hit the missionaries serving there. It was five o'clock before we were able to get him into the hospital. The incident seemed to be a fierce attack of the devil at the very outset of the classes. Illness also swept through the congregation. Though we were able to carry on with the classes, the Bible woman and I both caught the bug as well.

Yet God blessed those days. Sometimes young men came in after the classes to ask questions about Islam or Catholicism. We ended up teaching an afternoon class on prophecy. Interest proved high. One day we started calling on people in their homes at seven in the morning, had our breakfast at a little food stall, and kept going until noon. Another day we went visiting after the meeting and didn't get to the last home until 11:15 p.m. It was those contacts in the homes that I believe the Lord really used. No wonder I was exhausted and ready for furlough!

"Ye have compassed this mountain long enough. Go northward!" (Deut. 2:3). God gave these instructions to Moses at the end of Israel's forty years of meandering in the dessert. But as I read these words one day, they seemed alive as if the Lord were saying them to *me*. With the visa stamped in my passport marked "final," I was facing leaving Malaysia for furlough May 7th, likely never to return. I wondered if God were pointing me to Taiwan, the only northward country out of several countries that mission leaders had mentioned as possible alternatives.

After a short trip to Singapore, I traveled home on a chartered missionary flight via Rome, Amsterdam, and England. I was too tired to do any sightseeing. I just wanted to get home and "stay put" for a while. But I praised God for what was probably my most fruitful term of service yet. ଔ

Chapter 22

Final "Final"
Year in Malaysia

In February of 1971 my application for re-entry into Malaysia went into the mail.

By April I was looking fretfully for news of that visa day after day. In response the Lord said, "Sit still, my daughter, until thou know how the matter will fall." I wondered whether a visa would be granted for me for Malaysia or some new country like Taiwan or Indonesia. Scripture says, "He shall choose our inheritance for us. For this God is our God. He will be our guide even unto death." I was all set to go. I was just waiting for my marching orders!

One of the fascinating things that happened on my furlough was watching Apollo 14 go to the moon and return. It reminded me of missionary work. This is how I saw it:

<u>Launching:</u> The power for send off was not the men themselves or the crew that sent them. It was in the rocket that blasted the space ship into space. Our power is not in ourselves to serve the Lord and live pleasing to Him. The only power we have is the Holy Spirit.

<u>On the moon:</u> The men knew their job and did it. Home base could see via pictures and hear by tape, but could not go. They kept on working and watching, expecting the job to be done. I was about to take off, and I was very much aware of my need of many to pray for me.

<u>Splashdown:</u> If the Lord would tarry, I'd be coming back to report on what the Lord did through my prayer partners.

During my furlough I continued to keep in touch with my friends in Malaysia. I was saddened by news of Golden Lion's behavior. The devil was going all out to get this young man, using false teachings to lead him astray. I asked my friends to pray that the Lord would open his eyes and keep him from falling. Many were already praying for Golden Lion, even boys and girls.

And then in late May the good news came! My visa arrived, and I was once again off for Malaysia. The Lord gave me a very good journey, with the consciousness of His Own Presence all along the way. The night before I left, His message to me was a reminder: "Emmanuel, God with us." And part of the *Daily Light* reading the morning I left was, "Arise ye, and depart for this is not your rest.... Here have we no abiding city. (How true for me!) This one thing I do, forgetting those things which are behind. I press on toward the mark of the high calling of God in Christ Jesus. Until He comes...."

The Lord gave me a very happy and restful few days in Philadelphia while I waited for my passport. Friends very kindly took me to see our children's hostel in Ivyland, the retired workers' home and interesting Amish country in Lancaster County. One day I would be a resident there.

In London I visited with Malaysian fellow workers, was taken to the famous Westminster Chapel for Sunday morning worship, and to a Chinese service in the afternoon. The day we arrived was the Queen's birthday, and we drove past the palace and then home to watch the Trooping of the Colors on television.

My concern about overweight luggage was a wasted worry (as

most of my worries are). Although it was put on the scales, no one paid any attention to the reading. When I arrived in Kuala Lumpur, the customs lady asked me how long I planned to stay. When I replied, "I've come home," she said, "How long have you been in this country?"

I said, "Since 1955," and she waved me on. I did not have to open a case. Praise the Lord for all of His mercies and help!

I could hardly believe I was actually back again. A very warm welcome awaited me. My whole furlough seemed like a lovely dream.

When I visited the OMF office in Kuala Lumpur, I learned that at first my visa had been refused. At immigration Mr. Sadler from the OMF office had made a special plea. In response, the Controller of Immigration granted the visa, but said not to apply again. As I was expecting the Lord's return at any time, I didn't worry about the next year. I wanted only to be found faithful at His coming. If He should tarry, I believed He could work another miracle, even without our applying, and give me another visa. But if not, I knew the Almighty was still on the throne, and I was simply a servant ready to take His orders.

Since I had not brought any supplies with me, I spent the first days in Kuala Lumpur shopping. I had a marvelous time spending my farewell gifts on the necessary linens, stationary, books, supplies for my room, etc. How thankful I was for the givers of those gifts!

I began lesson preparation on a Monday morning. It was quite an effort to shift gears to studying in Chinese. I was preparing a series of studies on the book of James. I prayed that I would be quick to learn the lessons the Holy Spirit wanted to teach me.

One of my first trips was to the village of Sikinchang. Right from the start we had some difficulty. In spite of good attendance every night, so much jealousy raged among the church leaders that it seemed impossible for the Holy Spirit to break through. Yet He did. I searched my own heart daily lest there was something in me—a lack of faith or something—hindering the Lord's work.

The church was right in the middle of a large rice-growing area. Rats were in abundance. Some nights five or six were running around in front of the platform. They had made their home under the platform in the church. We never lacked for entertainment— or distraction!

When I visited this same village a few years before, I had stayed in the home of two brothers and their 17 children. It was wonderful to see them all again. The oldest daughter had married a Christian man and moved to the village. The oldest son had dedicated his life to the Lord and was having problems because his family wanted him to marry a Christian girl in the church, but he wanted to go to Bible school. The younger brothers and sisters were all grown up and taking an active part in teaching Sunday school and helping in youth work. They thoroughly enjoyed the lessons in James and did all the memory work. One of the leaders of the church said he thought they were the best classes they had ever had. Several nights two carloads of folk joined us from a village eight miles away, with between eight and ten people in each car. This was in spite of the fact that I had given the same lessons to that group the week before! There was a real hunger after the Lord. I felt sure that if they were seeking, they would be found of Him.

I wrote to Singapore Bible College to get the latest news about the young man Golden Lion. The reply: "He is clever, talented, tempted to be proud, but God is working in his life. He is full of [the false teaching of Herbert] Armstrong, but as he studies the Bible with men who are rich in experience and have a solid knowledge of history, church, and the Scriptures themselves, we hope he will see the falseness of Armstrong. He doesn't eat pork and the kids all laugh at him and call him a Muslim." I asked my praying friends to keep praying for him.

In September I visited Temerloh. There was no resident worker in the church, but the little group faithfully carried on their services. One of their young men, Fuk Choy, would soon be graduating from the Christian Training Center. The church was looking forward to his help. This church had been flooded out the past January. One family found a dead cow, dogs, and rats in their home when the water went down. The church was full of mud —including the dishes in the cupboard. During the troubles in Indonesia a few years previous, this very small church sent a donation to help the refugees. The Indonesian church heard of the floods in Temerloh and sent a gift to help them to replace Bibles, Sunday school materials, and the like. Wonderful evidence of Christ-like caring!

In another village, Gambang, the work had been so discouraging before I went home on furlough that I wondered if I would ever go back. The Lord took me back, however, and what a joy it was to see what He had done! The little room was filled each night. In fact, it was so full some nights that the church leaders decided they should knock out a wall and enlarge the meeting place. I wrote my prayer partners to ask them to pray that these village churches would be willing to support their workers and that the Lord would use me in the classes to present this need to the churches.

My next visit was to Srijaya, a new village that had been cut out of the jungle. They still had no electricity or running water. In the home I stayed the well in the kitchen had water the color of mud. The family ran the water through a big water butte with stones and sand to clear it. The outlet was a pop bottle cemented into the bottom of the barrel. "Just pull the cork when you want water!" they told me.

The latrine was a little house in the rubber estate used by one and all! To get to it, one had to walk through a duck yard, across a pile of boards, cross a flooded area on planks, and into the rubber plantation!

The place was extremely hot in the afternoon. Temperatures were around 100 degrees. For supper we sometimes had peanuts and pork, kidney, tripe or chicken soup; or it might be fresh crab that was still crawling when it went into the pot. The people showered us with the best of everything they could produce.

The little room was filled each night. At first we tried to cope without opening the front of the shop house that was used as a chapel. It was right on a main highway where logging trucks, taxis, cars, and motor bikes went racing past, blowing their horns as they went. It was so crowded and hot that in the end we decided we would rather have the noise and more people and air. What a thrill it was to introduce many of these folk to my precious Lord Jesus for the first time!

In October I really got an education in Chinese living! I was staying with a Christian girl who rented a room in a Chinese shop house. The whole building boasted only two windows, one at the front and one at the back. Three families lived there besides my hostess. The kitchen was shared by all. When I went out first thing in the morning, I would find several people squatting on the floor with a wash basin in front of them. Everyone brushed his teeth and spat on the floor. The wash water went all over the floor and down the drain in the middle of the room. At mealtime each one had a little one-burner gas stove, or maybe a charcoal stove, and all cooked away for all they were worth. After breakfast I would find the ladies back on the kitchen floor doing their washing. They soaked their clothes in soapy water and then put them on the floor and brushed them with a stiff brush. So much for the kitchen!

The whole lot of us shared one toilet and one shower room. Soon I learned that the neighbor lady was a relative of our landlord and had nineteen people in her house. They also used our shower room because our water was cheaper!

Our bedroom had no ceilings and no windows. A few glass tiles set into the roof let in the light also the sun, sending the temperature up to about 100 degrees. The walls were made of just a sheet of thin wallboard about eight feet high. Everyone could hear all that went on from one room to another. One Sunday while we were trying to rest, I heard one radio with a program from China on the "Thoughts of Mao Tse Tung" in Mandarin. The next room had their radio a little louder on "Cantonese Stories," and a third had very loud music. To drown it all out. I managed to get BBC in English.

Now let me introduce you to our in-house neighbors: Next to us was a couple who had been married the night before I got there. They did not have a honeymoon. The first two nights the man went out and left his bride at home. She went to bed and slept so soundly he could not wake her up when he came in. Instead he managed to wake up all the rest of us! Next to them was a couple with a month-old baby who often wailed his woes during the night as well as the day. Then there was a lady with three children whose husband lived up the street with a second wife. This woman attended the classes and said she believed. Time would tell if she was really born again. She had a very sad life. Also among our neighbors in the building were two older people with two grandchildren. Because the son had beat up the wife and she had left home, the grandparents were left with the kids.

The church in this village was made up of a group of young people. The church managed with no building, no pastor or resident missionary. Meetings were held in our bedroom. The advantage was that our neighbors could lie in bed and listen to the message! The first night we had strong competition from the radios, but after that the owners were quite considerate, and we made the noise with our singing. Some of the ladies in the house were quite interested, but were afraid to come. The man who had two wives had not been home for a long time, but came one night and sat through the service. Out of this little group of young people, one young man was about to graduate from the Golden Links Bible School. Another had had a year at Singapore Bible College, but dropped out. We were praying him back to finish his course. A third fellow was helping OMFer Em Stewart in the Christian book room. I was impressed with the percentage of Christian workers from one little shepherdless village church.

That week I received a letter saying that Golden Lion was really beginning to see the error of Herbert Armstrong's doctrine. "Praise the Lord and keep on praying," I wrote my prayer partners. Did God answer those prayers? Today Golden Lion¯Rev. Dr. Tan Kim Sai¯is principal of Malaysia Bible

Seminari, with a recent total student enrolment of 447. He visited me here in Lancaster a year or so ago.

The Scripture says, "The prayer of the upright is His delight" (Prov. 15:8B). I was sure the Lord received much joy from the ministry of my prayer team. I was grateful to them as well.

In the first session at the South Perak Missionary Conference the English-speaking folk discussed the Book of Ezra while I gave a message from the book to the Chinese-speaking congregation. I had a very poor interpreter. Though the lady was well educated, she did not know her Bible and did not understand spiritual terms. Fortunately most of the congregation were young people who understood my Mandarin. The afternoon communion service was conducted in three different languages. One man prayed in Chinese, and another read the Scripture in Tamil. OMFer David Uttley spoke in English, interpreted into the other two languages! I am sure it must have given the Lord real joy to see all the different races remembering His death together. How great it will be to get to Heaven to worship the Lord without any language barriers!

That was to be one of David's last meetings. A couple of weeks later he was killed in a car accident. He had come to the field just two years before with his wife and two little boys. When he was killed, his wife was close to delivering their third child. I could hardly keep from asking the Lord why he did not take me, an old worker at the end of her road. One young man said, "I used to think we do not know what tomorrow holds; now I know we do not know what the next hour may bring." I was able to step in and help with teaching those young people. Again the Lord reminded me that He was planning my work schedule. Meanwhile I kept on with my regular ministry.

I had much for which to be thankful: First, not a single meeting had been cancelled because of rain in spite of its being in the middle of the rainy season. In flooded areas, churches that had been half filled with water two weeks before dried out in time for the classes. Sometimes it rained during the day but stopped in time for folk to come to evening meetings. Other times it began to rain just after the service started, when we were all safely in church!

Second, while not quite as many were finding Christ as Savior as earlier, more were dedicating their lives to the Lord. I requested prayer especially for these individuals at Chinese New Year time, when non-Christian families would pressure some of them to worship the spirits. One Chinese lady dental surgeon dedicated her life to the Lord and was considering working with OMF. She had applied to the Discipleship Training Center. She was expecting opposition from her family. She would need much prayer that the professing Christian parents would come into new blessing and be willing to support their daughter.

Third, while I was in Raub, I saw the Hokkien lady I wrote about earlier. She was going on steadily with the Lord. I went out to visit her in Sungai Ruan (where I had lived my first years in Malaysia). Her eldest daughter was believing as well.

My greatest joy was seeing Leung Mei-Yee, the lady who worked for us. Let me refresh your memory about this dear lady. The day I took my last Cantonese exam the examiner had said, "No one will ever understand your Cantonese." I went home and that day had the joy of leading this woman to the Lord. The Lord showed me He could use my language, even though it was far from perfect. Mei-Yee came to visit me in spite of the fact that she had nine children and lived an hour's walk into the jungle. The family was running a vegetable farm for the Malays. When I asked if she ever came to church, she said, "It is too far to come with the children. We have Bible reading, prayer and singing in our home." What a thrill! How I prayed that their lives would be a testimony to the Malays!

If I tried to write all the interesting descriptions of the houses I lived in, churches I visited, and opportunities in travel, it would take another whole book.

The next four months I taught Bible classes mostly to young people. The Lord blessed, and several of these young people dedicated their lives to Christ, in spite of hardships and opposition. A number excelled academically and blossomed spiritually. One was a school teacher with a wife and baby and with the promise of a good future. He struggled fiercely before acknowledging Christ as Lord of his life. Another school teacher said, "I had such joy for two years after I accepted the Lord. Then I went to university, where I had a non-Christian girl friend who led me into a spiritual wilderness for five years. I want to come back to the Lord and serve Him."

Just recently I received a letter from another of the young people who took impressive strides during those months. Now a middle-aged, home-schooling mother of five, Chooi Sin ministers in a church in Hong Kong. What a joy to know that God continues to work in and through this precious disciple of Jesus Christ! She wrote May 5, 2005: "I shed tears as I think of you. Thirty-three years ago you spoke to my church friends and me in Kuala Kangsar, Malaysia. Since then you have written beautiful letters of encouragement to me. I shared this story with my children, and they were touched to hear about you. My youngest daughter Josephine cried when she heard about your pain and the words of your last letter to me.... I love you so very much. Thank you for being my spiritual mother and…for your prayers…."

I will always thank God for crowning my years among the Chinese with His wonderful working among Malaysia's young people. My prayer partners stood shoulder to shoulder with me in the battle to see Satan's plans defeated in these precious Asian lives. It was wonderful to see God freeing them to be all that He planned for them to be. ✺

Chapter 23

"Now What, Lord?"

With the denial of government permission to stay on in Malaysia, I faced the prospect of shifting to a new field and new people. Older, but not quite retirement age, and seeing this coming for some time, I had been working with OMF leaders to discover the answer to "Now what, Lord?"

Clearly God said, "Taiwan." My skills fit needs among the 200,000 Paiwan tribes people.

For a long time people had been praying for someone to do Bible teaching among the 60,000 Paiwan Christians. The result of a wildfire turning to the Lord years before, they were now scattered in fifty-six understaffed churches. They needed a fuller grasp of God's Word and its intended impact on their lives.

With rugged living conditions, unfamiliar customs, and unintelligible (to me) language, tackling this task among the Paiwan would be a tremendous challenge for me. I definitely needed much prayer. Changing work and fields at my age was far from easy. My natural self shrank from it. Yet I knew that God was able to make all grace abound.

In July of 1972 I said my tearful good-byes in Malaysia and moved to the island of Taiwan. I felt a heartfelt welcome.

In those remaining years overseas the Lord never failed me once.

They were hard years that included enduring typhoons, trudging through mud, sleeping on a stone bed, and riding perilously on the back of motor bikes along tortuous mountain roads. Hard battles in the heavenlies also sapped strength, but proved God faithful.

Three years after moving to Taiwan and forty years after first setting foot in China, I said my final good-bye to Asia. I arrived home safe, tired, but happy. My Michigan family had a wonderful homecoming for me. But again came the big question: "Now what, Lord?" I wasn't ready to just retire to a rocking chair. I was as much the Lord's servant as anytime.

In answer to my open heart, the Lord led me to start a prayer ministry for missionaries in the Grand Rapids area of Michigan. Over the years I had been infinitely grateful for people's prayers for me as I trekked to the far corners of the world. They had kept me connected to God's power. Only eternity will reveal the extent of God's working as a result. Now I felt God wanted me to help mobilize prayer teams for other "goers."

As I'd never driven a car in my *life*, I expected to travel from place to place by bus. In my earlier years buses went everywhere, and I would just hop on one and go. I couldn't believe it when I got home this time and discovered that buses no longer plied the highways between cities! I couldn't go by bus even from Grand Rapids to nearby cities of Zeeland or Holland! I was going to have to learn how to drive. Yes, *me!*

My brothers had warned me, "You can't live in Michigan and not have a car. You've *gotta* drive."

At first I said, "No way! I'm scared even to ride in cars. I'm never going to drive one. No way!"

But then reality settled in—I wasn't going to get anywhere if I didn't drive a car. So I started to pray, "Lord, if you want me to drive and do this prayer ministry, you will have to give me the courage because I'm scared to death. Also you'll have to provide the money for a car, because I don't have two dollars to rub together!

Now you're probably wondering, *You weren't afraid to get on a train and a boat and go to China. You traveled on all kinds of rickety vehicles on terrible roads up and down mountains, but you were afraid to drive a car in Michigan?*

Well, you must know that 28th street in Grand Rapids looked like a very dangerous place to me. Cars went whizzing by—lane after lane of them. *It is just too much,* I thought.

Besides, I didn't know the first thing about a car. I didn't even know where to put the key—and I didn't know the brake pedal from the gas pedal! I didn't know *anything* about a car.

"Now don't worry," my brothers promised, "we'll get you a good second-hand car."

I said, "No way. If I'm going to get a car, I'm going to get a new one."

My brothers thought I was absolutely nuts. But the next thing I knew, the Lord gave me money for a new car. I had a dear friend from Spring Lake, Michigan—from the Barber family. Barber was an old, old name in Spring Lake. The family at one time had owned an ice company called The Ice and Coal Company. When I went to China, their daughter Harriet had wanted to go to the mission field too, but was never accepted. Since she couldn't go herself, she took on the task of sending out missionaries' prayer letters. She sent out *all* my prayer letters from the day I went out. She paid for the postage and did all the typing and corrected all the grammatical mistakes. (That's why they were such good letters!) With Mr. Barber supporting their efforts financially, Harriet and her sister did this for 50 missionaries or so. Just when I needed the money, Harriet died and left me $10,000. Since it was just the right amount to buy a nice car in those days, I went out and bought a new Chevrolet.

My nephew Larry, who taught driver training for the local school, somewhat reluctantly volunteered to teach me to drive.

The first day he said, "Aunt Sadie, I couldn't get the driver training car, so you'll have to go in my van." Now, I was afraid to *ride* in a car; I certainly was not going to *drive* a van! (It was one of those big ones.) I didn't know *beans* about it.

But we went out. First we drove around the churchyard across from their home. I learned how to start the vehicle and how to stop it and how to turn around and back up and so on. Then we went out on the country roads and rode around. After that first time we had a driver-training car. I wonder what people thought when they saw this gray-haired lady with a driver trainer!

The only mistake I made occurred when I came back to the house. We turned into our circular driveway, and I put my foot on the gas instead of the brake. Larry hit the brake on the other side of the car. I said, "Lawrence, you're just like the Lord. When I need you, you're there!"

So that was my driver training. After that the Lord had me driving all around Michigan.

My brother John was already involved in prayer meetings. We started new meetings in Zeeland, Holland, and Grand Rapids. Mondays we went down to Ann Arbor, Wednesdays we went to Zeeland, another day we went to Holland and so on. I covered all the meetings in one week.

The first time in each place I would come armed with pictures and testimonies of our new workers from OMF's *East Asia Millions* magazine. I'd cut them all out and put them on the table and tell the people, "Now, you pray that the Lord will guide you to the one you're to pray for because this is not just choosing, this is obeying the Lord and doing what He wants you to do."

The only advice I gave them was a suggestion: "If you're a married couple, choose a married couple with children the age of your children. Get your children involved. If you're a school-teacher, choose a teacher. If you're an accountant, choose somebody in finance. Choose something that you're interested in yourself. It'll help you to pray, and it'll help your children fit in," I said. After praying about it, they would choose their missionary.

After that, each person/family had one special missionary with whom to correspond. When we would meet together, they would read the letters they received from that missionary and then pray for him or her. By doing it this way, they got to know the missionary and what his or her prayer needs were. If they got an urgent request, everyone would join in the prayer. They promised to pray until they received an answer. This was the way the prayer group in Zion, Illinois, prayed for me. I was just following their plan. At one time ten groups were meeting each week.

If a missionary was home on furlough, he or she could come for one week and visit all those groups. It was a lot of traveling and hard work. We were told that nobody worked missionaries like John and I did! Usually by Thursday we were through and could rest a couple of days before we went off to the next meeting. I did that for twelve years.

Unfortunately the older people who were involved in the prayer groups have died, and young people haven't come up to take their places. I'm not sure but that I made a mistake in making all the contacts to draw in new members myself. Maybe I should have had original members recruit others to fill up the ranks. I'll never know for sure and will have to trust that the Lord was pleased with what we did.

After twelve years of my doing this work, my sight deteriorated to the point that I could no longer drive. I sold the car to a retiring fellow worker from Malaysia for $1.00. She took it back to Canada and used it for at least ten years before giving it up because of *her* failing eyesight.

I left Grand Rapids after that and moved out to Lancaster, Pennsylvania, to OMF's retirement home for its "reassigned" (a. k.a. "retired") missionaries. I found plenty for me to do there. When I first moved to the home, for example, I read to those who couldn't see to read at all at Calvary Fellowship Homes nearby. I was still occasionally invited to speak about missions at churches in the area, but this vagabond's traveling days were over.

When I look back over my life now from my corner (literally!) of Calvary Fellowship Homes in Lancaster, Pa., a block from OMF's Lammermuir House, I am just amazed at what the Lord did with an ordinary farm girl. I would follow Him all over again if I could start over. His way is *perfect.* ❧

Epilogue

Letters from China

When the editing process of this book was well along, my niece received a letter from Frank Moore, son of Percy and Amy Moore and grandson of Arthur and Esther Moore, with whom I worked in China. Frank was a little boy when I first knew him. Today, white-haired and a retired schoolteacher, he teaches English to schoolteachers not far from where, more than six decades ago, I began ministry in Xin Ji. His letter thrills my heart. Obviously God didn't leave or stop working when we did.

Having spent all of yesterday out at Xin Ji, I have a strong feeling that God is answering prayers out there, and I'm sure that Sadie's fervor for Xin Ji is reaching the ear of the Almighty!

After a lecture at Nanzheng Middle School in the area where he grew up as a boy Frank Moore befriends some of the students.

Firstly let me describe Xin Ji to you. It's a typical, slightly down-at-heel Chinese market town.... You can walk from one end of the town to the other in about 15 minutes. It sits in the middle of a fertile plain surrounded by lovely mountains. I rattled along on an old bus for about an hour to get there.

I told the bus driver that I wanted to be let off at the Christian church. He waved his hands around eloquently and said that there were two Xin Ji churches now—which one did I want? I last went to Xin Ji in 2003 (I think), and at that time the pastor told me they were planning on a new church. However, it was all pretty vague.

I pushed the driver to tell me more of the new church. He said that as it was in the process of construction, I'd be better off going to the old one. So I did. The old church is called the Xin Ji/Gao Tai Christian Church. That's because it sits out in the fields about three miles from the township of Xin Ji, but in the middle of the G a o   T a i community. In this region the church seems to have revived after the virtual closure of the church during the dark days of the C u l t u r a l Revolution.

The Xin Ji town Christians have been attending this church since 1978. Now the c h u r c h   h a s

The old Xin Ji/Gao Tai church out in the country.

Frank Moore photo.

become strong enough to build a second church just outside the township of Xin Ji, again in a most stunning setting next to the Lian River and with a backdrop of fields and mountains. This new church will cater for the Christians in the town and from districts further to the south and west of Xin Ji. So it seems that remarkable things are happening!

When I got to the old church, I was warmly greeted by the gatekeeper and family, who contacted Pastor Luo Ye Ming. Pastor Luo was soon on the scene—a man about 50 with an eternally cherubic face.

I was then introduced to Men Juan, an 18-year-old girl who has been brought up within the church community since she was 12 years old. At that time her parents split up and went off in different directions, abandoning Men Juan. The church adopted her.... What a lovely, engaging, warm-hearted young woman she is! She's going to the

Men Juan and Pastor Luo make music.

Xian Bible College (the former San Yuan Bible College) in September and is being groomed for leadership in the church. She's very musical. She sat down at an electric organ and played and sang a hymn for me and then played the saxophone, trumpet and trombone in turn.

Pastor Luo arranged a car to drive us to the new church. After about a ten-minute run through the ripening fields of rape-seed and new rice, we drove through the town and out the other side. To my astonishment, there ahead rose a magnificent new church. Chinese church architecture is vaguely Greek Orthodox/Byzantine in appearance. ... While a bit ostentatious to our tastes, it sure makes an impact. In a landscape of rice fields and purple mountains this huge edifice rises, making a very big statement. To me it was saying, "Look, we Christians are a presence in this area! We intend to let you know we're here!"

Then I was told that the church will formally open in August 2005 and that they would like to invite me to be present. It seems absolutely right that I do so, God willing. [He did go—ed.] The long thread of connectedness to Sadie Custer and Bertha Silversides runs through me to the new Xin Ji church.

After lunch we went for a walk through the town. I asked Pastor Luo to take me to the old, original town centre and

Above: The mew Xin Ji church building under construction.

Below: Possibly the original church meeting place in Xin Ji town.

Frank Moore photos.

maybe we could try to identify where Sadie and Bertha had lived in the late 1930's onwards. The town has grown and the new parts of town are mostly nondescript shop buildings of two stories with white-tiled facades. We soon got down into the old quarter—much of it built with mud brick and half-moon tiles. Eventually we stopped in front of a house which Pastor Luo thought might have been the site of the old, original church. If so, Sadie and Bertha lived behind it.

More than 2000 Christians, plus interested friends, live in the district. This makes the Christian presence far and away the most powerful spiritual presence in the area. I saw no sign of Buddhist or Taoist temples. I guess the locals who are not Christians are probably typical of most modern Chinese who have been thoroughly confused by the events of the last 55 years.... Chairman Mao made it perfectly clear during the Cultural Revolution years that all religions were relics of feudalism and should be rejected. What happened then, as far as I can see, is that the people lapsed into age-old superstitions or, if they were young, took to material pursuits.

I returned last night to my little apartment in Hanzhong city, convinced that God has answered the prayers of Sadie Custer and Bertha Silversides and others who have prayed for the church at Xin Ji. What a remarkable movement forward since the first convert, still remembered at the church, a humble carpenter!

Concluding a precious long letter to me after an earlier visit to Xin Ji, Frank Moore had written:

...Christians at Xin Ji worship in a timeless way. They still sing old missionary favorites, "Blessed assurance, Jesus is mine" and "Holy, holy, holy." ...Their beginnings go back to the hard work that you and Bertha Silversides did as young women so long ago. I come bearing history to these people, and they know it in some vague and dim way. They know that once I lived here as a child and [that] there were others, missionaries, who brought the Gospel, people who are now part of the ancestral memory. I tell them again of their origins, and they listen, and their roots deepen. They understand that it is humans that tell the stories of the Gospel, humans impelled by the Holy Spirit. We humans are God's voice. ∞